Leveraging Digital Innovation for Governance, Public Administration, and Citizen Services:

Emerging Research and Opportunities

Nidhi Vij Mali
University of Mississippi, USA

A volume in the Advances in Electronic Government, Digital Divide, and Regional Development (AEGDDRD) Book Series

IGI Global
DISSEMINATOR OF KNOWLEDGE

Published in the United States of America by
IGI Global
Information Science Reference (an imprint of IGI Global)
701 E. Chocolate Avenue
Hershey PA, USA 17033
Tel: 717-533-8845
Fax: 717-533-8661
E-mail: cust@igi-global.com
Web site: http://www.igi-global.com

Library of Congress Cataloging-in-Publication Data

Names: Mali, Nidhi Vij, 1983- editor.
Title: Leveraging digital innovation for governance, public administration, and citizen services : emerging research and opportunities / Nidhi Vij Mali, editor.
Description: Hershey PA : Information Science Reference, [2020] | Includes bibliographical references.
Identifiers: LCCN 2017043234| ISBN 9781522554127 (hardcover) | ISBN 9781522590774 (paperback) | ISBN 9781522554134 (ebook)
Subjects: LCSH: Public administration--Technological innovations. | Public administration--Citizen participation--Technological innovations. | Public administration--Cross-cultural studies. | Internet in public administration.
Classification: LCC JF1525.A8 L48 2020 | DDC 352.3/802854678--dc23 LC record available at https://lccn.loc.gov/2017043234

This book is published in the IGI Global book series Advances in Electronic Government, Digital Divide, and Regional Development (AEGDDRD) (ISSN: 2326-9103; eISSN: 2326-9111)

British Cataloguing in Publication Data
A Cataloguing in Publication record for this book is available from the British Library.

Advances in Electronic Government, Digital Divide, and Regional Development (AEGDDRD) Book Series

ISSN:2326-9103
EISSN:2326-9111

Editor-in-Chief: Zaigham Mahmood University of Derby, UK & North West University, South Africa

MISSION

The successful use of digital technologies (including social media and mobile technologies) to provide public services and foster economic development has become an objective for governments around the world. The development towards electronic government (or e-government) not only affects the efficiency and effectiveness of public services, but also has the potential to transform the nature of government interactions with its citizens. Current research and practice on the adoption of electronic/digital government and the implementation in organizations around the world aims to emphasize the extensiveness of this growing field.

The Advances in Electronic Government, Digital Divide & Regional Development (AEGDDRD) book series aims to publish authored, edited and case books encompassing the current and innovative research and practice discussing all aspects of electronic government development, implementation and adoption as well the effective use of the emerging technologies (including social media and mobile technologies) for a more effective electronic governance (or e-governance).

COVERAGE

- E-Government in Developing Countries and Technology Adoption
- ICT within Government and Public Sectors
- ICT Infrastructure and Adoption for E-Government Provision
- E-Citizenship, Inclusive Government, Connected Government
- Emerging Technologies within the Public Sector
- Online Government, E-Government, M-Government
- Adoption of Innovation with Respect to E-Government
- E-Governance and Use of Technology for Effective Government
- Urban Development, Urban Economy
- Electronic Government, Digital Democracy, Digital Government

IGI Global is currently accepting manuscripts for publication within this series. To submit a proposal for a volume in this series, please contact our Acquisition Editors at Acquisitions@igi-global.com or visit: http://www.igi-global.com/publish/.

The Advances in Electronic Government, Digital Divide, and Regional Development (AEGDDRD) Book Series (ISSN 2326-9103) is published by IGI Global, 701 E. Chocolate Avenue, Hershey, PA 17033-1240, USA, www.igi-global.com. This series is composed of titles available for purchase individually; each title is edited to be contextually exclusive from any other title within the series. For pricing and ordering information please visit http://www.igi-global.com/book-series/advances-electronic-government-digital-divide/37153. Postmaster: Send all address changes to above address.

Titles in this Series

For a list of additional titles in this series, please visit:
https://www.igi-global.com/book-series/advances-electronic-government-digital-divide/37153

Learning Cities, Town Planning, and the Creation of Livelihoods
Idowu Biao (University of Botswana, Botswana)
Information Science Reference • copyright 2019 • 312pp • H/C (ISBN: 9781522581345) • US $215.00 (our price)

Global Campaigning Initiatives for Socio-Economic Development
Luísa Cagica Carvalho (Instituto Politécnico de Setúbal, Portugal & Universidade de Évora, Portugal) and Maria José Madeira (University of Beira Interior, Portugal)
Information Science Reference • copyright 2019 • 325pp • H/C (ISBN: 9781522579373) • US $195.00 (our price)

Constitutional Knowledge and Its Impact on Citizenship Exercise in a Networked Society
Ana Melro (University of Aveiro, Portugal) and Lídia Oliveira (University of Aveiro, Portugal)
Information Science Reference • copyright 2019 • 332pp • H/C (ISBN: 9781522583509) • US $195.00 (our price)

Private Sector Innovations and Technological Growth in the MENA Region
Maryam Ebrahimi (Azad University, Iran)
Information Science Reference • copyright 2019 • 217pp • H/C (ISBN: 9781522570868) • US $195.00 (our price)

Multi-Level Governance in Developing Economies
Tugba Ucma Uysal (Mugla Sitki Kocman University, Turkey) and Ceray Aldemir (Mugla Sitki Kocman University, Turkey)
Information Science Reference • copyright 2019 • 303pp • H/C (ISBN: 9781522555476) • US $195.00 (our price)

Security Frameworks in Contemporary Electronic Government
Ryma Abassi (Carthage University, Tunisia) and Aida Ben Chehida Douss (Carthage University, Tunisia)

For an entire list of titles in this series, please visit:
https://www.igi-global.com/book-series/advances-electronic-government-digital-divide/37153

IGI Global
DISSEMINATOR OF KNOWLEDGE

701 East Chocolate Avenue, Hershey, PA 17033, USA
Tel: 717-533-8845 x100 • Fax: 717-533-8661
E-Mail: cust@igi-global.com • www.igi-global.com

Table of Contents

Preface

The continually changing outlook of existing practices in digital innovation in public administration creates a prerequisite for information resources that will empower experts, academics, educators, researchers, and industry advisors all over the world. Leveraging Digital Innovation for Governance, Public Administration, and Citizen Services: Emerging Research and Opportunities is a pivotal research volume that will meet these needs by exploring the most up-to-date reporting on all facets of the digital divide, economic development, management, and technology adoption from different fields covering topics such as e-government, e-participation, electronic payment and netnographic analysis.

This academic resource is arranged into seven chapters contributed by international professionals who draw on their experiences, observations and research surrounding economic development, e-business, and the digital divide. A short description of each of the chapters can be found in the subsequent paragraphs.

In Chapter 1, "A Framework for Longitudinal Analysis of University Spin-Offs" by Fernando Almeida (Oporto University, Portugal) and Eugénio Cunha (Oporto University, Portugal), the authors provide an in-depth study on the establishment of a framework for longitudinal analysis that could identify and characterize the evolution and performance of Portuguese university spin-offs.

In Chapter 2, "Coupling of Economy Development and Technology Diffusion for Inclusive Growth to Meet the Challenge of Technology Implementation in Perspective" by Nirmalendunath Ghosh (independent Researcher, India), the author explores a model that shows a link between technology and infrastructural and economic development and also looks at how strategies can be developed to meet the challenges of joining the two together.

In Chapter 3, "Data Analytics for Better Branding of E-Governance and E-Business Systems: Case of 'Digital India' Campaign" by Rajan Gupta (University of Delhi, India), Saibal Kumar Pal (DRDO, India), and Sunil Kumar Muttoo (University of Delhi, India), the authors examine e-governance and how it leads to a stronger democracy which is achieved through higher trust, visibility, and transparency in the system, which can be acquired through effective branding of different government programs.

In Chapter 4, "Digital Divide and Its Dimensions: A Study in India" by Vasantha Gouri Prathapagiri (National Institute of Rural Development, India), the author provides an overview on the digital divide and how the gap differs between high income countries where at over 90% of the population is able to access the internet and lower income countries were less than 10% of the population has access to the internet.

In Chapter 5, "Digital-Locker Services in India: An Assessment of User Adoption and Challenges" by Sumangla Rathore (Sir Padampat Singhania University, India), the author gives a summary of the digital locker program that launched in India in 2015 and discusses the awareness level of citizens regarding the service, identifies problems and challenges associated with its implementation and also looks at factors that affect adoption of such services and makes recommendations to the stakeholders.

In Chapter 6, "Learning and Developing With Each Other: Case of Collaborative Innovation Through ICT in India and Canada" by Rajan Gupta (University of Delhi, India) and Saibal Kumar Pal (DRDO, India), the authors discuss how ICT (information communication and technology) is a powerful tool and can be used to enhance both India and Canada politically, socially and economically through tools such as chat/instant messaging, knowledge portals, groupware workflow, best practices repository, and expertise locator.

In Chapter 7, "Participatory Mapping, E-Participation, and E-Governance: Applications in Environmental Policy" by Pragati Rawat (Slippery Rock University, USA) and Juita-Elena Yusuf (Old Dominion University, USA), the authors focus on public engagement using information and communication technology, namely participatory mapping, known by a variety of terms such as participatory GIS (PGIS), public participation GIS (PPGIS), and voluntary GIS.

The range of research included in this academic reference publication is sure to provide a heightened understanding of all issues, research, and findings related to e-government and e-participation. Furthermore, the work included in this volume will be influential in the development of knowledge offerings in the field. This publication will help to inspire readers to contribute their own research and insight into this vast field as they look forward to the future.

Chapter 1
A Framework for Longitudinal Analysis of University Spin-Offs

Fernando Almeida
https://orcid.org/0000-0002-6758-4843
INESC TEC, Faculty of Engineering, Oporto University, Portugal

Eugénio Cunha
INESC TEC, Faculty of Engineering, Oporto University, Portugal

ABSTRACT

The creation of university spin-offs plays a fundamental role in the technology transfer process between universities and the business field. Universities have developed for themselves internal processes within their technology transfer offices in order to collect this information. However, this data is only available locally and often outdated. Furthermore, the number of frameworks that allow the study and simultaneously access to this data in an integrated way is still small on a global scale, and in Portugal, there isn't a repository which contains this information. This study proposes the establishment of a framework for longitudinal analysis that could identify and characterize the evolution and performance of Portuguese university spin-offs. The repository is built exclusively in open source technologies and offers the potential to characterize and analyze the evolution and performance of university spin-offs in different perspectives, such as individual factors; organizational factors; institutional factors; and scientific, educational, and commercial outputs.

DOI: 10.4018/978-1-5225-5412-7.ch001

INTRODUCTION

Today's most advanced economies are based on the greatest availability of knowledge. The competitiveness of the society, people or companies is based on their ability to access to knowledge, in order to meet the challenges of contemporary society. In this new paradigm, universities perform a central role, because they are important producers of new knowledge that have direct and indirect impact in the educational formation of society and competitiveness of companies.

At the same time, frequently, the knowledge created within universities will have a commercial application and a commercial value which can be exploited through commercialization activities (Perkmann et al., 2013). Nevertheless, only fairly recently universities have serious invested in expanding to this new role. Universities have been playing a critical role in society because alongside their traditional roles as training and research institutions, they also help to foster economic and social development. But this economic role has been primarily a function of their first two roles – the training and education of students and the generation of new knowledge. The Universities that in many parts of the world have started to invest in the creation of internal mechanisms aimed at supporting academic entrepreneurship in its different forms (Fryges & Wright, 2014) have witnessed that these internal, university-level mechanisms and policies have contributed significantly to the professionalization of activities that encourage the exploitation of research results (Baldini et al., 2014). In addition to the traditional mandates of teaching and research, knowledge transfer has become a third mission in which academic institutions engage.

In general, the concept of the third mission encapsulates many of the rising demands of the university to take a more visible role in stimulating and guiding the utilization of knowledge for social, cultural and economic development (Carot et al., 2012). In order to embrace the third mission, universities needs to readapt and reorganize in order to perform new activities, such as IPR and patenting, licensing, carry out entrepreneurship training, internal incubation, support spin-off creation and help them in the market (Reichenfeld, 2010).

In this paper, we propose the establishment of a framework for longitudinal analysis of University spin-offs in order to facilitate the mission of knowledge transfer offices that, could they easily identify and characterize the evolution and performance of university spin-offs along several years of analysis. This is the first repository for longitudinal analysis of university spin-offs in Portugal that offers great potential to characterize, discuss and mitigate open issues in literature related to several dimensions of spin-offs analysis. Furthermore, the repository is exclusively built on open source technologies, can be accessed by Web and mobile devices and offers interactive features that let users easily understand the main events and occurrences associated with each university spin-off. The paper is organized as

Table 1. Definitions of university spin-offs

Author	Definition
Shane, 2004	"…university spin-off as a new company founded to exploit a piece of intellectual property created in an academic institution."
Libaers et al., 2006	"...university spin-out companies, defined as firms that have been spun off from academic departments or research centers within a university with the aim of commercializing technology invented at the university."
Wright et al., 2007	"…university spin-offs as new ventures that are dependent upon licensing or assignment of an institution's IP for initiation."
Muller, 2010	"...new firms created to exploit commercially some knowledge, technology, or research results developed within a university."
Rasmussen, 2011	"a university spin-off is defined as a new venture initiated in a university setting and based on technology developed at a university."
Fini et al., 2011	"We define an academic spin-off as a company that has either a university or at least one academic (full, associate, or assistant professor; or Ph.D. candidate, research fellow, or technician) among the founders, regardless of the presence of a formal commitment from the parent university"

follows: First, we clarify the adopted concept of spin-off and we perform a revision of literature in university spin-offs by highlighting the contribution made by the main results on this subject. Then, we present a list of similar initiatives conducted by other universities and R&D institutions. Subsequently, we present the approach adopted in the development of this project. After that, we discuss the contributions made by our project. Finally, we draw the conclusion of our work.

LITERATURE REVIEW

The Concept of University Spin-off

There are many different expressions used interchangeably to refer to university spin-offs, namely by combining the words "university" or "academic" with "spin-off" or "spin-out". In addition to the fuzziness generated by several distinct terms to represent the same concept, there are also different definitions for the same term. Table 1 summarizes the main definitions of university spin-offs identified in the literature.

These different definitions of university spin-offs share common characteristics, such as (Pattnaik & Pandey, 2014):

- The parent organization from which the innovation emerges has to be a university or academic institution;
- The output that is a university spin-off has to be a separate legal entity and not an extension or controlled body of the university;
- The new entity has to exploit knowledge produced from academic activities or academic pursuits;
- The spin-off should be aimed at profit generation and commercialization of technology.

The spin-off term is also associated in literature with both the outcome and the process that generate an outcome (Borges & Filion, 2013). As a process, it refers to the fact that the new firm, its entrepreneurs or the technology used in the new venture was developed in a pre-existing organization (university or R&D center). The result of this process is the creation of a university spin-off.

In the context of our work, we define a university spin-off as a "new company based on knowledge developed at university, polytechnic or research center (home institution), whose founders have met in the content of the home institution". This concept is less restricting and doesn't require that the home institution is a shareholder of the spin-off company.

Studies Perspectives on University Spin-Offs

There are currently a significant number of studies regarding university spin-offs. These studies have been undertaken at several levels, including the university and its Technology Transfers Offices (TTOs), the spin-off venture, the contextual environment, and the academic entrepreneurs involved. There is currently an emphasis on longitudinal studies rather than cross-sectional section at a single point in time. According to Fitzmaurice et al. (2011), a longitudinal study typically refers to an investigation where participant outcomes and possible treatments or exposures are collected at multiple follow-up times.

The traditional rationale for academic entrepreneurship considers that it helps to enhance the commercialization of university research and also serves as a source of revenue for the university. The early reviews of the academic entrepreneurship literature focused mainly on analyzing the performance and establishment of metrics for university technology transfer offices, such as the establishment of TTOs, patents, licenses and spin-offs. Two of the most predominant studies that review and highlight the main dimensions, explaining the performances of TTOs were conducted by Rothaermel et al. (2007) and Markman et al. (2005). These studies identified the following dimensions: financial resources, scientific and technological resources, organizational structure, the development of capabilities, and incentives.

There are significant contributions based on quantitative methodologies. Among them, we highlight the study conducted by Mustar et al. (2008) that adopts a multi-level approach in order to understand the university spin-off creation and development in environments outside the high-tech cluster of the US. Chapple et al. (2005) have addressed the issue of efficiency in technology transfer by employing non-parametric (DEA - Data Envelopment Analysis) and parametric (SFE - Stochastic Frontier Estimation) approaches to compute the relative efficiency of TTOs.

In literature, we can also find contributions based on qualitative methodologies. Among them, we highlight the study conducted by Siegel et al. (2004) that identified the key organizational issues in promoting successful knowledge transfers based on 55 structured interviews of 98 university/industry technology transfer (UITT) stakeholders associated with five US research universities.

However, the previous approaches have largely not considered all dimensions of the new entrepreneurial ecosystem, which should reflect the wider social and economic benefits of academic entrepreneurship to the university ecosystem. The perspective of analysis typically includes the rise of property-based institutions such as incubators and science parks, the role of entrepreneurship education, the establishment and growth of entrepreneurship centers, the commercialization process and start-up creation, and the role of the alumni community in the entrepreneurial ecosystem.

The quality of the entrepreneurs is essential in explaining spin-off creation and success (Clarysse et al, 2011). Furthermore, Rasmussen & Wright (2015) considered that university context plays an important role both in relation to the individuals starting university spin-offs and their ventures. However, it is still not totally clear how different university-level factors and conditions influence spin-off creation and development. In fact, there are universities in the US that are highly successful in creating new ventures based on research, but there are also universities that have most numbers. In Europe the number of firms created is lower than in the US, but is progressively growing. However, these numbers are highly skewed in favor of fewer institutions (Wright et al., 2007).

There is significant consensus in literature that the potential benefits of creating university spin-offs are substantial. Van Looy et al. (2011) demonstrated that most empirical research shows that entrepreneurial activities in universities are associated with higher scientific productivity and strengthen. However, some critics have also appeared by claiming that a too heavy commercial orientation would endanger the university as an independent knowledge producer and some conflicts of interest may appear (Blumenthal et al. 1997).

Quantitative research studies have been conducted by several authors in order to determine and evaluate the impact of different dimensions of the entrepreneurial ecosystem. Bonaccorsi et al. (2014) intended to understand how far in space does university knowledge flow to breed the creation of knowledge-intensive firms, depending on the nature (codified or tacit) of this knowledge. Lejpras & Stephan (2011) looked if there are differences in R&D and innovation behavior between established academic spin-offs and otherwise created firms. Stephan (2014) analyzed if academic spin-offs are more innovative than other knowledge-intensive firms and also looks if academic spin-offs are more successful in attracting public innovation support.

Qualitative research studies have also appeared, but in minor number. Among them, we highlight Huyghe et al. (2014) that conducted a case study analysis to understand and explain how hybrid TTOs engage in boundary spanning activities that help early spin-off companies move through the pre-spin-off process. Rasmussen et al. (2014) adopted a case study over UK and Norway, in order to examine how the university department context influences the spin-off process from the perspective of both the spin-off venture and the department.

Another important challenge to be addressed is the severe lack of longitudinal data. Most large- scale survey-based studies are based on cross-sectional data and therefore pose limitations in terms of inferring causal relationships between variables. For instance, it is unclear whether individual research performance is enhanced by spin-offs or in (a reversed causality) spin-offs are themselves a mere consequence of high research performance. On the basis of existing evidence it is difficult to establish temporal patterns or how outcomes in one period are linked to activities in a prior period. While a new generation of studies using panel data on academic patents and publications has started to take into account the time dimension (Stuart and Ding, 2006), this has yet to be accomplished by research using survey data, the main source of information on academic engagement. The only studies acknowledging the longitudinal dimension are qualitative contributions (Kenney and Goe, 2004; Shinn and Lamy, 2006; Jain et al., 2009). Therefore, it is advised that future research on this topic conducts surveys repeatedly, or at least administer subsequent surveys containing some identical questions, across a comparable population of academic researchers.

Finally, sampling procedures should as far as possible, ensure population representativeness and avoid sampling bias. To date, most studies focus on specific disciplines whilst others address populations of academics at particular universities, we plan to develop research ensuring population representativeness and also limiting selection bias. The key operational challenge for researchers – successfully addressed by some studies (Abreu et al., 2009) – is to generate large lists of researchers that are either reflective of the whole population, or a random non-biased sample.

SIMILAR INITIATIVES

Unlike the US, where there has been a systematic effort to assess the impact of government policies and legislation (Shane, 2004), and mechanisms and policies implemented by universities to support the commercial exploitation of research results (Becker & Niebuhr, 2010; Allen & O'Shea, 2014), in Europe, both per se and conditional to local context specificities, the effects of universities' interventions are still generally unknown with the notable exception of Italy and, to a lesser extent, Norway and the UK. In the context of our work we will focus our attention on the most complete and extended projects and, therefore, we excluded from our analysis some local initiatives, such as TRIC project (UK) that only examines spin-offs derived from Imperial College scholars, FORNY (Norway) that is mostly a funding mechanism for academic entrepreneurship, and the PROKNOW (EU) that is a strictly academic project with no expected managerial implications and, in this sense, distinct from the previously mentioned projects.

Spinouts UK

Spinouts UK is a project developed by the Young Company Finance, which has collected data on companies created from university spin-offs. The project initially started by collecting data from Scotland, but has gradually expanded to include other territories such as England and more recently the entire UK. The project provides a listing of spinouts and startups from universities and Higher Education Institutions (HEIs) with information about their origins, their activity, their growth, and their current status, providing a regularly updated continuous time series of data. However, only universities listing and companies listing are freely available to the public. In order to get information regarding market sector, company status, and turnover information, the user must have a premium subscription or pay for a database download. This information is provided in a searchable online database and an Excel spreadsheet.

Spinouts UK is the first survey for the whole UK area, to investigate this field of knowledge by taking a cumulative bottom-up approach, compiling data company by company and updating it regularly. The project is now in its sixth year, benefiting from previously cumulative recorded data.

Project TASTE

Project TASTE (Taking Stock: External Engagement by Academics) aimed at offering such information in a structured and longitudinal way (http://www.project-taste.eu). TASTE has been and continues to be carried out within the Department of Management of the University of Bologna (UNIBO). Starting in the year 2000, TASTE systematically collected information on the population of 95 Italian universities, including multilevel-longitudinal data on their personnel, internal policies, departments, patenting and spinout activities, and the characteristics and entrepreneurial support mechanisms of the 20 Italian regions.

TASTE extensively contributed to improving the knowledge of academic entrepreneurship by providing evidence about (a) the social-cognitive determinants of academics' enterprising behaviors; (b) the impact of knowledge-commercialization activities on academics' cognitions and behaviors; and (c) how and to what extent the engagement in knowledge-commercialization activities are changing academic institutions and their constituting logics.

TASTE takes a multilevel approach, structured on three different levels of analysis: 1) Individuals. Relying on a representative sample of Italian academics, it analyses academics' cognitive characteristics and human capital, as well as the depth and breadth of knowledge-commercialization activities in which academics engage in; 2) Organizations. This is meant to characterize the population of Italian academic spin-offs (i.e., firms established to commercialize knowledge developed inside public research institutions), identifying their founding and management teams, as well as assessing their developed technologies and market performances; 3) Academic institutions. It characterizes the Italian public research institutions, analyzing their constituting logics as well as the whole set of mechanisms (e.g., internal policies, technology transfer offices and university incubators) put in place to support knowledge-commercialization activities by academics.

SESTAT

SESTAT (Scientists and Engineers Statistical Data System), initially designated as NCSES, was established in 1993 as a unique source of information on education and employment of the college-educated US science and engineering (S&E) workforce. The platform provides an integrated data system that is a unique source of longitudinal information for the US market. The data available in the platform are collected through biennial surveys: the National Survey of College Graduates (NSCG), the National Survey of Recent College Graduates (NSRCG) that was discontinued after 2010, and the Survey of Doctorate Recipients (SDR).

The NSCG is the core of SESTAT and covers the entire college graduate population residing in the United States. It provides information on individuals educated or employed in S&E fields as well as those educated or employed in non-S&E fields. The SDR further supplements SESTAT with the stock and inflow of US-degreed doctoral level scientists and engineers.

The SESTAT data are available for download through the SESTAT tool, which allows the dynamic generation of information, letting users to generate their own data tables.

Global Entrepreneurship Monitor

The Global Entrepreneurship Monitor (GEM) is one of the most recognized study of entrepreneurship. GEM began in 1999 as a joint project between Babson College (US) and London Business School (UK). The initial aim of this project was to understand why some countries are more "entrepreneurial" than others.

The GEM monitors two areas:

- The Adult Population Survey, which tracks the entrepreneurial attitudes, activities and aspirations of individuals;
- The National Expert Survey, which monitors entrepreneurial framework conditions (e.g., infrastructure, cultural norms, etc.).

GEM includes currently 17 years of data, has data from more than 100 countries and includes more than 300 academic and research institutions. The platform is a wide-scale initiative with large data collection, but not specifically dedicated to academic spin-offs, more targeting entrepreneurial and technology transfer activity, respectively, in general. Besides that, the public data are displayed with some considerable time delay.

APPROACH

Data Structure

The proposed framework has a double educational and knowledge production purpose. From an educational point of view, this framework aims to promote the environment for advanced training, including the support of young researchers pursuing master and doctoral degrees and postdoctoral studies. This will benefit a new generation of young researchers, increase human capital and expand research specific to the topic of academic spin-offs. From a scientific perspective, the application aims to collect data over the course of several years (3 to 5 years) about spin-offs and academic entrepreneurship, which will, on one hand, foster validation and replication efforts of previous research and, on the other hand, will allow the collection of primary data to examine new research questions and address literature gaps.

Figure 1. Conceptual framework of academic entrepreneurship
(Perkmann et al, 2013)

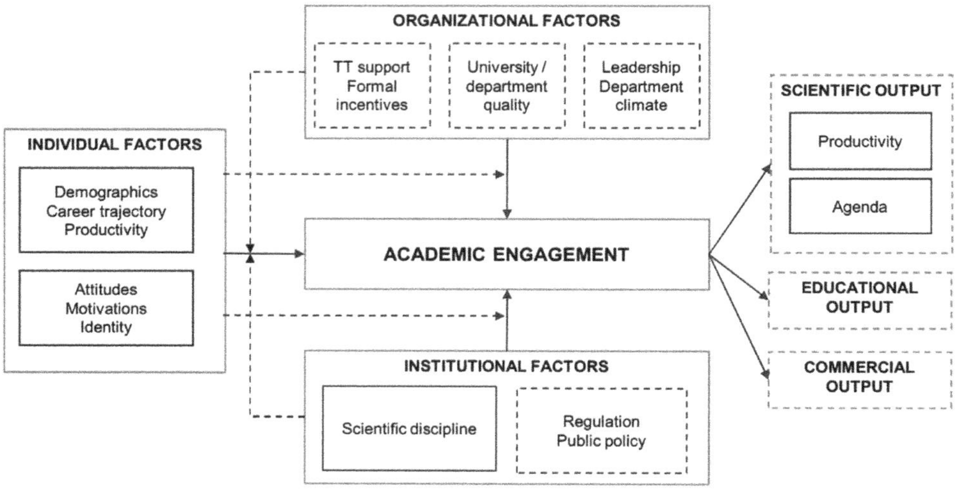

The framework is built on the work performed by Perkmann et al (2013) to map what is known in the literature by now and what which is still lacking a systematic analysis. The authors proposed a conceptual framework (Figure 1) to understand the several antecedents of academic entrepreneurship (individual, organizational and institutional factors) and the main consequences of spin-offs including scientific, educational and commercial outputs.

Individual level factors, including demographic characteristics, career trajectories and psychological features seem to be associated with engaging in academic entrepreneurship. Organizational factors are mid-level variables as characteristics of the University/Department, including peer influence, climate and leadership. In institutional factors two macro-level variables are included: the affiliation to a scientific discipline and the effect of specific national regulations and public policies. Both factors inform academic engagement as they shape the norms and rules relevant for researchers, either because they are official government regulations or because they are the more implicit structural rules of conduct. For Perkmann et al (2013) consequences of academic entrepreneurship engagement were proposed to be scientific outputs, educational outputs and commercial outputs.

Furthermore, we added several factors that have not been contemplated in Perkmann et al (2013) analysis, but which we consider fundamental to better understand the barriers and outputs of university spin-offs. In particular, high-quality educational training (individual factor), departmental team processes (organizational factor), incubation models (organizational factor) and when assessing at the consequences

Figure 2. Corporate actions structure and levels

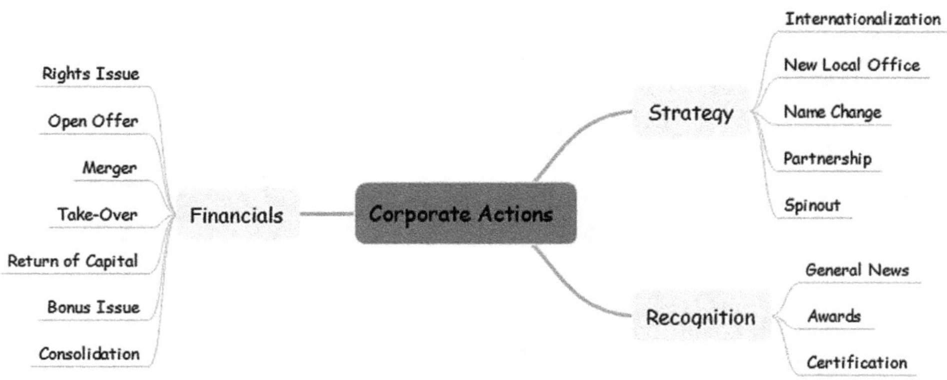

of academic entrepreneurship, we endorse it is critical to evaluate the socioeconomic outputs at the regional and national level where the spin-offs operate. Additionally, we recorded the corporate actions of the company in order to trace the evolutionary path of a company. These corporate actions are aggregated in three levels: financials, strategy and recognition (Figure 2).

Corporate actions were established considering the corporate actions addressed and discussed by Groves (2008) and Parnell (2013). Additionally, we included three corporate actions related to the notoriety of a company in a third category (recognition).

Functional and Non-Functional Requirements

The project is divided into two main modules: *Frontend* and *Backend*. The *Frontend* module only intends to display the content to the public. This means that any user / visitor can freely browse the various Web pages that provide this information. On the other side, the *Backend* module allows the administrator of the platform to perform various maintenance tasks, such as insert and update of new data, export data to an external statistical program, etc. These operations are only available to the platform manager(s), being necessary to perform their authentication in the system for this purpose.

Having regard to the purpose of both modules, a requirements specification analysis was made to determine the set of features (functional requirements) that should be available on the platform. Two of the most important features provided by the platform are the display of data in real time and the graphical analysis of information. A full list of companies is available to the user. More detailed information regarding each company (e.g., institutional address, contact form, founders' information, and

Figure 3. Detailed information and associated events to 3Decide' company

associated events) is also freely provided to the user (Figure 3). There is also a feature that lets the user see statistical data regarding the data available in the database (Figure 4). Besides that, an interactive map of Portugal counting the number of companies by district is also given. This information is always provided to the user in real time.

The application should also attend some non-functional requirements, such as usability, portability (support for mobile devices), performance, maintenance (easy to add new features), and interoperability (API to import financial data from external agencies, API to export views from multiple tables, API to export data to CSV files).

Figure 4. Statistical information regarding the number of spin-offs created by year

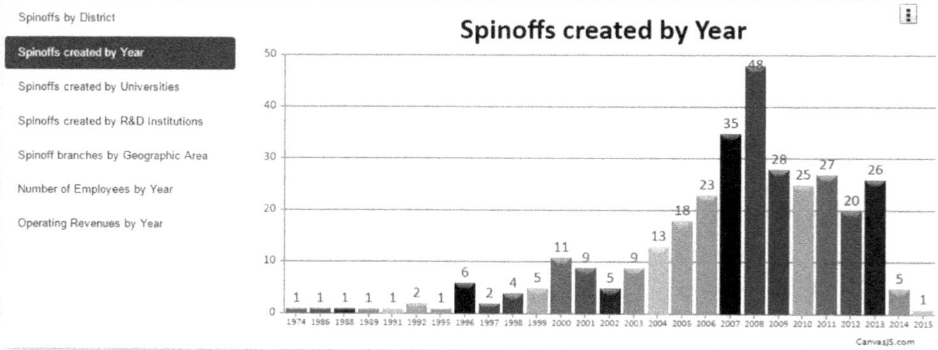

Technological Architecture

The proposed framework is based exclusively on open source technologies and adopts a multi-layer architecture composed of three levels (presentation, business and data). This model is designed to take into account the flexibility and reuse of modules, facilitating code change process and avoid total rewrite of the application whenever the adjustment of any component or the introduction of new functionalities required.

The presentation layer is responsible to present the user interface. It is implemented using the HTML, JavaScript and CSS. Whenever possible, this layer avoids processing data, since this task is responsible for the business layer.

The business layer, also known as logical layer, is responsible for processing data received so as to send to the database. In this layer, PHP implemented services are invoiced, allowing that processing is done on the server side. This approach avoids the use of device intensive resources, which particularly important for mobile devices that typically have lesser processing capacity.

Finally, the data layer, is responsible to store all the required information for the project. In addition to the respective information itself, it also incorporates a management system that will allow access to the records, defining what services will be available for this purpose.

The connection between the data layer and business layer is ensured by a sub-layer called the Data Access Layer (DAL), which is responsible for the establishment of a connection between the available services to perform the required queries and insert/update of records. In its turn, the presentation layer, which builds the structure (layout) of the pages that the users can access, should be implemented taking into account the use of a responsive design approach, in order to cover the largest possible number of heterogeneous devices and equipments. This approach also lets that the display space (viewport) will be automatically established, without requiring dependence of different implementation for each case in order to standardize the code.

The Figure 5 represents a deployment diagram, which lets to visualize how the several layers and components are related and interconnect between them.

DISCUSSION AND PERSPECTIVES FOR ANALYSIS

The repository is organized in 21 relational tables with around 5MB in total. The database records information regarding 416 university spin-offs. 67,5% of the university spin-offs are located in the three more populated Portuguese districts (Porto, Coimbra and Lisbon). Table 2 shows the number of attributes, records and size of the core tables of the system.

Figure 5. Logical architecture of the application

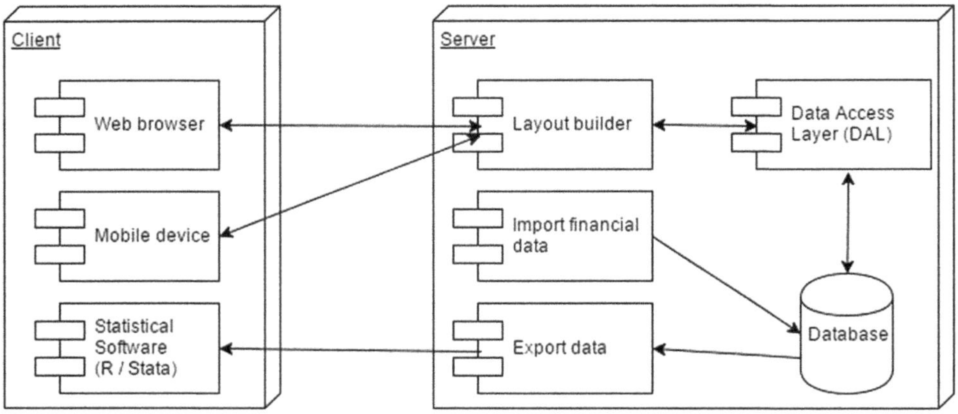

Next we discuss the information recorded regarding the four dimensions of the proposed framework. Additionally, we will look how the recorded information could help to improve the knowledge and open issues regarding university spin-offs for each dimension.

Individual Factors

A fundamental table in the repository is "Founder", which is responsible to store information regarding the founder's name and his/her nationality. A spin-off may have one or more associated founders. For each founder we collect information about his/her fiscal tax number, social security number, date of birth, professional experience and academic degree. In order to perform longitudinal studies, we store the start date and end date of each activity perform by the founders. On the other side, for each academic degree achieved by founders, we store the name of associated institution and

Table 2. Organization of the core tables

Table	No. of Attributes	No. of Records	Size
Spin-off	21	416	576kb
Institution	7	116	128kb
Founder	6	372	142kb
Sector	3	69	96kb
Location	4	30	92kb
Account	14	3390	700kb

the year of the conclusion. Finally, for each founder we store information regarding the top skills acquired along its professional and academic path.

There are essentially three open issues regarding the individual dimension:

- Age has been shown to have mixed effects; some studies find a positive relationship, while others find a negative relationship or no relationship at all. The negative impact of age found by some studies may reflect a training effect: individuals who were trained in earlier periods when universities' engagement with industry was less relevant or even discouraged, may be attached to norms not compatible with collaboration with private companies (Bercovitz and Feldman, 2008). The existence of information since more than 20 years will let us understand how the behavior of age had a positive or negative impact in the establishment of new academic spin-offs in Portugal. This also will let us understand if this path in recent years is different from more older years;
- Evidence presented by research on the attitudinal and motivational aspects of both academic engagement and commercialization is very slim. There is some evidence about the attitudes of US academic researchers towards 'university entrepreneurship'. Most members of the faculty were in favor of transfer activities, but objected to the most radical forms of commercialization such as start-up assistance to new technology firms, and equity investment by universities. Few other studies show that academic engagement tends to be viewed by academics as a natural extension of publication-driven 'open science', while commercialization is seen as a distinct type of activity. In order to understand this situation we need to combine information from individual and organizational dimensions. It would be relevant to analyze the differences between the number of spin-offs founded by each university and understand why it happens. The information available in the repository isn't complete to understand completely this situation, and it should be complemented by a qualitative study that let us understand the vision and motivation of the academic staff from each institution;
- Research critically needs to differentiate between having a motivation to engage in spin-offs versus having the ability to do it, in particular having the skills and competences at a global managerial level to successfully undertake this enterprise. The role of expertise and competence of academic entrepreneurs has been severely neglected in the literature and it is likely as a strong barrier to both engaging with and maintaining sustainable spin-offs. Therefore, our framework proposes to investigate how professional experience, academic path and skills of the founders have an impact on the process of gave more competencies to the founders of university spin-offs.

Organizational Factors

Information regarding organizational factors is mainly in our framework collected looking to the home institution of each university spin-off. In order to differentiate each home institution, we divided it into three groups: universities, polytechnic institutions and R&D centers. We don't make any difference between public and private institutions. Associated to each institution, we have information regarding its location.

The open issues associated with organizational dimensions are essentially:

- Research about organizational factors has been mostly restricted to the impact of TTOs and other facilitators of knowledge transfer. Nevertheless, mid-level factors at the departmental (team) level and University organizational culture has been overlooked as promoting vs. inhibiting spin-offs development. In order to address this issue we collected information regarding the faculty and department. This will let us to collect quantitative information regarding mid-level factors;
- There is no consensus in literature about the relevance of academic participation in the shareholding structure of a spin-off. Therefore, it would be relevant to understanding if a more academic engagement and connection between the spin-off and home institution have a positive impact on the outcomes of the spin-off.

Institutional Factors

In order to understand the physical environmental conditions of the territory we record information regarding the location of each university spin-off. For that, we store the NUTS classification of Portuguese territory: NUTS 2 that contains basic regions for the application of regional policies; and NUTS 3 that has small regions for specific diagnoses. Additionally, we also store information regarding the districts of Portugal that will allow us to create the dynamic map of Portugal organized by each district. Furthermore, we record information regarding each technological park in Portugal (TTO and its location).

There are essentially two open issues regarding the institutional dimension:

- In social sciences, knowledge seems to be transferred through personal contacts and labor mobility. The conceptions about and concrete actions towards academic entrepreneurship in social sciences remain unexamined. In our framework we propose to analyze this issue by looking to the professional, academic and top skills acquired by spin-off founders;

- Studies conducted by Sanni et al. (2009) and Moudi & Hajihosseini (2011) found that technological parks have a positive impact in the early phases of a spin-off company. However, it is not clear how much is this impact compared to others spin-off and what is the importance the physical distance between science parks and home institutions. The information about the location of each spin-off, technological park and institution will help us to understand this research question;
- In terms of the role of national policies, comparative empirical evidence is limited. Most studies focus on North American and European countries, including the UK, Spain, Germany and Sweden while little is known about other geographical contexts. Research on academic engagement has rarely addressed the role of institutional environments and national policies, partly because it has enjoyed less attention from policy-makers than commercialization. Currently, the repository doesn't provide data about national policies, but in future we intend to perform comparative analysis between different European countries.

Scientific, Educational and Commercial Outputs

"Spin-off" table is a central point for the analysis of outputs from each university spin-off. In this table, we store basic institutional information regarding each spin-off such as designation and contact forms. Besides that, we store information about incorporation date, extinction date (if applied), shareholders structure, number and location of branches, capital stock and legal form. There is also a very important field that is used only for visualization purposes that is responsible to store the last update date. This lets the visits of our platform to know when the information of each spin-off was updated. Another central table in our model is the "Accounts". This table is responsible to look for the financial outcomes of each spin-off. There we store information about cash flows, total assets, EBITDA, costs of employees and financial ratios (ROE, ROCE, ROA, etc.) for each available year. Finally, the table "Events" stores relevant news about the path of a spin-off in terms of financial outcomes, strategy dimension and recognition notices.

There are several open issues that look to the consequences of academic entrepreneurship:

- The impact of academics' engagement with industry on teaching is not clear and the question has not been addressed in the literature. The only exception is Lin and Bozeman (2006), who observe that academics with industry exposure support more students. Our framework doesn't provide direct data on this issue, but let us to identify the number of academics that are simultaneously founders of university spin-offs. This will let us analyze if academics from those universities encourage their students to open their own start-up businesses;

- There is no consistent empirical evidence about the economic and market performance of academic spin-offs or the extent to which academic spin-offs improve the human capital pool of the regions and countries in which they operate. In our framework the information collected in "Accounts" table will let us analyze the financial outputs of each company organized by location (NUTS) and district. This information can also be compared with institutional data about the financial performance of each region;
- It would be important to analyze the role of spin-offs in Portuguese exports and in attracting new investments in Portugal. For that, the "Accounts" table stores a percentage value of incomes obtained by spin-offs in international market. Additionally, we intend to understand if there is a positive correlation between the emergence of new spin-offs and attraction of foreign capital inflows in Portugal;
- The analysis of the university spin-offs contributions for the employment rate of each region is another factor to be analyzed. There are already some studies (Müller, 2006; Rodeiro et al., 2012) that analyze the relationship between human capital and the success rate of spin-off, but there is a lack of more detailed studies to assess if the existence of spin-offs in a given region allow to capture young people to develop a local career away from major urban centers;
- Studies conducted by Jackson (2013) and Piterou & Birch (2014) demonstrated the role of internships in building employability and entrepreneurship skills. Therefore, it would be important to measure if this impact will be more relevant in big companies, government agencies, SMEs or spin-offs companies;
- It would be important to study the impact of the current economic crisis in Europe, and corresponding austerity policies, had in terms of creation and closure of university spin-offs. In order to respond to this research question we have two fields: incorporated date (which is mandatory) and extinction date that will be filled when a spin-off gets out of the market.

FUTURE RESEARCH DIRECTIONS

The study of university spin-offs is an emerging area in the business and management fields. This is a research area that offers immense potential, since university quality indicators refer to the technology transfer as one of the most important elements to assess the scientific quality of a higher education institution.

In this sense, there is a need to deepen the research on the support policies that could be applied to encourage the appearance of new university spin-offs. However, it is not enough to support the launch of new business, but also to ensure a set of support mechanisms throughout the various phases of the business. It is also important to study what kind of link should exist between universities and university spin-offs, since it is desired that these companies have a link with the mother institution, but it is also fundamental to enable them to grow autonomously in the global market.

Finally, another topic that needs to be explored in order to explore the challenges and difficulties of university spin-offs is to perform a comparative analysis among several countries. It is important to know what support measures are taken by various governments and local institutions, so that these good practices, with the appropriate adaptations, could be applied in other contexts.

CONCLUSION

University spin-offs are important elements in the knowledge-based economy by offering a potential for economic growth, generation of new jobs and increase the interconnection and relationship between industry and the academy. Our proposed framework for Longitudinal Analysis of University Spin-offs intends to offer an excellence tool for researchers and policy makers in order to understand the dynamics of university spin-offs creation, organization and development path.

The framework is technically implemented as a repository using exclusively open source technologies. It was developed a descriptive and a longitudinal database of spin-offs initiatives in Portugal that offers a public front-end interface that allows users to search information regarding each spin-off organized per university and per region; and private back-end that allows the inclusion, update and exportation of data. This framework will allow researchers to examine the generalizability of the main results about individual, organizational and institutional antecedents of academic entrepreneurship in the Portuguese context. Additionally, this tool can be used by universities themselves, public authorities and governments, which will help them to launch new projects and adapt current processes that will support those companies to become more competitive in the market.

As future work we plan to include the adoption of external available APIs that could help us to receive automatic data about the founders, financial and events, decreasing the human effort associated to its maintenance. Furthermore, we plan the adoption of semantic Web technologies combined with big data tools that could help to detect new association patterns between spin-offs, founders and institutions.

REFERENCES

Abreu, M., Grinevich, M., Hughes, A., & Kitson, M. (2009). *Knowledge Exchange between Academics and the Business, Public and Third Sectors*. Centre for Business Research and UK~IRC, University of Cambridge. Retrieved July 19, 2016, from http://www.cbr.cam.ac.uk/pdf/AcademicSurveyReport.pdf

Allen, T., & O'Shea, R. (2014). *Building Technology Transfer within Research Universities: An Entrepreneurial Approach*. Cambridge, UK: Cambridge University Press. doi:10.1017/CBO9781139046930

Baldini, N., Fini, R., Grimaldi, R., & Sobrero, M. (2014). Organisational Change and the Institutionalisation of University Patenting Activity in Italy. *Minerva*, *52*(1), 27–53. doi:10.100711024-013-9243-9

Becker, S., & Niebuhr, R. (2010). *Cases in Technology Innovation: Entrepreneurial Successes and Pitfalls*. Hershey, PA: Business Science Reference. doi:10.4018/978-1-61520-609-4

Bercovitz, J., & Feldman, M. (2008). Academic entrepreneurs: Organizational change at the individual level. *Organization Science*, *19*(1), 69–89. doi:10.1287/orsc.1070.0295

Blumenthal, D., Campbell, E., Anderson, M, Causino, N., & Louis, K. (1997). Withholding research results in academic life science - evidence from a national survey of faculty. *Jama-Journal of the American Medical Association*, *277*(15), 1224-1228.

Bonaccorsi, A., Colombo, M., Guerini, M., & Rossi-Lamastra, C. (2014). The impact of local and external university knowledge on the creation of knowledge-intensive firms: Evidence from the Italian case. *Small Business Economics*, *43*(2), 261–287. doi:10.100711187-013-9536-2

Borges, C., & Filion, L. (2013). Spin-off Process and the Development of Academic Entrepreneur's Social Capital. *Journal of Technology Management & Innovation*, *8*(1), 21–34. doi:10.4067/S0718-27242013000100003

Carot, J., Carrión, A., Hämäläinen, K., Pausits, A., Marhl, M., Soeiro, A., . . . Vidal, J. (2012). *Needs and constraints analysis of the three dimensions of third mission activities. European Indicators and Ranking Methodology for University Third Mission (E3M)*. Retrieved June 21, 2016, from http://e3mproject.eu/Three-dim-third-mission-act.pdf

Chapple, W., Lockett, A., Siegel, D., & Wright, M. (2005). Assessing the relative performance of U.K. university technology transfer offices: Parametric and non-parametric evidence. *Research Policy*, *34*(3), 369–384. doi:10.1016/j.respol.2005.01.007

Clarysse, B., Tartari, V., & Salter, A. (2011). The impact of entrepreneurial capacity, experience and organizational support on academic entrepreneurship. *Research Policy*, *40*(8), 1084–1093. doi:10.1016/j.respol.2011.05.010

Fini, R., Grimaldi, R., Santoni, S., & Sobrero, M. (2011). Complements or substitutes? The role of universities and local context in supporting the creation of academic spin-offs. *Research Policy*, *40*(8), 1113–1127. doi:10.1016/j.respol.2011.05.013

Fitzmaurice, G., Laird, N., & Ware, J. (2011). *Applied Longitudinal Analysis*. Wiley. doi:10.1002/9781119513469

Fryges, H., & Wright, M. (2014). The origin of spin-offs: A typology of corporate and academic spin-offs. *Small Business Economics*, *43*(2), 245–259. doi:10.100711187-013-9535-3

Groves, F. (2008). *Corporate Actions - A Concise Guide: An introduction to securities events*. Petersfield: Harriman House.

Huyghe, A., Knockaert, M., Wright, M., & Piva, E. (2014). Technology transfer offices as boundary spanners in the pre-spin-off process: The case of a hybrid model. *Small Business Economics*, *43*(2), 289–307. doi:10.100711187-013-9537-1

Jackson, D. (2013). Student Perceptions of the Importance of Employability Skill Provision in Business Undergraduate Programs. *Journal of Education for Business*, *88*(5), 271–279. doi:10.1080/08832323.2012.697928

Jain, S., George, G., & Maltarich, M. (2009). Academics or entrepreneurs? Investigating role identity modification of university scientists involved in commercialization activity. *Research Policy*, *38*(6), 922–935. doi:10.1016/j.respol.2009.02.007

Kenney, M., & Goe, W. (2004). The role of social embeddedness in professorial entrepreneurship: A comparison of electrical engineering and computer science at UC Berkeley and Stanford. *Research Policy*, *33*(5), 691–707. doi:10.1016/j.respol.2003.11.001

Lejpras, A., & Stephan, A. (2011). Locational Conditions, Cooperation, and Innovativeness: Evidence from Research and Company Spin-Offs. *The Annals of Regional Science*, *46*(3), 543–575. doi:10.100700168-009-0356-x

Libaers, D., Meyer, M., & Geuna, A. (2006). The role of university spinout companies in an emerging technology: The case of nanotechnology. *The Journal of Technology Transfer*, *31*(4), 443–450. doi:10.100710961-006-0005-9

Markman, G., Phan, P., Balkin, D., & Gianiodis, P. (2005). Entrepreneurship and university-based technology transfer. *Journal of Business Venturing*, *20*(2), 241–263. doi:10.1016/j.jbusvent.2003.12.003

Moudi, M., & Hajihosseini, H. (2011). Science and Technology Parks, Tools for a Leap into Future. *Interdisciplinary Journal of Contemporary Research in Business*, *3*(8), 1168–1176.

Müller, B. (2006). *Human capital and Success Academic Spin-off*. Retrieved July 12, 2016, from ftp://ftp.zew.de/pub/zew-docs/dp/dp06081.pdf

Muller, K. (2010). Academic spin-offs transfer speed: Analyzing the time from leaving university to venture. *Research Policy*, *39*(2), 189–199. doi:10.1016/j.respol.2009.12.001

Mustar, P., Wright, M., & Clarysse, B. (2008). University spin-off firms: Lessons from ten years of experience in Europe. *Science & Public Policy*, *35*(2), 67–80. doi:10.3152/030234208X282862

Parnell, J. (2013). *Strategic Management: Theory and Practice*. New York: Sage Publications.

Pattnaik, P., & Pandey, S. (2014). University Spinoffs: What, Why, and How? *Technology Innovation Management Review*, *12*, 44–50. doi:10.22215/timreview/857

Perkmann, M., Tartari, V., McKelvey, M., Autio, E., Broström, A., D'Este, P., & Sobrero, M. (2013). Academic engagement and commercialisation: A review of the literature on university–industry relations. *Research Policy*, *42*(2), 423–442. doi:10.1016/j.respol.2012.09.007

Piterou, A., & Birch, C. (2014). The role of Higher Education Institutions in supporting innovation in SMEs: University-based incubators and student internships as knowledge transfer tools. InImpact. *The Journal of Innovation Impact*, *7*(1), 72–79.

Rasmussen, E., Mosey, S., & Wright, M. (2011). The Evolution of Entrepreneurial Competencies: A Longitudinal Study of University Spin-Off Venture Emergence. *Journal of Management Studies*, *48*(6), 1314–1345. doi:10.1111/j.1467-6486.2010.00995.x

Rasmussen, E., Mosey, S., & Wright, M. (2014). The influence of university departments on the evolution of entrepreneurial competencies in spin-off ventures. *Research Policy*, *43*(1), 92–106. doi:10.1016/j.respol.2013.06.007

Rasmussen, E., & Wright, M. (2015). How can universities facilitate academic spin-offs? An entrepreneurial competency perspective. *The Journal of Technology Transfer*, *40*(5), 782–799. doi:10.100710961-014-9386-3

Reichenfeld, L. (2010). The Barriers to Academic Engagement with Enterprise: A Social Scientist's Perspective. In R. Howlett (Ed.), *Innovation through Knowledge Transfer 2010* (pp. 163–176). New York: Springer.

Rodeiro, D., Calvo, N., & Fernández, S. (2012). Opportunities for Managing Human Capital in University Spin-offs: A dynamic analysis. *Universities and Knowledge Society Journal*, *9*(2), 329–346.

Rothaermel, F., Agung, S., & Jian, L. (2007). University entrepreneurship: A taxonomy of the literature. *Industrial and Corporate Change*, *16*(4), 691–791. doi:10.1093/icc/dtm023

Sanni, M., Egbetokun, A., & Siyanbola, W. (2009). A Model for the Design and Development of a Science and Technology Park in Developing Countries. *International Journal of Management and Enterprise Development*, *8*(1), 62–81. doi:10.1504/IJMED.2010.029761

Shane, S. (2004). *Academic Entrepreneurship: University Spinoffs And Wealth Creation*. Cheltenham, UK: Edward Elgar Publishing. doi:10.4337/9781843769828

Shinn, T., & Lamy, E. (2006). Paths of commercial knowledge: Forms and consequences of university enterprise synergy in scientist-sponsored firms. *Research Policy*, *35*(10), 1465–1476. doi:10.1016/j.respol.2006.09.024

Siegel, D., Waldman, D., Atwater, L., & Link, A. (2004). Toward a model of the effective transfer of scientific knowledge from academicians to practitioners: Qualitative evidence from the commercialization of university technologies. *Journal of Engineering and Technology Management*, *21*(1-2), 115–142. doi:10.1016/j.jengtecman.2003.12.006

Stephan, A. (2014). Are public research spin-offs more innovative? *Small Business Economics*, *43*(2), 353–368. doi:10.100711187-013-9539-z

Stuart, T., & Ding, W. (2006). When do scientists become entrepreneurs? The social structural antecedents of commercial activity in the academic life sciences. *American Journal of Sociology*, *112*(1), 97–144. doi:10.1086/502691 PMID:17526160

Van Looy, B., Landoni, P., Callaert, J., Van Pottelsberghe, B., Sapsalis, E., & Debackere, K. (2011). Entrepreneurial effectiveness of European universities: An empirical assessment of antecedents and trade-offs. *Research Policy*, *40*(4), 553–564. doi:10.1016/j.respol.2011.02.001

Wright, M., Clarysse, B., Mustar, P., & Lockett, A. (2007). *Academic Entrepreneurship in Europe*. Cheltenham, UK: Edward Elgar Publishing. doi:10.4337/9781847205575

KEY TERMS AND DEFINITIONS

Application Programming Interface (API): Routines developed to allow two software programs to communicate with each other.

Big Data: Very large sets of data that can only be stored, used, and analyzed with the help of technological tools and methods.

Cascade Style Sheets (CSS): Language used to define the presentation of web pages built with markup language, such as hypertext markup language (HTML).

Comma-Separated Values (CSV): Comma separated values file which allows data to be saved in a table structured format.

Earnings Before Interest, Taxes, Depreciation, and Amortization (EBITDA): Financial indicator that represents how much a company generates of resources through its operational activities.

JavaScript: Client-side programming language. It is used to control HTML and CSS, in order to implement dynamic behaviors on the page.

PHP: Programming language widely used for Web development that can be embedded within HTML.

Return on Assets (ROA): An indicator that measures how profitable a company is relative to its total assets.

Return on Capital Employed (ROCE): Financial ratio that measures a company's profitability and the efficiency with which its capital is employed.

Return on Equity (ROE): Represents the amount of net income returned as a percentage of shareholders equity.

Technology Transfer Offices (TTOs): Technology transfer center or unit offered by a higher education institution that is established to facilitate the commercialization of the university's scientific and technical research findings for the benefit of the community.

User Interface: Represents the user interaction layer, that is, everything that is visually perceptible on some platform and leads the user to a positive interaction.

Chapter 2
Coupling of Economic Development and Technology Diffusion for Inclusive Growth to Meet the Challenge of Technology Implementation in Perspective

Nirmalendunath Ghosh
Independent Researcher, Kolkata, India

ABSTRACT

The chapter is devoted to clearly analyze economic development in the country that will usher economic growth in all goods and services to benefit all people for inclusive growth. The discussion justifies the concept by logical reasonings that technology acts as catalyst in accelerating economic development. A model has been shown to link technology, infrastructural development, and economic development with a mathematical model that establish a relationship between per capita income, capital investment, labor, and economic growth. For this purpose, economic resources and infrastructure development have been discussed with logical sequence by exemplifying the economic status of different states in respect of energy sector which is the main driving force of the economic development. Finally, strategy for implementation of technology diffusion in the system has been developed to meet the challenge of coupling technology with economic development.

DOI: 10.4018/978-1-5225-5412-7.ch002

INTRODUCTION

The present population in India of 1.21 billion (Census India, 2011) is increasing at 2.3. %,(Average), in 2050, the total population in India will reach around 2billion. It is a challenging task to meet the growing demand of the food and shelter requirement for this growing population, in addition to this, other basic necessity for energy, education, health care, communication and transport across the country need be looked into. Economic development is necessary in order to meet the requirement of the population for better standard of living, economic growth in country implies better standard of living by increasing productivity in economic resources with development of infrastructure Economic resources are industrial and agricultural sector that provide employment and generate income of the population. Economic growth at 7.8% was pegged at Indian economy during 2016 ("NCAER", 2016). But Income of people across the population is not equal that varies interstate and intrastate across the country that is barrier to reach benefit of economic growth to all in rural and urban area. This difference in income per capita across the country is attributed to non uniformity in infrastructural development and productivity of industrial and agricultural sectors. The non-uniformity of economic development in vertical and horizontal level of the society is manifested by inequality of income, educational level, health benefits and communication services. There is considerable disparity in access to benefit of services because of difference in purchasing power of the population across the country interstate and intrastate. Since 1991, trade liberalization, the impact of economic development in global economy on the economic scenario in India is manifested by application of information and communication technology and massive computerization of different administrative, financial and business activities. It is obvious fact that economic growth becomes stagnant when the infrastructural capacity augmentation is stopped. The quality, production capacity and time of any work can be efficiently improved by application of technology. Therefore, economic development in India need technology application in functioning of economic resources and other social dimensions. Technology diffusion in the process of economic development act as catalyst to increase production, reduce cost of production, increase supply chain activity for employment generation to boost up income inter alia purchasing power of population. The infrastructure growth along with economic growth needs a concurrent effort consistently in order to meet basic services to all across the country. Thus the strategy invigorate the dual activity of maintaining flow of hard and soft technology to support supply of commodity and simultaneously increasing purchasing power capacity by agricultural work and self help programme. Economic resources are agriculture, industrial and service sector that are supported by energy and communication and transport infrastructures. There is linkage between supporting services with development of economic resources which are changing with new development of technology. Simultaneously the economic resources need be actuated to operate in the changed technological environment. This technology change is adapted in the growth of economic resources in order to maintain sustainability of growth as well as to increase growth of production within the limit of existing resources. But it is necessary to keep in mind that sustainability of resources principle will not at all compromise with environmental regulation.

BACKGROUND

Purpose

The chapter is devoted to analyze inclusive growth of economic development by technology application, and then derive the ways to meet the challenges for implementation of technology infusion in the system. The major challenge to implement technology is the environment of the specific locality of application. The environment encompasses the political, regulatory framework, the behavior of the people who are targeted to be beneficiary of technology based development and the socio-economic status of population. The chapter addresses these issues in respect of technology application in economic resources of agriculture and industry associated with technology change in infrastructure consisting of different dimensions of energy, communication and road. The objective of this study may further be explained by ascertaining how technology adoption can change the way of growth in production of economic resources, equitable distribution of services and products, effective communication and knowledge dissemination in order to spread the benefit of development within the reach of all people. The purpose of this study is to ascertain economical utilization of resources for production by application of technology, because loss factor in the resources need be minimized for efficient transformation of input resources into output product. Therefore, the purpose is to know about selecting right technology at least cost at right time that will assure best quality of resources, the efficient processing mechanism and efficient transformation into final product to carry out efficient distribution within affordable price to reach all people .

Analysis Outline

The study in this chapter emphasizes on analysis about core issue of economic development which is infrastructural development. It is obvious that Technology application and infrastructure development is correlated. Therefore, analysis must be directed to know how infrastructure development is possible. First and foremost essentiality in analysis is to know the catalyst of accelerating the growth of development. Thus analysis has focused on application of technology in energy sector explaining in detail supply, demand and losses which is controlled by technology application, because energy is driving force for all the economic sources that need be sustainable as well as reliable for uninterrupted supply of electricity. The study also looked into acceptability criterion among the people, how to negotiate with the people, what are common issues of obstruction in implementation, how to overcome such constraints. The growth of economic resources is depended on infrastructural development across the country. It is obvious that Technology application and infrastructural development is correlated. The technology deployment specific to infrastructural development work is decision making strategy in management. There are several options of available technology for connectivity issues, in the case of electricity generation, transmission and distribution, communication, education and health sector, the emerging technology that appear to be more compatible with existing system now is likely to change in the future which may create problem of obsolescent of the existing infrastructure affecting efficiency of the system operation and financial status. So, analysis is focused on effectiveness of vision for application of technology. How Infrastructural development reduces poverty and impact of technology on jobs and better living facilitates is the pertinent issue of this analysis. The study is also directed to identify pattern of energy utilization by assessment of end use and productivity, supply efficiency and fuel mix (World Energy Council, n.d.) and which are basic input to industrial and agricultural development, then focused on the issue of resources flow to underdeveloped area. Next case studies of west Bengal and Maharashtra has been studied. The economic development in the states of Maharashstra is assessed on the basis of the report of Human Development Indicator report (Maharashtra Human Development Report, 2012), Year wise development index is then compared with the technology application index [technology application/HD and inclusive growth ***indicator[16]It has been observed that flow of resources to the rural areas are restricted due to lack of basic infrastructures like electricity, transport and communication and irrigation facilities .Thus the study resort to find out whether the economic development in these states is technology deprived and what is the characteristics of management. There is basic notion that privatization of organization will benefit the system in terms of more capital flow and technology related knowledge propagation. This study attempt to evaluate whether this notion is justified by case study whether the economic development is inclusive in these states is enumerated by analysis of the economic indicators like energy consumption per capita income, energy intensity (ratio of energy consumptions per GDP and the access to basic services, literacy and crop intensity, food consumption per capita, internet, mobile and telephone facilities

Dimensions and Indicator

First of all, the analysis is directed to find out whether existing socio-economic status in macro and micro level is adequate to cater benefit of the economic development equally reaching to all. For this purpose, indicator of inclusive growth has been assessed as well as access to benefit of services (Ghosh,2012). Therefore, the study begins from the findings of the prior work to identify the states where access to benefit of services is above or below normal. Access to basic services is defined as the ratio of Purchasing Power (p1) of consumer at prices according to their income and the actual demand of services of the consumer in existing market price (p2). Therefore,

1. 1. Indicator for Inequality, Access to Basic Services (abs)

Abs = p1/p2 0 < p1/p2< 1

It has been observed that there is difference in abs between rural and urban population and differences in between lower income docile and upper income docile. Some state like Gujrat, AP, Karnatak and Tamilnadu have abs near 1 whereas Jharkhand, Odissa, UP states have abs near 0 (Ghosh 2012)

2. Human Development Indicator (HDI)

This is actually developed by UNDP that relates three dimensions education, health and income in Human Development Indices(HDI), 0 <HDI < 1.low rate of development is near zero and perfect human development is 1(Maharashtra Human Development Report, 2012)

3. State Gross Domestic Product (SGDP)

The economic indicator is SGDP; the ratio of SGDP of a state to all India GDP will express the economic development achievement

4. Per Capita Income

per capita income across the country is different that depends on the economic growth of agricultural and industrial productivity There is inequality of income per capita interstate and intrastate depending on educational attainments, specialization in specific vocation and skill. Therefore, income of people without any specialized knowledge or skill will be much lower than a person with skill and knowledge by education. The education of higher learning or professional qualification will remain out of reach of lower income group people and income per capita will remain in equal. ("Planning Commission", 2012-2017)

5. Monthly Per Capita Expenditure (MPCE)

There is inequality in MPCE between rural and urban area as well as in horizontal level because of disproportionate availability of income through economic resources, i.e, agriculture and industrial development. [MOSPI]

6. Energy Intensity

It is ratio of energy consumption to SGDP, this indicator represent the growth of electricity in a state that drive the economy of the state [Govt. of India web portal]

7. HH Electrification

This indicator actually indicate the progress of electricity distribution in a state, electrification of HH will improve education of people and literacy

The study then take account of the NSDP at current prices statistics [15] to observe the relative change of NSDP value of the states with the All India value of NNI. Besides, the statistics on per capita district domestic product (DDP) is an indicator of income generating employment status of the states. Purchasing power of the population is correlated to NNI and the actual demand of basic services is relative to the growth of DDP per capita in the surrounding region of the area. That method of analysis then corroborated with Human Development Indicator report [4] which justify the choice of the states UP and Orissa, Maharashtra and west Bengal for case study

Evidence based study on this topic rests on analysis of socio- economic data in respect of the states UP and Orissa which are marked as poverty driven economy states in India [2],[3], The data has been compiled from MOSPI [9]and Government of India directory Web Portal (n.d.)[1].

MAIN FOCUS OF THE CHAPTER

Model of Economic Growth

Economic growth = growth of productivity

= Qt2 - Qt1

Where Q is productivity of economic resources i.e, industry and agriculture and services

Q t2 is productivity at time t2 and Qt1 is productivity at time t1

If efficiency of production system at time t1 is ή1 and efficiency of productivity at time t2 is ή 2, then

Economic growth = ' ή 2t1 - ' ή 2 t1

= ' ή 2[C2 +L2] -' ή 2[C1+L1] ... (1)

If economic growth is represented by am, then

X (m2-m1) = ' ή 2eta'2[C2 +L2] -' ή 2eta1'[C1+L1]

Or x = ' ή 2[C2 +L2] - ή 2[C1+L1] / (m2-m1) ... ... (2)

When economic growth in country is fully in consistence with access to benefit of services, where access to benefit of services is defined as the ratio of actual consumption by the population to actual demand of services, then it is assumed that benefit of economic growth has reached to all. Actual consumption of services is presented by p1*Q and actual demand of services is represented by p2*Q

Here p1 is price that can be afforded by people to pay for services Q and p2 is price of service for full requirement of the desired service by the people. Then,

X (m2-m1) = p1/p2 ... (3)

Or

x = ψ.p2 {' ή [C2+L2] - ' ή t0 [C1+L1] / P1 (m2-m1) ... ... (4)

Now differentiating rate of change of income per capita with variable p and p2 to know about change in economic growth

∂m / '$\partial p1 \partial p2 = p2\psi/p1$ [(z2) - (z1)]

$=1/p1 - p2/p1^2$

$=1/p1$ [1 -p2/p1]

At maximum growth situation $\partial m / \partial p1 \partial p2 = 0$

p1=/= 0, so p2 / p1 =1

Or

p2 =p1

Substituting in eq. (3)

$x = \psi$. {' ή t1 [C2+L2] - ή t0 [C1+L1]} / (m2-m1) .... (5)

Eq. (5) implies as the differences in income per capita reduce, economic growth increases. The mathematical model signify that technology as represented by ή t2 and ή t1 will have relation

ή2 > ή1

Or, it can be interpreted as technology factor increase at time t2 will have greater impact on economic growth, thus economic development is coupled with technology implementation in the system.

ISSUES, CONTROVERSIES, PROBLEMS

Technology, Economic Development and Employment

Economic development is coupled with technology change in the system. Economic resources productivity growth is linked with economic development. According to the mathematical model, the linkage between economic growth and technology is expressed as x =' ψ... {ή2t [C2+L2] - ή1't0 [C1+L1]} / (m2-m1)

Efficiency ή is taken as proxy to technology factor, because technology change always improve cost of production, reduces time of operation and enhances quality of product. Therefore, rearranging the eq.,the relation between labor status and technology diffusion effect can be explained

'ήt0 = x (m2 -m1) /'psi'*[C1+L1]

As ' ήt0 ----> ήt2; C+L -----> > C2+l2

m2 > m1

This relation between technology, economy growth and capital labor implies job opportunity will decrease with more technology change, because of diminishing value of capital and labor in denominator, but difference between per capita income before and after technology change will increase. The Job will require more technically skilled person to operate new technology driven hardware or more intelligent staff to perform more demanding complex function of system. However, existing routine type of job opportunities will be replaced by technology based jobs. Capital investment (C) will tend to reduce because of cost reduction. Automation, information and communication technology application in the system need more training of personnel and knowledge disseminations through workshop, seminar and tutorials of the organization in related work. Foreign Direct Investment has opened the scope of knowledge transfer through import of software and hardware in the system. Since technology improve the productivity, it will be necessary to monitor performance of the system to ascertain rate of growth with input of capital and labour. If economic growth of economic resources remain stagnant or manifest a trend to financial loss, then management should take an option for technology change in the system.

Development of Economic Resources

The major driving engine for advancement in economic resources is energy that needs efficient performance to deliver quality product and uninterrupted services. Since independence load growth in domestic, industry and agricultural sector has reached considerable level(MW).The reliability and productivity of energy supply is dependent on advanced technology based operation. According to eq. (5), economic growth is dependent on capital and labour, thus investment with trained manpower will improve the productivity. In energy sector automation is replacing routine work and information and communication technology application has enhanced reliability in supply. The complexity in transmission and distribution of power require a technical change periodically that has been manifested in changing the intrastate transmission network to interstate power grid.

Infrastructure

Energy Sector

There is tremendous impact of technology on development of energy sector. The ever increasing demand requires expansion of capacity in generation, Transmission and distribution sector. But capacity addition in generation is spread over a couple of years by that time demand will increase, so technology application is required to match demand growth with capacity addition. The two main approaches for solution of this problem are to implement energy efficiency technology in generation and in distribution sector as well as technology implementation. Present energy scenario in India project low energy intensity in different category of consumers.

The trend of curves related to growth of per capita electricity consumption and growth of GSDP per capita is not of same pattern .This trend of curve signify per capita consumption of electricity (%) is not following change in growth of per capita GSDP (%).In other words, economy of the states is dominated by contribution of service sector and industry sector where use of solid state equipments is more. Energy efficiency measures in these economic resources have been improved by application of technology.

The data on energy intensity (energy consumption/GSDP (at constant price) indicate energy intensity is gradually decreasing, whereas rate of growth of GSDP at constant price show an increasing trend. Therefore, the data implies that economic growth is increasing. The reason of this rate of variation of the indicators is attributed to energy efficiency measures with advance technology. However, energy consumption, income per capita and technology penetration in consumer durables is interrelated. When per capita income rises, energy consumption increases or more technology based appliances are used. As for example, rural people change over to LPG in substitution of kerosene or fuel wood is substituted by kerosene. Urban people of around 71% population and rural people of only 17% population uses LPG. This difference in energy use portray inequality in countryside. Urban people use more electronic gadget or use electricity for longer period. But the major driving engine of economic development, energy is not up to desired level in rural area .HH Electrification in rural area is 57% completed in rural areas 91% HH uses kerosene, particularly for lighting.(Millennium Development Goal, 2011)

The barrier for energy sector growth is technical and commercial losses. This losses accounted for retardation of growth by 25% to 35% .The technical loss are attributed to dilapated conductor, insufficient capacity of distribution transformer and configuration of substation as well as communication deficiencies. Commercial losses are accounted for deficiency in billing, metering and accounting procedure. All these issues are addressed by implementation of technology based programmes. Informtaion and communication technology is now widely applied in many discom and transmission system. Generation of electricity is now also experiencing technology change, transmission of electricity has been transformed to interstate grid from intrastate transmission line, many new technology based application has improved power flow through grid, thus relieving the system from grid failure. Distribution system has also undergone technology change where ICT based operation has dramatically changed the working system and enhanced quality and reliable power supply. Computerisation and automation has rapidly changed the metering, billing and accounting procedure. AT & C losses in utilities are now gradually declining to acceptable level. The available information indicates the reduction of AT & C losses in west Bengal, Maharashtra, Karnataka and Gujarat where technology based operation is in progress. Electricity utilities have focused on technology based operation to move on energy efficiency measures that include customer indexing & GIS database, supervisory control and data acquisition, distribution and grid automation, automated meter reading, enterprise resource planning and smart grid distribution sector, whereas, in transmission sector, power grid has introduced gas insulated substation, remote control substation and HISL technology is gaining momentum for implementation that will effect high density transmission corridor (MW/meters) [4].

The cause and effect of technology change that indicate technology change in energy sector is solution to problem of meeting challenge of demand rise.

It has been observed from Power Finance Corporation (n.d.) report on performance of power utility- 2008-09 to 2010-11 that Maharashtra, MP, Gujrat, UP and Rajasthan generation was low at around PLF of 59% to 76% that necessitates growth of power purchase 13% - 21%[11].The major coordinating agency central and regional load dispatch centers will be at risk because of congestion of power through grid when states with inadequate owned installed capacity attempt to overdraw power to meet increasing demand. In state sector, there is lagging capacity addition of 15616 MW ("Planning Commission", 2012-2017) due to lack of coordination between implementing agencies. But the delay in capacity addition at state level will have impact on bridging demand -supply of power in the state. There is difference in strategy adopted for implementation of Power plant projects in central and state sectors; the later is mostly lagging in implementation. It has been observed that many states could not implement the planned project of capacity addition in their own sector because of financial constraint; land acquisition process and the policy issue that varies from state to state. There is necessity of an integrated plan to strengthen distribution system that derives revenue in power supply system. If there is deficiency in infrastructure at receiving end of power system, then the power supply system will lose stability due to wastage of energy through distribution sub system. Since distribution sub system is major source of revenue to maintain financial stability in power system, the analysis is now focused on the performance of DISCOM in private and public sector specially projecting technology based achievement. Most of the electricity Utilities and DISCOM are operating at losses. A sizable cross section of states in northern, western states are dependent on purchase of power from interstate grid because of inadequate capacity to generate power out of its own installed capacity which has impact on interstate grid turning network system vulnerable to congestion in case of absence of monitoring power flow instantaneously. Therefore, transmission line infrastructure needs continuous monitoring regarding Operation of mechanism through IT and automatic system. Most of the States utilities that are selected for analysis are reeling under financial losses, .AT&C losses decreases in Northern and Western states by 0.75 and 3.58% respectively between 2009-10 and 2010-11[plan], whereas eastern and southern states show increase by 4.3% and 0.21% respectively. The states were selected for analysis on the basis of their performance in order to compare activities of private and state owned DISCOM. UP PashVVNUP, Some specific examples are cited here to show difference in performance due to technology diffusion with others who have not implemented technology diffusion in the system. Pashimanchal Vidyut Vitaran Nigam limited has achieved improvement in distribution system by implementing advanced technology of Automatic meter reading, use of electronic meters, MRI based billing and sustained drive in minimizing losses. NDPL is a private distributing company in Delhi that has achieved success in reducing AT&C losses by corporate management and application of advanced technology in metering, billing and operation process.MP Paschim VVCL is state managed DISCOM which has high AT&C losses and absence of IT enabled services and advanced technology, Profit after tax and gap between ARR and ACS indicate high losses.BSEB Yamuna Delhi, a state managed DISCOM has recovered from losses in 2010-11 by application of IT. Tamilnadu DISCOM is Govt. managed which has incurred losses and Gap between ARR and ACS is appreciable [PFC 2011-13]. The state has not implemented advanced technology in metering, billing and in operation. Overall performance Report [peck] of the states in India reveal Delhi, Karnataka, Gujarat, AP, WB and Kerala achieve Profit whereas Tamilnadu, UP, MP, J&K, Punjab and Bihar incur losses[PFC]. The observation of available data reveal Private distribution company performed better because of application of advanced technology and better monitoring and corrected programme on the basis of feedback. Bihar, Tamilnadu, MP, Chattisgarh, Pumjab, Assam have not implemented APDRP program properly, thus incurred loss with low improvement of AT&C. Whereas, Delhi, Gujrat, AP has implemented the program with application of IT and achieved profit with reduction of losses[govt. of India directory]. It is also observed that the more technology intensive application in APDRP will have impact on the profit accrual after tax[PFC]. The observation on the performance of Delhi Surat and Ahmadabad, Andhra Pradesh and Gujarat clearly indicate that SCADA and DMS is most effective technology to reduce losses and increasing revenue. It has been emphasized in National electricity Policy to implement a time bound programe of SCADA and Demand management system. But so far none of the states except Delhi and Gujarat has implemented technology in distribution system whereas; Tamilnadu, Chhattisgarh, Bihar, Karnataka, Orissa and Punjab neither have make much progress in improvement losses nor have applied technology[GOI directory]

The salient feature of observation of above analysis is

1. To speed up implementation of SCADA, DMS, Remote metering without further delay
    a. Tariff regulation by regulatory commission on its own without external interference.
    b. Application of advanced technology in infrastructure development.
2. Development of efficient management system

Renewable energy technology is gradually penetrating into grid electricity in some economically advanced states in India. Bio mass energy accounts for 89% of household energy consumption in rural area and 37% in urban area. The biomass energy is efficiently utilized in bio power development to supply of electricity for HH and agricultural work purpose. Total renewable energy resource installed capacity as on 31.2016 is 42849 MW out of total installed capacity of 3,02,088 MW, growth rate renewable energy capacity in 2015- 2016 over 2014 -2015 is 19.77% and CAGR from 2006 -07 to 2015-16 is 18.63%. CAGR: Compound Annual Growth Rate =((Current Value/Base Value)^(1/nos. of years)-1)*100[MOSPI energy statistics 2017]. AP, Gujrat, Karnataka, MP, Maharashtra, Tamilnadu and Rajasthan has achieved major progress in grid interactive renewable power infrastructure by installing 1431,4037,2869,2141,4564,7613 and 3993 MW respectively. It is interesting to observe that these states have achieved much success in economic growth. There are some factors behind progress of Bio power and wind energy has maximum achievement in the abovementioned states, this renewable technology application has favored SGDP growth. Total installed capacity in Bio power and wind power categories is 4831 MW and 26866 MW respectively; almost 100% villages were electrified in these states [MOSPI]. The rate of consumption of energy in rural area is an indicator of economic growth that corresponds to increase in agricultural

Table 1. Comparison between economic growth and renewable power

State	Growth of GSDP (%)	Growth of Renewable Energy (MW)		Human Development Indices (%)
		Bio Power	Wind Power	
AP	12.03	12.03	1431	0.473
Gujrat	16.26	16.26	4037	0.527
Karnataka	14.24	14.24	2869.15	0.519
MP	16.86	16.86	2141	0.375
Maharashtra	11.69	11.69	4654	0.572
Tamilnadu	14.34	14.34	7613	0.570
Rajasthan	11	11	3993	0.434
UP	13.18	13.18	0	0.380
WB	13.35	13.35	0	0.492
Orissa	13.86	13.86	0	0.3

(Data Source: MOSPI & GOI directory)

productivity. According to available data on Growth of GSDP, the economic growth in the following state is interesting to note.

Communication

While energy is considered as driving engine of economy growth, Communication technology is considered as fuel to economic growth. Information and communication technology has immensely penetrated into economic resources and development of infrastructure.

Rural area needs best development of ICT infrastructure where 70% of total population earns their livelihood in agricultural occupation. In order to maintain inclusive growth, penetration of ICT into village is expected by good regulatory framework and skilled human resources that constitutes the requirement for access to this technology. (World Bank, 2007). Communication infrastructure development need financing the programme through high allotment of fund in the budget for infrastructural development in rural areas. Private partnership will yield best result within a regulatory framework. Many states in India specifically Orissa, UP, Jharkhand, Bihar and Chhattisgarh, rural area are deprived of basic services in comparison with the service benefits access in the urban area. The basic deficiency is energy poverty and access to ICT Economy of some rural area is lagging behind the improved growth pattern of urban area. Employment opportunity need be enhanced to support income generation among the rural people, most of whom are land less farmer and unskilled labor by best connectivity across the state. "Over a period of 12 years, internet subscriber base had increased by 97 fold from 0.21 million in 1999 to 20.33 million in 2011. The 20.33 million Internets subscribers at the end of June-2011 as compared to 19.67 million at the end of March-2011 registered a growth of 3.33% within a period of three months. Number of Broadband subscribers increased from 11.89 million at the end of March-2011 to 12.35 million at the end of June-2011, registering a quarterly growth of 3.89% and Y-O-Y growth of 30.37%. Apart from this, 346.67 million wireless subscribers have subscribed to data services, as reported by the wireless service providers". [India country report, 2011]

Economic Resources

Industrial Resource

Industrial growth or productivity is essential for all around economic growth in the country. But policy of the government, labor availability, land acquisition and governance in the state is the dominant factor for capital investment. According to the eq. (5), capital and labor are interrelated variable for economic growth. Skilled manpower with educated and vocational trained work force is more favorable for capital investment. Secondly lower wages benefit with production of goods at competitive rate is also attractive to capital investment. Thirdly, best availability of infrastructure is major requirement for capital investment. According to eq. (5), economic growth is related to ψ factor which stands for infrastructure development. Energy is one of the major driving inputs, which have been discussed in previous section. Connectivity between places of resource to industrial site and market delivery point through highways and roads are important issues in infrastructural development. Also required Information and communication technology support for logistical development of industrial operation. The next issue in industrial growth that contributes to GSDP is the technology change that is penetrating slowly in Indian economy. The impact of advance technology is reduction of labor in the area of routine work and increased requirement of skilled and specific knowledgeable manpower. Therefore in employment scenario, there is reverse effect on job security. The technology enabled Tax system is also conducive to growth of industries. The GST is such a step by government to ensure cent percent tax collection from the business activities. The industries on the other hand is relieved of paying multiple end tax that benefit industrial finance environment. According to available information ("NCAER", 2016), major barriers are corruption, initial approval on different issues for setting up industry, availability of NET connectivity which are addressed by technology based infrastructure. How technology is affecting contribution of industry to GSDP is portrayed in Andhra Pradesh where manufacturing sector contribute only 15% to industrial output because of limited diversification and low adoption of technology[ADB] Digitization is driving engine of industrial transformation. New technology in the area data analysis, apps for consumers, digital delivery system of product, robotics, power storage, sensors have expanded scope of industrial activities. There are needs for higher flexibility in supply chain that can be possible by technology defining boundaries of flexibility from supply at right moment sensing signal of demand in the system.

Agricultural Resource

Agricultural productivity growth is a major criterion for inclusive economy growth because 70% of population in rural area depends on agriculture for their livelihood. The basic necessity in policy formulation is to increase productivity which is possible by technology infusion in farming and allied products, but productivity growth is not possible when productivity reach at maximum of potential growth. Technology infusion will be effective in case of high productivity land .warming is another climate related issue that need technology oriented approach to deal with productivity growth. Technology applied in irrigation will enhance productivity. Irrigated land has increased from 20% in 1981 to 35% to date ("Planning Commission", 2012-2017). During 11th plan period low rainfall below 95% of long average period as compared to 15 previous years had reduced productivity as shown table 2, the reason is attributed to policy of sticking to existing technology rather than switch over to new technology

12th plan emphasize greater stress on technology application in specific crop production. Public distribution has adopted end to end computerization for tracking food grain movement and lifting of food grain at distribution end by infusion and disseminations of Information and communication technology. Technology of digitization has been introduced in land record and GIS mapping has enhanced land use efficiently.

Service Sector Resource

Service sector experienced digital revolution in transforming manual work to on line in hotel, restaurant, railway and bus utilities. Shopping is now at the fingertip of consumer that enhanced business activity. This growth in service sector productivity has contributed to GDP more than industrial and agricultural sector. The following table illustrates the growth pattern

Table 2. Growth rate of Agriculture and allied sector

V Year Plan	Share of Agriculture in Economy (%)	Growth Rate of Agriculture & Allied Sector (2004-05) (%)	Growth Rate of Total Economy (%)
9th	23.4	2.5	5.7
10th	19	2.4	7.6
11th			
2007-08	19	5.8	9.3
2008-09	15.8	0.1	6.7
2009-10	14.7	1.0	8.4
2010-11	14.7	7.0	8.4
2011-12	14.0	2.8	6.5
XIth plan average	15.2	3.3	2.9

(Data Source: State of Indian Agriculture 2015-16)

The analysis of data indicates share of agriculture to GDP is least of all economic resources. The declining share of GDP is attributed to variation of favorable climate and technology infusion. Actually during 11th plan new technology was not infused keeping the old technology in operation. Industrial

Strategy of Technology Implementation

The technology deployment in the system involves two stages, first stage is the strategy development and second part is strategy implementation. This chapter will focus on strategy

Implementation part. There are several issues in implementation stages out of which leadership, database development, analysis of data and monitoring feedback after every milestone with objective set up are important.

Study on Objective

The chapter attempted to emphasize coupling of technology with economic growth in the country. Therefore, objective of the work is to quantitively and qualitatively formulate strategy to develop economy of the country so that the entire region down to block level can manage decent standard of living. The infrastructural development of economy and social level need technology deployment in order to achieve high efficiency with best quality of work within the time frame of completion. The concept of strategy development on a specific issue is based on R&D about a

Table 3. Sector wise share of GDP

Year	Agriculture (%)	Industry (%)	Service (%)
2004-05	19	27.9	53
2005-06	18	28	53.7
2006-07	17.4	28.7	54
2007-08	16.8	28.7	54.4
2008-09	15.8	28.1	56.1
2009-10	14/.6	29.3	57.1
2010-11	14.6	27.9	57.5
2011-12	14.4	28.2	57.4
2012-13	13.9	27.3	58.8
2013-14	13.9	26.1	59.9

(Data source: ("Planning Commission", 2012-2017))

problem experienced during operation of the system which is referred to institution in collaboration with industry. This work is dependent on data collection and analysis to focus on the problem. The study then corroborate with advanced technology relevant to address the issue. The research study is then forwarded expert committee for implementation.

Database Management

After the research study is finalized, for the purpose of implementation of technology, the workshop is organized involving participation of all stakeholders that constitute a committee for execution. First phase of the work is focused on data collection and analysis of the system. For example, in a distribution system loss reduction and efficiency improvement, data on consumer end consumption, load factor and demand and supply pattern is collected and analyzed. In case of resource planning, fuel and financial resource management data is collected and analyzed. The baseline data region wise and state wise on economic scenario in respect of economic resources and infrastructure need be analyzed. Such data include information on growth of industrial productivity and agricultural productivity, distribution of resources to industrial and agricultural sector, connectivity standard and distribution of product up to grass root level. On the other side, social infrastructure data related to education, healthcare, electricity and petroleum product, communication need be scientifically managed. Data management needs information and communication technology to form a network that can be accessed by every stakeholder in the implementation process. This database management need a hierchial set up to include

Central data bank which can access to the performance data at panchayat level. Data analysis is the next step after framing database; data analysis will attempt to identify the exact field, appropriate capacity and target for improvement

Gap and Barriers

Strategy on roadmap for technology deployment that has been approved by the expert committee is reviewed and the existing scenario of the system is studied with the required standard attainment of the system. The difference in the value of the attribute is then matched with the expected value to reach by implementation of technology. In this course of work at this stage, barriers to implement technology are assessed. These constraints are addressed by suitable re -engineering of the implementation process.

Action Items

First Step: Cost-Benefit Analysis

The cost -benefit analysis will portray the probable benefit to the organization who will implement the technology by comparing different option of technology available. Cost benefit analysis will determine pay back period as well as verify whether its benefit outweigh the cost and how much. This step will ensure confidence of the organization management about benefit of implementing the technology.

Second Step: Decision on Appropriateness of Technology

Technology infusion necessitates technology evaluation to match with existing infrastructure. If the existing infrastructure is insufficient in skill and knowledge of the manpower, then suitable training programme need be arranged to acquaint the staff with new technology and arrange feedback their views about the operation process and production efficiency.

Development of milestone in execution of work, each milestone will indicate per cent of achievement in terms of overall completion of the works

Third Step: Tracking of Progress in Implementation Is Done by Reviewing the Following Indicators

- Production efficiency
- Technology cost
- Time of completion of phased work
- Benefit in terms of overall economy

For example, in case of energy efficiency improvement the following indicator are monitored

- Consumption of energy
- Energy intensity
- Use of CFL or LED lamp by consumer
- In case of distribution of end use appliances
- Distribution and stock of appliances
- Substitution of conventional appliances by energy efficient appliances

In case of resource planning

- Number of new technology introduced
- Capacity addition
- Operational efficiency
- Cost of capacity addition
- Type of technology used
- Productivity growth

Fourth Step: Reviewing Feedback From the Organization Focusing on the Appropriateness of Technology in the Overall Performance of the Organization

The progress of work is compared with milestone of the implementation programmatic there is any deficiency, then that is addressed by necessary adjustment of technology infusion in the system.

CONTRAST OF ECINIMIC DEVELOPMENT IN BETWEEN SELECTED STATES

The study on economic development in reality in respect of some states has been attempted to ascertain whether economic development has achieved economic growth in all respect to provide a standard of living with access to education, energy, employment to generate income. In order to study on this issue, West Bengal, Orissa, Maharashtra and UP states has been selected on the basis of strategic importance in India.

West Bengal

West Bengal with population of 9.13 crore (Census India, 2011) Comprises of 76.76% literates out of which 72.13% of population inhabits in rural area .per capita NSDP at current price of (2004-05 TO 2014 -15) is Rs 78903cr. Which is above all India average of Rs 74380cr. Most of the rural population in north and south Bengal depends on agriculture for their livelihood .Per capita income at current price is Rs 61352.But, some districts are economically better than other districts according to 2010-11 data (GOI directory, states), per capita income of Rs 53682 and Rs 46277 in Bardhaman and 24-Parganas (N) respectively appear to be higher than low per capita income in Purulia and west Dinajpur and North Dinajpur that is Rs 31670 and Rs Rs 28597 respectively. The employment opportunity in Bardhaman is better because of 29339 nose of small scale industries and 491 no's of factory in this district are offering employment to 171756 and 77854 nos of people, besides, agricultural productivity in Bardhaman is high because of 50% of total 698770 ha area is irrigated. The monsoon is active in this area with rainfall around 1322 mm. whereas in 24-parganas (N) district, 10661 no's of small scale industries has employed 82374 no's people. The agricultural productivity in total cultivable area of 271845 ha is high because of net irrigated area of 167128 ha. Therefore income generation in these two districts out of all 19 districts in WB is on higher scale indicating better economy than other districts.

But when the study is focused on Purulia district, where 89% of population is of rural area, the economy is in lower level where per capita income low because of scarce existence of industries with insufficient infrastructure of local pisciculture and poultry business. The agricultural productivity is low having mono crop area of large area, only 17% of net cropped area is multicropped area. Only 31.24% of rural population is cultivator and 35.09% population are agriculture labour. The irrigated area of cultivable area is not sufficient. The climate in this region is not favorable for agriculture work with low amount of rainfall. The major portion of BPL population is economically supported by NRGEA scheme. Thus overall

Table 4. Economic growth in West Bengal

Per Capita Income	Rs
Economic Growth During Decades Macro Level	
2004-05	22648.91
2012-13	61352.35
Annual Growth Rate of Domestic Product at Constant Prices (2004-05)	
2005-06	6.29%
2012-13	6.50%
Annual Growth Rate of Domestic Product at Current Prices	
2005-06	10.35%
2014-15	13.35%
Net Domestic Product by Industry of Origin at Current Prices	
2010-11	47245.49
2004-05	22648.91
Per Capita Income	
2004-05	Rs 22648.91
2010-11	Rs47245.49
Economic Growth in Micro Level	

economic status is below the standard of living. The literacy level in this district is 56% where 53.82% of rural population is literate. Looking into other area in Uttar and Daskhin Dinajpur, web portal is not organized to provide data. Only available information is 90% of total population is inhabitant of rural area in Uttar Dinajpur, contribution to state economy is low. Climate in west Bengal is moderate but natural disaster in monsoon months cast a shadow on economy of the districts in Hooghly, 24-parganas, Howrah and Midnapur. Thus economic development get set back even all round effort is initiated for economic growth in these area.

The information in Table 4 suggest Growth is uneven across the district, there is high level of per capita income in some districts while other district like Purulia, Birbhum, Uttar Dinajpur and Dskhin Dinajpur have lower income level. Employment generation by setting up small scale industries and increasing agricultural productivity by technology based mechanism with infrastructural development is the only option to support the population to increase purchasing power. Simultaneously technology driven development system need be introduced to provide education, electricity, medical care and drinking water.

Besides, climate is another factor that has impact on economic growth. The application of technology is the only option to meet this challenge. The available data in table appended in appendix visualizes state of economy during last decades and economic growth pattern

Income

Maharashtra

Maharashtra with population of 1, 12,374 000 nos. (Census India, 2011) has achieved per capita state income of Rs 147399 at current price during 2015-16 in comparison with all India figure of Rs 94178 where literacy rate is 82.3%.Gross state domestic product at market price is Rs 2001223 Crain comparison with all India figure of 13675331 Cr during 2015-16 at annual growth rate of 8.5%. The climate is favorable with rainfall 94.9% to normal. Agriculture production contributes 9.82% of total state income while industry production and service sector contribute 28% and 48% to state economy. Gross irrigated area is only 20% of gross cropped area. The state has per capita electricity consumption of 1038. The state is converging next generation technologies across the infrastructure sector. In Energy sector, the state has reduced AT & C losses to 19.7% with zero load shedding. Infrastructural development in transport sector has achieved progress while improving infrastructure of school in education sector. The state has achieved score of 0,752 in Human Development indices during 2016-17 (Maharashtra Human Development Report, 2012),the percentage of people engaged in cultivation is 37.1% of total population while 44.3% of population earn their livelihood by manual labour. There are economically lagging districts like Nandurbar, Hingoli, Washim, Gondia, Bhandara, sindhudurg and osmanabad where infrastructure is insufficient to reach benefit of economic development according to data of 2015-16 [Goidirectory].All the economic development indicator are showing satisfactory trend with best infrastructure enabling economic growth. Employment generation in this state is high because of industrial growth that in turn has increased purchasing power of the population. Some pockets of under developed area are existing in this state; the reason is attributed to poor climatic condition and under developed infrastructure. In this state also there are happenings of natural disaster affecting cores of population, because of its geographical location in coastal region. But overall economic developments appear to be prospective because of technology based infrastructural development. [GOIDIRECTORY]

SOLUTIONS AND RECOMMENDATIONS

Economic development in the country is self propelled because people need economic growth to maintain decent living standard. At the same time the economic growth will be inclusive to reach benefit of economic development within the reach of all. This problem is addressed by implementation of infrastructural developmental programme with technology diffusion to bring quality, reduction of coat and completion within time frame. Employment generation by increasing industrial investment and agricultural production is essential to increase purchasing power of the people. Local self help group development and promotion of local arts and handicrafts will assist the people to increase their purchasing power, Information and communication technology penetration in remote villages is necessary to facilitate better connectivity with modern India. Banking services need be extended to rural interior parts in order to cover all population within the fold of ambitious central government yojonas. HH electrification should be completed in all respect and village electricfication must be complete to operate agricultural pump sets, lighting in heath centre and educational institutions. Proper monitoring with advanced technology will help to accelerate the work.

CONCLUSION

Economic development and economic growth both need technology support for better achievement. While economic development is directed to development in infrastructure, health security literacy of the area for general wellbeing of the public, economic growth is mean changes in social value over a given period of time. Infrastructure growth need hard and soft technology that maintain flow of supply of goods and maintains services as well as invigorate increasing purchasing power by improving economic resources. The discussion in this chapter is initiated with the objective of to find ways and means to meet the challenges of implementation of technology that depends on environmental issues. The study also aims to reduce loss factor by efficient transformation of resources into final product. The analysis attempt to correlate technology application with infrastructural development. More stress were given in analysis of energy sector contribution to economic growth There is some negative impact of technology diffusion, because technology of present day may obsolescent in future because of new emerging technology, in that case the infrastructure will become un productive unless the system is modernized with new technology Employ generation is an issue associated with economic development and the effect on improvement of standard of living is manifested by economic growth. Technology support always help to maintain flow of resources and develop purchasing operate study developed a mathematical model that establish linkage between technology, income per capita, capital investment and labor force. that is then equated to access to basic services which is ration of purchasing power and actual demand of service to meet at greater prices. The model highlights that technology supporting greater efficiency n the system production is coupled with economic development.

Technology economic development and infrastructural development are aat the apex of system that acts on GDP growth while, education, communication and energy are three arms of the system that support the GDP growth.

The mathematical model also shows linkage between Technology, economic development and employment. It is imperative to say that employment generation should be prime objective of the country but development of industrial and agricultural productivity. While discussing on energy sector renewable energy progress has been discussed with facts and figures to high light the progress of renewable energy capacity addition in India. Then the study discussed on communication system to show marked improved of technology diffusion towards economic growth. Next the study highlight on economic resources that comprises industrial and agricultural and service sector. The technology diffusion in this sector has been highlighted Next case studies on west Bengal and Maharashtra about economic development and economic growth bring out the relevance of technology diffusion and economic growth. Maharashtra has all round technology implementation in different industrial, agricultural activities that has impact on growth of precipitate GSDP and per capita income. The Maharashtra ha also performed better in industrial investment that increase employment generation, West Bengal has not so much impressive industrial investment but service sector has well performed to maintain Per capita Gross GSDP. Next the study discussed on the strategy for technology implementation that include step by step approach objectives, database management Gap and barrier in implementation of Technology and action to be taken Specific instances of energy efficiency improvement programme and integrated resources planning has been discussed that that assign importance in tracking progress of implementation by reviewing indicators and periodical workshop, seminar and discussion need be arranged.

REFERENCES

Asian Development Bank. (n.d.). Retrieved from https://www.adb.org/sites/default/files/linked-document/48434-002-ssa.pdf

Census India. (2011). Retrieved from http://www.censusindia.gov.in/

Government of India Web Portal. (n.d.). Retrieved from www.goidirectory.gov.in

Maharashtra Human Development Report. (2012). *Yashwantrao Chavan Academy of Development administration.* Pune: SAGE Publication Delhi. Retrieved from https://mahasdb.maharashtra.gov.in/docs/pdf/mhdr_2012.pdf

Millennium Development Goal. (2011). *India Country Report 2011. Central statistical organization.* Ministry of Statistics and Programme Implementation. Retrieved from Govt.of India: www.mospi.gov.in

NCAER State Investment Potential Index N-SIPI 2016. (2016). *Study supported by foreign and commercial office. British high commission India.* National Council of Allied Economic Research. Retrieved from http://www.ncaer.org/uploads/photo-gallery/files/1482230277Mythili%20Bhusnurmath.pdf

Nirmalendunath, G. (2012). *Driving growth in Indian industry unlocking transformational value with technology, confederation of Indian industries.* Springer. Retrieved from https://www.pwc.in/publications/publications-2014/driving-growth-in-indian-industries.html

Performance of State Power Utilities, Power Finance Corporation. (n.d.). Retrieved from www.pfc.gov.in

Planning Commission. (n.d.). *12th Five Year Plan (2012-2017).* Retrieved from www.planningcommission.nic.in

State of Indian Agriculture. (2015-16). Ministry of Agriculture and Farmers Welfare. Department of Economics and Statistics. Retrieved from https://eands.dacnet.nic.in/PDF/State_of_Indian_Agriculture,2015-16.pdf

World Bank. (2007). *Building knowledge Economies advanced strategies for development.* World Bank Publications. Retrieved from www.library.britishcouncil.org.in

World Energy Council. (n.d.). *A report on transmission and distribution in India. A joint initiative of power grid and WEC-IMC.* Retrieved from http://wecindia.in/webportal/index.php/publications/weci-publications

Chapter 3
Data Analytics for Better Branding of E-Governance and E-Business Systems:
Case of "Digital India" Campaign

Rajan Gupta
https://orcid.org/0000-0002-9851-4047
Department of Computer Science, University of Delhi, India

Saibal Kumar Pal
DRDO, New Delhi, India

Sunil Kumar Muttoo
Department of Computer Science, University of Delhi, India

ABSTRACT

Efficient e-governance leads to stronger democracy which can be achieved through higher trust, visibility, and transparency in the system, which can be acquired through effective branding. Various techniques of data analytics can help in achieving trust and transparency in the system. The objective of the study is to resolve various issues in the public sector through analytics-based improvement of different parameters of branding, namely, communication, consistency, clarity, and competition. The research design of the study is a combination of both qualitative and quantitative techniques like descriptive statistics. The main techniques emerged for data analysis includes rating and ranking analysis of government apps, social media analytics, text and speech analytics, media analytics, statistical analytics and data mining, telecom analytics, and people demographics for government programs. It was found that the "Digital India" campaign under e-governance initiative was highly successful based on different kinds of analytical methods found in the study.

DOI: 10.4018/978-1-5225-5412-7.ch003

INTRODUCTION

Many countries are working well on the democratic structure but digitization of the government services through introduction of E-Governance has impacted their system. To improve the E-Governance services, government needs to improve the branding of their services so that citizens can be engaged well. To improve the branding, various government departments need to understand the dynamics behind the campaign and data related to it. But which data analytical techniques can be helpful is a difficult question. This study helps in understanding various such techniques and uses the case study of "Digital India" campaign in India to understand the application of the various data analytics techniques.

Digital India Campaign

Digital India was launched by the Prime Minister of India Narendra Modi on July 1, 2015 to empower the people of the country digitally. The digital India campaign was launched with the aim of bridging India's Digital segment and to solicit investments in the technology sector. Digital India campaign focuses on E-Governance and seeks to transform India into a digitally empowered country (MyGov, 2016). The campaign involves knowledge-based transformation. The programs aim to provide high speed internet services to the citizens and to make services available through online mode and through mobiles. It also emphasizes on providing broadband services, tele-medicine and mobile healthcare services to villages and transforms ease of doing business in India (Panwar, 2015). Through this campaign, the prime minster aims to make the governance more participative. The Ministry of communications and IT is responsible for the implementation of the campaign.

- Digital India program has introduced schemes such as Digital Locker, e-education, e-health, e-sign and national scholarship portal in which investment of over Rs 1 lakh crore has been made.
- Digital India campaign has also introduced BharatNet in 11 states and Next Generation Network (NGN).
- The Digital India campaign ensures that people get advantage of latest information and communication technology and that they receive government services electronically.
- Various apps introduced under Digital India campaign are Digital India Portal, MyGov Mobile App, Swachh Bharat Mission app and Adhaar Mobile Update App (Panwar, 2015).

Apart from this, Pillars of Digital India have been stated in the program. These are access to phones for all, universal broadband access, participative governance, e-Kranti (electronic delivery of services), electronic manufacturing and information access to all (Panwar, 2015).

Success of Campaign in India

Various national campaigns have been launched under the Government of India after the 2014 elections. Campaigns such as Swachh Bharat or Clean India Mission, Make in India, Digital India and Start-up India have been launched in the recent years. The campaigns, launched by Narendra Modi, have been quite popular and are known to the public. These programs are promoted through TV commercials, radio commercials and newspaper ads. The campaigns are promoted through advertisements for a short period of time and then move towards a societal communication to induce change (Choudhary. 2014).

A social media campaign by the current government titled 'NDA government in action' showing how NDA government is better than UPA, has run successfully (where NDA refers politically to National Democratic Alliance, which is a Bhartiya Janta Party led coalition group in India; UPA refers politically to United Progressive Alliance which is a Indian National Congress party led coalition group in India). PM Modi's campaigns has spellbound investors and made women feel safe and independent. The Ministry of Information and Broadcasting in consultation with PMO has prepared 60-slide bilingual presentation which highlights that NDA government has launched successful campaigns which has resulted in India's growth and ease of doing business. The campaigns have also improved the land bill to help farmers and outshined countries like US, Japan, china and Australia. Investment projects have also been skyrocketed due to the successful campaigns launched under Modi government (Sharma, 2015).

These campaigns launched under NDA government have been advertised through various sources and branding has been done for such campaigns to increase their success rate. The Prime Minister - Narendra Modi has been associated with the campaign promotions that improved its success rate (Mujtaba, 2015). For instance, the success of 'Make in India' campaign is attributable to brand India as investment destination.

Branding of a Nation

Nation branding refers to the branding of country's intangible assets that has no explicit relation with any product. It is sometimes related to the country of origin effect or place marketing (Kotler, 2002). Nation branding involves applying branding and marketing procedures to promote a country's image. It is concerned with branding of almost all aspects of a nation's character.

Branding of India has been a work in progress for quite a long period of time. However, this has gained momentum after the launch of 'Make in India' and 'Incredible India' campaigns. These two campaigns have gained enough attention and are considered remarkable in the process of branding India. India is now considered a place for doing business rather than for tourism (Mujtaba, 2015).

- *Swachh Bharat*- Swachh Bharat campaign was launched at a national level and was marketed through TV commercials, politicians and celebrity endorsements. Narendra Modi became the face of the TV commercials and various celebrities have been chosen as brand ambassadors of the campaign.
- *Make in India*- Make in India was launched at a global level to attract foreign investment to boost manufacturing sector of India. Global level branding, design and innovation were introduced to promote the brand in countries globally. 'Make in India is the biggest brand India has ever created', Modi said at the launch of Make in India campaign.
- *Digital India Campaign*- Digital India aims to provide Digital Infrastructure as a Utility to Every Citizen as well as Governance & Services on Demand. It also targets to enhance Digital Empowerment of Citizens. For the achievement of its goals, the campaign has been promoted through conversations about the initiatives. Google India is another step taken by the Modi government to accelerate the promotion of Digital India campaign.

The focus of nation branding has shift from branding India as a tourist destination to a business destination. The recent campaigns focus on branding India as a business destination and build its 5 Ts- technology, trade, talent, tradition and tourism (Shaikh, 2014). The prime minister's vision is that of 'Brand India' to compete the globalized world by building the 5 Ts. The emphasis of the government is to develop the weak segments and areas to create a brand image of the nation in the global society.

Data Analytics in Public Sector

The data analytics contribute to gain normal insights in the public sector. Government sectors of many countries have been using data analytics to collect extensive information and create data warehouse from where information can be extracted when required.

For example, in the United States of America, 90% of the citizens interact with the government through government websites and 75% of them prefer online transactions for government related procedures. Data analysis in E-Governance enhances trust and transparency. 67% of people were found to have more trust when they can interact with the government through online mode. According to a McKinsey research, the governments across the world save USD 1 Trillion annually by digitizing the procedures and government service delivery mechanism (Deloitte, 2015a; Deloitte, 2015b).

Use of analytics would provide unique digital identity to citizens, digitization of financial transactions, easy access to Common Service Centre, seamless integrated information for governance and service, enable service digitally and on time, ease of making financial transactions electronic, authentication and authorization of documents and certificates. A collaborative digital platform can be made available for governance (Deloitte, 2015a; Deloitte, 2015b).

As the digital technology emerges and grows, the use of data analytics innovates brand marketing approach used by entities in the recent times. The use of data analytics infuses brand marketing campaigns to improve interaction with target customers and market. In the public sector, brand marketing strategy infused with data analytics allows government to gain insights in developing better programs and citizen responses. Data analytics also helps in analyzing whether a brand marketing approach is bringing desirable results and encouraging participation from the public (Burby and Atchison, 2007).

This usage of Data analytics with Bran-ding techniques is studied in this research work. As branding for public sector and campaigns can improve the branding of a nation, therefore if branding can be improved using data analytics, it can have long term consequences on the development of a nation. The next section discusses the literature review with its focus on Branding theories and work done by researchers in past. It is followed by methodology description for this research work. Then analysis of various parameters is done by collecting secondary information and last discussions are done to evaluate the analytics approach.

LITERATURE REVIEW

Brand Orientation

The concept of brand orientation was introduced by Frans Melin and Mats Urde in the 1990s (Urde, 1994). It was introduced to create a better understanding that brands are not only add-ons to a product or service but a strategic resource. It also adds knowledge about how to successfully manage a brand when brands are managed by the marketing departments of the company. The existence of brand orientation is based on the role of brands and their perception with respect to existing concept of market orientation. The brand-oriented approach generates a desire for creating and communicating an identity to the brand. Due to this importance of brand, it takes precedence over product, and conveys emotional value and symbolic meaning to the consumer. The concept has been defined by many researchers. One of the proposed definitions say that Brand orientation is a deliberate approach to brand building where brand equity is created through interaction between internal and external stakeholders, where brand management is perceived as a core competence, and where brand building is intimately associated with organizational development and superior performance. Brand orientation is the degree to which an organization considers itself as a brand. It is the extent to which the organization aims to reinforce distinctiveness from other organizations (Gromark, & Melin, 2013).

Need for Branding in Public Sector

Brand orientation has been practiced in private sector for a long time. But, brand orientation has penetrated well into the public sector institutions also. From Indian perspective, all the major government departments like Indian Railways, Indian Postal services, Indian Tourism (through Incredible India campaign), etc. are using lots of branding activities to give their respective departments a clean image, so that citizens can be engaged effectively. There has been a considerable interest in brand orientation of non-profit sector as they can improve their resource acquisition with the help of marketing (Bennett & Sargeant, 2005). Also, it has been the found that "Institutional Performance" is the lagging area in the non-profit sector. There has been a lack of theoretical and empirical research about brand orientation in public sector.

Public sector has been considered an integral part of non-profit sector (Ewing & Napoli, 2005; Napoli, 2006). Brand orientation in the public sector has been discussed in the literature at a general and aggregate level which means that public sector heterogeneity has not been considered (Schmidt, 2017; M'zungu et al, 2017; Leijerholt et al, 2018; Ashworth & Kavaratzis, 2018). There exist similarities between public sector and non-profit organizations such as profit motive and complexity in the shareholder's models. Differences also exist such as governance, transparency and accountability. There is a need of introducing brand orientation in the public sector due to the following stated reasons.

- Public sector in all countries is very important such that it contributes almost half of the GDP. Public sector organizations also have their own identity and brands, names and logos that people recognize.
- Public sector is going through transition of identity which makes it crucial to promote the brand (Brunsson & Sahlin-Andersson, 2000).

- Brands were not promoted in the public sector earlier because these were not perceived to be strategic resources for the public sector and were equivalent or an extension of market orientation.
- Brand develops positive associations related to the company/institution's brand that enhances the acceptance of products and services of the company by the society.

This ignorance of brand orientation in the public sector decreases the importance of brand orientation in bridging the limitations of market orientation in the public sector.

Branding exerts three main functions as suggested by Laidler-Kylander & Simonin (2009). These are information purpose, risk-reduction purpose and an image purpose. Branding helps the public-sector organizations to obtain public trust which helps them to accomplish their mission and goals. It has been discussed that greater brand trust results in developing brand equity which is a need for the public-sector organizations.

Antecedents of Branding Orientation

Hankinson (2001a) suggested factors that can be called as antecedents of brand orientation. These are categorized as mangers' related factors and environmental factors. Managers' personal vision, experience and education about brand, supportive organizational culture and environmental factors have been discussed as antecedents of brand orientation. Apaydin (2011) elaborated the antecedents to be personal vision of managers, relevant experience and education of managers related to brand, communication skills of managers and managers' ability to develop and maintain relationships with the stakeholders. The organization related factors such as culture, structure, resources, type of organization also influence brand. These mediators of brand orientation are external environment where the organization is operating and the internal environment of the organization.

Outcome of Branding Orientation

Wong and Merrilees (2007) have discussed that implementation of brand-oriented strategy leads to better organizational outcomes. Brand-oriented strategy build up brand values and provide a framework for planning and is the basis for other strategies. Brand oriented strategy helps them to develop values in the organization and keep it in line with the mission and vision of the organization. The performance of the organization with respect to goods and services, social capital and policy impact is impacted by the branding. Performance is measured by the efficiency in the use of scarce resources. Social capital is the impact of the organizational activities on the community it operates in. Policy impact is the advocacy impact and this dimension helps the public sector to contribute to the society. Reputation is another outcome of branding orientation and is considered as an expression of esteem or high regard in the eyes of the stakeholders including customers. Brand orientation helps in enhancing the reputation of the organization and creates a positive association in the minds of the people. Another outcome performance dimension discussed is resource acquisition. Resource acquisition in the form of funds from the government is the outcome of brand orientation.

Branding Theories

Various other branding theories have also been proposed by researchers discussing the importance of branding in the performance of the organizations. Some of the branding theories and their relevance for organizations are discussed as follows.

Aaker's (1996) theory of brand equity suggests the important characteristics of strong brand such as brand name, brand awareness, perceived quality, brand associations and brand loyalty. Aaker defined brand equity as assets and liabilities related to brand such as its name and symbols that add value to the product offered by the organization. This model examined the relationship between components of brand equity and performance of the brand. The model suggested that brand equity increases as brand loyalty increases, perceived quality increases, brand awareness rises, brand associations become stronger and brand related proprietary assets increases. Aaker and Keller (1990) suggested that organizations can create positive beliefs and favorable attitudes by building strong brand names in the society and its application was seen in study by Wallin Andreassen (1994) and Becker-Olsen & Hill (2006).

Keller (1993) also developed a brand equity model. The model was customer based that depicted the process of building a stronger brand. Keller defined brand equity as *'the differential effect that consumer's brand knowledge has on their response to the marketing of that brand'*. This model recommended some steps that need to be taken in fixed order. The various dimensions of brand equity that the model advocates are brand salience, brand performance, brand imagery, consumer judgments, consumer feelings and brand resonance. When the highest level, that is, brand resonance is achieved, brand equity at that stage is highest. Resonance is achieved when the consumer achieves the highest level of awareness and familiarity with the brand and grasps some strong brand associations in his/ her mind. It was visible in the studies by Haywood-Farmer (1988) and Kurniawan and Sidharta (2016).

The service branding model developed by Berry (2000) examined brand equity for services. He defined brand equity as "*the differential effect of brand awareness and brand meaning combined on customer response to the marketing of the brand*"

(p. 130) which is a version of Keller's (1993) definition of brand equity. The only difference between the service and product model of brand equity is of the degree, according to Berry (2000). He argued that unlike as in the case of products where the brand equity is established depending on the performance of machines, in case of services it the human performance that makes a difference to the brand equity. In Berry's (2000) model, brand equity is a product of brand awareness and brand meaning where brand meaning has a greater influence on brand equity than of brand awareness. Service branding has been found suitable in nations, as analyzed in various studies (Tomkinson, 2017; Dinnie, 2015).

Brand Asset Valuator model (BAV) is another branding model developed by an agency called 'Young and Rubicam'. According to this model, brand is measured under two broad heads. These are: Brand Vitality and Brand Stature. Brand Vitality is defined as the potential of a brand for current and future growth and Brand Stature is the power and influence of the brand. These two heads of brand can be further categorized into differentiation, relevance, esteem and knowledge aspects. Differentiation is defined as the ability of the brand to be different from that of the competitor's brand. Differentiation aspect is further categorized into three aspects- different, unique and distinctive. Relevance is the association of the consumer with the brand's offerings. Esteem is the perception of the consumer about the brand and its popularity. Knowledge is the level of awareness of the consumers about the brand and the information the consumer possesses about what the brand stands for and the message it conveys to the consumers.

Issues with Public Sector Campaigns

The public-sector campaigns do not get popularity due to non-participation from the citizens' side. Citizens do not show much interest in the national campaigns as they have a negative perception of the public sector related campaigns. The public-sector authorities require understanding of reasons behind the lack of interest and non-participation of citizens towards the national campaigns. Lowndes, Pratchett, & Stoker, (2001) identified four issues with the public-sector campaign as per the citizens' perspective.

- *A negative view of the Local Authority:* The citizens, especially, the young ones, have a negative perception of local council, its services, officers and members. Such views are usually based on personal experience but sometimes prejudice also deliver such perception.
- *A lack of awareness about opportunities to participate:* The citizens believe they have very few opportunities to participate in the campaigns. The communication infrastructure of public sector is weak and therefore, not

all information is received by the public. People who are even willing to participate are not able to take part in the activities of the campaign due to lack of information about the campaign.

- *Lack of response:* The perception of the citizens that the government would not respond to consultation is the biggest deterrent of participation. These views are based on prejudice, hearsay and on personal experience. There is a lack of clarity of the outcome and reasons for the decisions of the government.
- *Social Exclusion:* Many people do not involve in the campaigns because they feel participation is not meant for them and simply suited for particular set of people. People expressed a clear sign of exclusion based on their identity. Generally, young people and single parents are reluctant to participate as they feel their opinion would not matter to the council (Lowndes, Pratchett, & Stoker, 2001).
- *Lack of trust:* The lack of trust can have two possible reasons. One is government's low performance and the other is rising expectations. Government has not completely embraced E-Governance and has not developed partnership to deliver services which creates distrust among citizens. The efficiency and effectiveness of the public sector are low, government fails to deliver its promises and to perform are the reasons for the decline of public trust (Van de Walle, Van Roosbroek, & Bouckaert, 2008).

The usage of analytics has been found for improvement of Public Sector (Van Dooren et al, 2015; Vedung, 2017; Pollitt & Bouckaert, 2017), but the improvement using branding is found to be less in the Public Sector. Majorly, the usage of analytics has been studied in various sectors like healthcare or international relations within the public sector, but overall usage of analytics has been found to be less. The issues mentioned above have not been addressed through usage of data analysis.

Branding Benefits to the Public Sector

Branding is usually associated with private sector. Public sector organizations should be aware of how they are being perceived by the society and should also improve the responsiveness towards public needs. Public organizations have been asked from the past 15 years about process improvements and organizational cultural shifts. Branding would enable the public organizations to address the behavior of current users and serve as feedback mechanism. Branding orientation in the public sector enhances the level of awareness and acceptance of the operations and allows the organization to become more visible, distinct and relevant. Branding needs to be introduced in the public sector due to the reasons like Competence supply, legitimacy development, Revenue generation, and effectiveness improvement (Dahlqvist & Melin, 2010).

Stronger brands fulfill the need for powerful internal development of government organizations. Branding reinforces the capacity for development in the organization and successfully attracts motivated and competent employees. Government organizations with social responsibility benefit from branding in the form of greater legitimacy. Strong brands results in greater effectiveness, especially, in service organizations. Also, competent service providers can generate greater revenues by establishing their brand. Brand orientation provides an identity to the organization to compete in the globalized world. Branding provides institutions and organizations the value of being well-known and gives them a strong position to negotiate, leads to grater legitimacy, credibility with investors, politicians and other stakeholders. Branding also enhances trust in the organization which is reflected in its esteem and reputation (Brunsson & Sahlin-Andersson, 2000).

The public campaigns' branding creates awareness among the people and communicates the desired information. It helps in popularizing the event and encourages participation. Branding can also create differentiation in the campaigns that helps in their promotion and generates active participation from the public. Branding also conveys the relevance of the campaign goals to the public. With branding of the campaigns, the participation of the public in the program enhances which in turn improves loyalty of the public towards the government initiatives and performance of the program (Whelan et al, 2010).

Key Parameters Leading to Branding

- **Communication**: Communication is a part of marketing that helps in providing information to the consumers about the product. Communication involves crafting messages and sending them to internal and external audiences. Communication is an important part of the execution strategy of marketing. Communication plays a vital role in enhancing company's ability to develop and disseminate its strategy. It helps the company to build ethical relationships with its key constituencies (Botan, 1997). Apart from helping to implement the strategy, communication also aids in building company's reputation and brand. Branding is closely related to communication as communication strategy forms long term relationship of company with its stakeholders and shape the organization's image and reputation (Foreman & Argenti, 2005).
- **Clarity**: Brand recognition and differentiation start with brand clarity. Brand clarity helps the audience to identify the brand and organization and connect the customers with the brand. Clarity involves informing targeted customers about what the brand is all about, what does it talk about and what message does the brand wants to convey to the audience. Consumers must have clarity

about what the brand signifies, the objectives of the company and the message the brand conveys. Being clear and overt about brand proposition, helps in proper execution of branding strategy.

- **Competition**: Competition in the global world has increased and this makes the success of the brand difficult. Competition requires the company to position the brand in the global market. It helps in creating a unique identity and differentiates the products in the global market (Shimp, 2008). The global brand name of the company depends on the competitive advantage desired by the company (Bever, & Lallemand, 2011). The level of difficulty in positioning the product due to competition encourages the company to build a brand image in the market.
- **Consistency**: Consistency is another important key to build a strong brand. Consistency with the message conveyed to people and goals of the organization helps in building a brand image. Focus should be on the consumer and their perception about the brand. Usage of same logo, marketing channels and same branding strategy provide consistency in marketing and establish a brand name. This results in recognition of the brand and increase brand trust among consumers. Without consistency, brands can lose their luster. Brand meaning needs to be supported over time and reinforcement of messages is required to strengthen brand equity. The logic of consistency applies to bring about a strong brand and develop brand equity (Kay, 2006).

RESEARCH FRAMEWORK

Much research has not been conducted based on branding as an important part of marketing of public campaigns. Very few studies have discussed Digital India and the role of branding in its promotion. There is little talk about data analytics and its use in branding of Digital India campaign. No study discussed the key parameters of branding in context of the Digital India campaign as stated in the current study. Therefore, the current study focuses upon role of branding in the success of various public-sector campaigns especially Digital India. Research framework is shown in Fig. 1.

Brand is responsible for building trust in the public sector and associated institutions. Public sector image can be developed through trust, visibility, distinctiveness and transparency. These features can enhance the usage of public programs and leads to success of government campaigns. The present study focuses on the 'Digital India' campaign and its enhancement through the usage of data analytics. Stakeholders such as citizens and foreign investors must be focused, and a humanistic approach must be followed to ensure the success of the program. Electronic interaction between

Figure 1. Research Framework for the current study
Source: Author's illustration

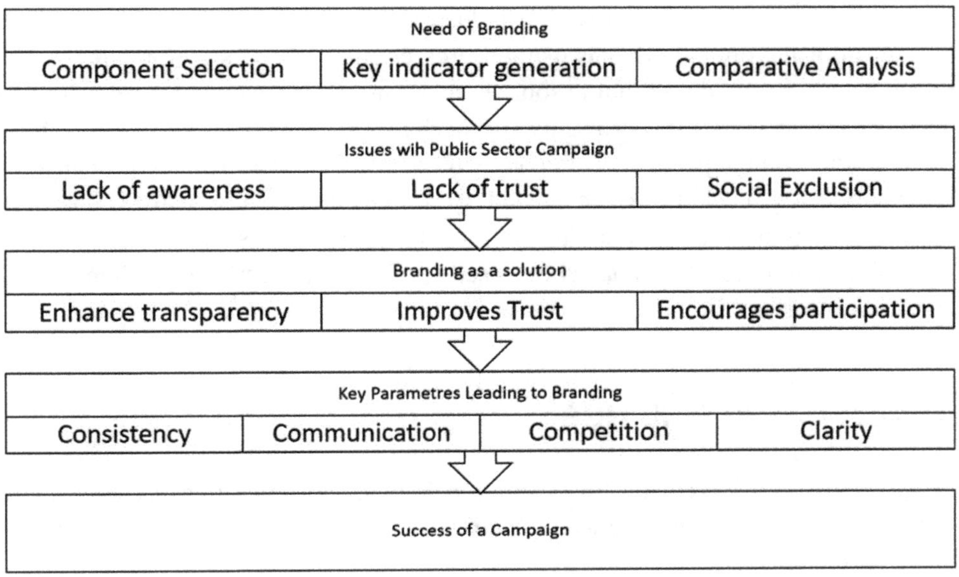

citizens and government is important to enhance the achievement of the campaigns. The assessment of interaction between citizens and government in the various areas like human capital index, infrastructure management, services, telecom presence and electronic participation needs to be assessed. Security and social presence are important parameters for assessment. The assessment of such features leads to world level key indicators that help in comparative analysis resulting in transparency and accountability in the system. The Digital India campaign must be promoted through branding to enhance the trust of foreign investors in the program. Therefore, the current study analyses the role of data analytics in branding of 'Digital India' campaign and other public-sector institutions.

The current research is an online desk research which maps available data points to the theoretical constructs to prove the that Data Analytics can enhance branding which can in turn lead to better Campaigns and Public Institution's image. The desk

Figure 2. Factors of success of Campaign
Source: Author's illustration

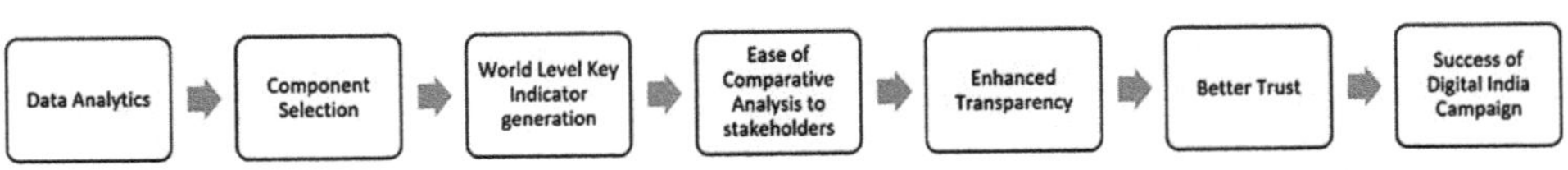

research requires specific information to be searched online as it requires surfing of billions of pages on internet. There are two approaches of fetching out information, one is direct that involves browsing industrial, marketing and business sites to dig out information and other is using search engines like Google or Yahoo. The present study is based on reliable sources such that the information is relevant and promising. It follows direct browsing approach in which specific information about Digital India campaign and branding is searched. This is a desk research because all information is collected through secondary sources online. The analysis has been done for "Digital India" campaign using the descriptive statistics. Mean, Standard Deviations and Percentages have been used to present the results in both graphical and tabular format.

ANALYSIS AND FINDINGS

Firstly, it will be discussed that how various techniques can be applied on Government Campaigns to attain key parameters leading to better branding and then campaign metrics are analyzed.

Communication

Rankings and Ratings of Government and Their Services/Apps Websites and Mobile Apps (Ranking and Rating Analytics)

Various mobile apps have been introduced by the government for numerous platforms such as android (Live and Demo), Java (Live and Demo), Apple and Windows. These apps have been launched under domains such as Agricultural, Electoral, AADHAR, Health, Indian Post, Municipal corporation, Social Sector, and Transport. The status suggests that the number of live applications is 728, demo applications is 63 and number of downloads till date is 519,333. The department of Electronics and Information Technology provides details of the app and reviews about it. There are other portals such as Google Play Store where ratings and rankings of such government applications is available, but their usage is limited as compared to non-governmental applications. But these government services and applications should be assessed and reviewed more to identify the problems associated and what limits its usage and popularity among users (Department of Electronics and Information Technology, 2014).

Social Media Analytics (Sentiment Analysis on User Generated Content on Official Pages)

Microblogging is a common tool for communication these days among internet users. Millions of people share their opinions regarding everyday life and new government policies through websites such as Facebook, Twitter and Tumblr. Political parties are also interested in knowing whether people support their activities and programs or not. These opinions can be positive, negative or neutral (Dalmia et al, 2015). For example, Bhola (2014) analyzed political orientation of twitter users in Indian General Elections of 2014. The volume of tweets everyday were analyzed and was found that the number of tweets increased as elections approached near and political parties in India like AAP, BJP and Congress were mentioned quite a lot. It was also found that Arvind Kejriwal and Narendra Modi were most talked about and their political behavior affected their popularity in India. Among the 1000 profiles assessed in the analysis, 613 instances were true positive, and 425 instances were not belonging category.

The social media has a game changing impact on the Indian political scenario. 300 million people are connected to social media and participate in political activities, campaigns and programs through this medium. The voting population has increased, and these greater numbers of votes are of people of age 25 or below and this demographic profile of new voters is same as those who are active on social media. The empowerment of people in expressing political opinions has increased with the increase of political campaigns and promotion being done though SMS and audio video campaign.

The Facebook page and Twitter account of PMO, India suggests that PM Modi has attracted numerous followers and is one amongst the most popular leader of the country. The PMO has 10.3 million followers on twitter and 10,609,085 likes on Facebook till end of 2015. Many people have started showing interest in politics after the Lok sabha election 2014 was announced because of PM Modi's participation. This suggests the importance of presence and participation of the leaders in social media activities to gain popularity among the users, to promote activities and campaigns through it and get public opinions of the programs launched by the government. Fig 3 shows the key statistics related to PMO, India.

Figure 3. Social Activities of PMO India
(Source: Official PMO profile on Twitter and Facebook)

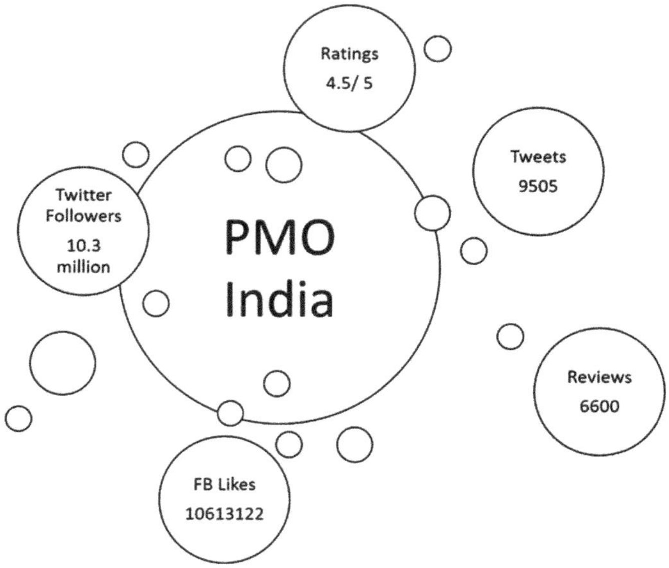

Clarity

Channel Selection for Communication (Media Analytics)

Communication of the launch of a campaign or achievements of the government is often done through multimedia marketing. The government creates awareness among the masses through radio, TV broadcasting, mobiles, audiovisuals and recently the internet platform. Apart from this, traditional sources are also used such as street plays, wall paintings and puppet show (Vasanti, 2012). However, with the advent of Modi government, social media has played a vital role in promotion and providing information to the general-public. With the increased social presence and online promotion of campaigns, a modern approach to communication has been adopted. Digital campaigning has gained importance and social media is now used for listening. During the campaign, online tools, from Google hangouts to Facebook, have been used to gauge public opinion (Chilkoti, 2014). Thus, clear communication occurs through appropriate Channel selection and target audience reach decides which channel should be used to communicate a clear message.

Event Conduction for Communication and Press Release (Media Analytics)

The major events of recent times include Lok Sabha elections held in May 2014 when BJP took charge of Government of India. In the same year, the prime minister conducted events to launch their programs such as Digital India, Swachh Bharat Abhiyan, Make in India and Saansad Aadarsh Gram Yojana. Also, Prime Minister of India launched the biggest ever cleanliness drive in which students, government employees and celebrities participated. Narendra Modi himself cleaned the road at Rajghat (Phukan, 2015).

The 25th Convergence India 2017 will be organized to support the 5 ambitious Digital programs launched by the Modi government- Make in India, Smart Cities, Digital India, Skilling India and Startup India. The focus areas of the program are broadband and internet, 4G/LTE, Big Data Analytics, Manufacturing, Cloud, Media, Electronics, Smart Devices and E-Commerce (Convergence India, 2016). Once the campaigns are launched, they must be clearly communicated through official press release and by addressing appropriate audience at appropriate place.

Speech Evaluation of Orators and Written Speech (Text Analytics)

Speeches and social media activities of political leaders and celebrities can build or destroy the brand. Speech analytics has been used in consistent product branding and brand management in businesses for years and has become a trend in politics branding also. Text analysis has been used to analyze speeches of famous personalities like Barack Obama, David Cameron, Nick Clegg and Narendra Modi. The speaking styles of these personalities show their personality and influence on the listeners' mind. The analysis shows that these personalities use positive emotions and present tense and avoid negative emotions that highlight optimism and honesty and creates an image in the minds of audience. Also, it was found many speakers aims to develop a personal relationship with their audience and use interpersonal style to connect with them. This socio-emotional style enhances a positive image of the leader and creates branding (Pennebaker and Chung, 2012). Narendra Modi's image and in-your-face messaging has created a brand and has overshadowed all other brands. Personal rhetoric has been used to create Brand Modi.

Speech analysis of Narendra Modi shows that he makes use of motivating and positive words such as he addresses audience as 'Brothers and Sisters, and as 'Countrymen' and, talks about 'development' and importance of 'Youth' and uses action-oriented words like come, Move, Work etc. He stresses on the participation of people. His speeches are forward looking, action oriented and deeply connects with the issues of common people. PM Modi is an excellent orator and his speeches

Figure 4. Number of E-Transactions in India
(Source: Deloitte, 2015)

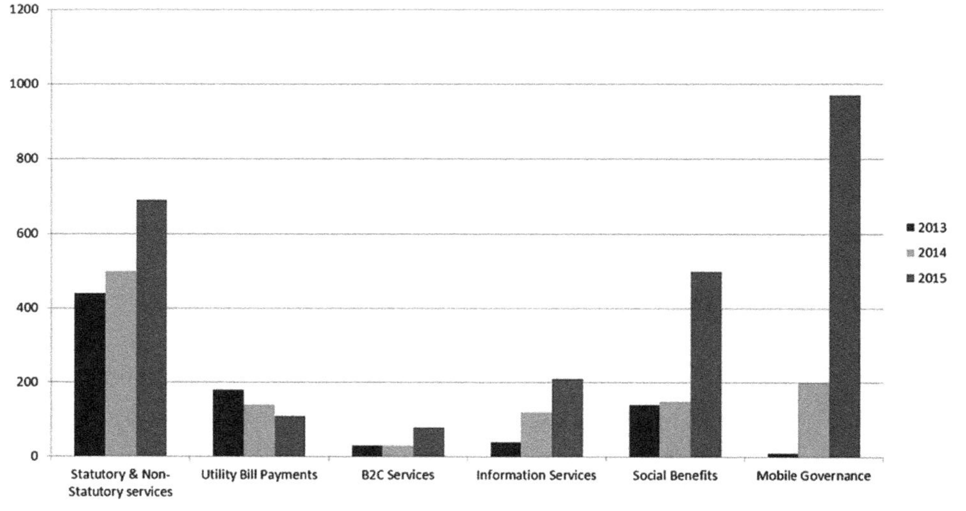

has been quite influential and moved many people to make him as their idol (Pande, 2014). For clarity of communication, positive speeches and other material should be prepared.

Competition

Scheme/State/Ministry Comparison Based on Electronic Participation: E-Taal Website (Statistical Analysis and Data Mining)

The electronic participation in National and State level government projects have increased over the years. The number of e-tractions has increased by 200% from 840 million in 2013 to 2580 million in 2015. The highest number of E-Transaction was witnessed in May, 2015 to be 1,300,000,000. The number of E-Transactions occurred in Delhi since January, 2015 are as high as 35,049,614. The State with high number of E-Transactions per 1000 population is Telangana (5490.10) and Sikkim has least E-Transactions (6.30) for the year 2016. This implies that although E-Participation in government and State level projects is increasing, few States still lack behind. However, the overall participation is rising implying the recent branding efforts of the government are fruitful and encouraging participation. Fig 4 shows the E-Transactions for various states of India.

The comparative analysis amongst the various states and schemes through public participation can help in finding out high and low rankers which may lead to different strategies and policies for handling of all these states and schemes.

Consistency

People should get access to same message on all channels. For that first thing to analyze is *Infrastructure available for Digital Messaging (Internet facility, Mobile phones, Broadband connection, rural kiosks). This infer to practicing Telecom Analytics.*

The growth in internet traffic is continuous mainly due to increased use of IP video, virtualized computing and data centers. Telecom infrastructure in India is expected to improve from the efforts of both government and private sector. Public as well as private sector has planned huge investments in high speed networks and for the establishment of National Optical Fibre Network (NOFN) and Government User Network (GUN) to connect optic fibre across the country. The concerned project will facilitate connection between 25000 Gram Panchayats with 100Mbps speed, provide community W-Fi at Gram Panchayat level and access to broadband connectivity at Gram Panchayats, schools and health centres. National Optical Fibre Network (NOFN) will also help in providing E-Governance services such as Tele-medicine, Tele-Education, E-commerce, E-entertainment and even financial services. The government aims to reduce the digital divide between rural and urban India in adoption of digital services. Urban India first adopted digital technologies like mobile telephony, DTH services, broadband and mobile internet while in rural India adoption was later. This was because the low level of literacy, technical knowledge, income, and high cost. This gap can be overcome through creating awareness by the government, provide affordable smart phones with digital India initiatives such as NOFN and connected Panchayats.

People Demographics (Census Analytics Across States and Regions)

The smartphone penetration has increased from 10% in 2014 to 13.4% in 2015 and the usage of mobile internet has also risen rapidly. The share of mobile users with smartphone has increased from 21.2% in 2014 to 29.8% in 2016. This share is expected to grow to 39% in 2019 (Statista, 2016). In 2014, India contributed to 9% of the global downloads, being third largest downloader after China and US. But the revenue generation of app market of India is low due to the price sensitivity of Indian customers, low level of digital literacy and lack of locally relevant apps. India stands at second position globally with respect to telecom market with over 937 million wireless subscribers. The young population, between the age of 18-14, are more active internet users and the people in this age accounts for more than half of the app users in India. 29% of the users lie in the age of 25 to 35. Also, in a study it was found that an average Indian spends 3 hours and 18 minutes using smartphone and almost one-third of this time is spent on usage of apps. According to the survey conducted by Deloitte in 2013, 64% people were planning to buy a smartphone in the next 12 months. Expansion of 3G network coverage and introduction of 4G network in 2015 is expected to increase usage and sale of smartphones and number of smartphone users are expected to rise to 200 million in 2016 from 120 million in 2014. India has third largest number of internet users with 259 million users. People using 3G mobile networks are expected to rise to 250 million by the end of 2016 and as the rollout of 4G internet in India, the demand for video and rich media content will grow the demand for apps.

Once infrastructure and people are studied across regions, different strategies can be adopted for the same message to be delivered which will enhance consistency.

Digital India Campaign Analysis

Under the umbrella of Digital India program, government has launched various apps to help people participate in the Digital India program. Digital Locker, Digital India app, E-health and E-education are some of the apps introduced under this campaign. These apps are downloadable from government sites and from Google Play store as well. Ratings and reviews have been provided by the users on these sites that can be used by the government authorities to improve such apps.

Digital India campaign was popularized on social media and received a lot of attention on social media platforms like Facebook and Twitter. The Prime Minister of India, Narendra Modi and CEO of Facebook Mark Zuckerberg changed their Facebook profile picture in support of Digital India campaign. Many people expressed their support for Digital India by changing their Facebook Profile pictures (India Today, 2016).

The Digital India campaign has been promoted through various media platforms. Social media platforms such as Facebook and Twitter were used, and offline efforts involve Statewide Digital Empowerment campaign is set to be launched by students of Kerala. A mega launch ceremony of Digital India was conducted in September 2015 in the presence of chiefs of the companies including Microsoft CEO Satya Nadella, Chairman Mukesh Ambani (RIL), chairman Cyrus Mistry (Tata Group) and chief Azim Premji (Wipro). Apart from this, 600 districts in the country organized various programs to sensitize and inform people about Activities under Digital India campaign (Siddhanta, 2015).

The launch of Digital India campaign by the prime minister was a big event where big Indian companies such as Aditya Birla Group, Bharti Group, Reliance Group, Tata Group and Vedanta Group committed investment of more than Rs. 4.5 lakh crore (US$68 billion) for the campaign. Many other technology companies such as Amazon, Google, Microsoft and Oracle in support of the campaign and have invested in the campaign. Facebook also made efforts to sponsor 100 Wi-Fi hotspots in rural western and southern India. The 24th edition of Convergence India 2016 expo was conducted at Pragati Maidan, New Delhi in January 2016 to showcase the technologies that would contribute towards Digital India campaign and how this will lead to digital transformation. Convergence India 2016 expo was conducted to showcase the latest technologies and solutions and to demonstrate the potential of ICT market. It was organized to highlight the key pillars of digital Revolution Innovation, wireless technologies, Mobility, Security, Big Data Analytics, Infrastructure and network solutions, Cloud and Satellite Communications and Services, etc. (Convergence India, 2016).

Government has made efforts to launch and promote Digital India campaign through various means and platforms and used branding to ensure the success of the campaign. This is the way, other campaigns should be designed and branded where parameters like appropriate communication, clarity, and consistency was followed.

DISCUSSION AND CONCLUSION

Role of Analytics in Improving Branding

Data analytics is generally used in public sector to gain normal insights and can also be used to improve branding of the campaigns and programs. Government sectors of many countries use data analytics to collect data and extract information which is useful.

Analytics is used to provide facilities to the public such as unique digital identity to citizens, digitization of financial transactions, easy access to Common Service Centre, document authentication, and ease of making financial transactions electronic. Data analytics has helped in branding of entities in the recent times. The use of data analytics improves interaction with the target customers and market that improves branding. In the public sector, data analytics is used to develop brand marketing strategy that helps government to gain insights in developing better policies and campaigns and allow citizen participation. The influx of data analytics provides information that helps in branding of government authorities which in turn results in delivering specific services to the public and attracts public participation. Big data analytics helps in improving digital marketing strategies that will bring the government closer to the public.

Data analytics provides information to the public that increases transparency, facilitates comparison and increases public trust on the government and its activities. This enhanced trust on the public-sector policies enhances branding of the sector and results in the success of the campaigns launched by the government.

Various initiatives have been launched under digital India campaign that provides information and transparency to the public (such as applications, broadband and 4G services, digitization, cashless transaction) and therefore, improves branding and increases chances of success of the campaign. This study found that through data analytics solution can be derived where different components of electronic interaction between citizens and government can be assessed. Areas like human capital index, infrastructure management, online availability of the services, telecom presence, and electronic participation have been found as the important parameters for the assessment. Feature like security and social presence are also considered important for the assessment and these assessment parameters helps in conducting comparative analysis. This brings in transparency and accountability in the system along with the substantial visibility which is marked by numbers and figures. The digital India campaign can be launched with more substantial numbers behind the campaign which brings in investor's trust towards the country.

How It Can Fill the Gap in Research

Stronger democracy can be achieved through creating better trust and transparency which makes citizens and other entities use the system. The current study analyzed how different types of data analytics schemes can be useful in developing trust and transparency among citizens and enhance branding of the public organization. The study focused on the Digital India campaign and explained how analytics have led to more visibility and distinctiveness in the procedures which would increase public trust and participation and would result in branding of the campaign. This transparency and enhanced trust would result in further success of the campaign. Therefore, theoretically the role of analytics for branding has been established which was not prominently discussed in the literature.

Conclusion

Since it was found that data analytics can improve branding of the campaign, recommendations can be made for the government to improve the visibility of the program. People must be made more aware about the program and its benefits to enhance public participation. The digital India campaign should be launched with more substantial numbers behind the campaign which brings in investor's trust towards the country. The government should focus on digital literacy of rural Indians, the enhancement of their technical knowledge and build locally relevant apps to support local facilities. The lowering of the cost of the facilities promised under the campaign must be focused upon as the public is price sensitive. To ensure success of the program, the government should focus on the modern approaches of communication apart from the traditional approaches. Also, a review and rating system of their apps must be developed to understand the perspective of the users and to improve the apps. Moreover, the infrastructure and network must be built in rural areas and it must be improved in urban areas for better enforcement of the program and ultimately, its success.

With Public Sector Branding, Analytics can play a crucial role and it is not something additional to the regular activities done to promote a campaign. It only requires careful examination of the communication and thus can help the Public Sectors to revamp their image.

REFERENCES

Aaker, D. A. (1996). Measuring brand equity across products and markets. *California Management Review*, *38*(3), 102–120. doi:10.2307/41165845

Aaker, D. A., & Keller, K. L. (1990). Consumer evaluations of brand extensions. *Journal of Marketing*, *54*(1), 27–41. doi:10.1177/002224299005400102

Apaydin, F. (2011). A proposed model of antecedents and outcomes of brand orientation for nonprofit sector. *Asian Social Science*, *7*(9), 194. doi:10.5539/ass.v7n9p194

Ashworth, G. J., & Kavaratzis, M. (2018). The Roles of Branding in Public Administration and Place Management: Possibilities and Pitfall. In *The Palgrave Handbook of Public Administration and Management in Europe* (pp. 425–439). London: Palgrave Macmillan. doi:10.1057/978-1-137-55269-3_22

Becker-Olsen, K. L., & Hill, R. P. (2006). The impact of sponsor fit on brand equity: The case of nonprofit service providers. *Journal of Service Research*, *9*(1), 73–83. doi:10.1177/1094670506289532

Bennett, R., & Sargeant, A. (2005). The nonprofit marketing landscape: Guest editors' introduction to a special section. *Journal of Business Research*, *58*(6), 797–805. doi:10.1016/j.jbusres.2003.12.001

Bever, M., & Lallemand, S. (2011). *A study of factors affecting a firm's global brand name strategy*. Halmstad University. Retrieved July 15, 2016 from http://www.diva-portal.org/smash/get/diva2:439827/fulltext01.pdf

Bhola, A. (2014). *Twitter and Polls: Analyzing and estimating political orientation of Twitter users in India General Elections2014*. Cornell University Library. arXiv preprint arXiv:1406.5059

Botan, C. (1997). Ethics in strategic communication campaigns: The case for a new approach to public relations. *Journal of Business Communication*, *34*(2), 188–202. doi:10.1177/002194369703400205

Brunsson, N., & Sahlin-Andersson, K. (2000). Constructing organizations: The example of public sector reform. *Organization Studies*, *21*(4), 721–746. doi:10.1177/0170840600214003

Burby, J., & Atchison, S. (2007). *Actionable web analytics: using data to make smart business decisions*. John Wiley & Sons.

Chilkoti, A. (2014). *Narendra Modi to be India's first social media prime minister, India*. Retrieved March 11, 2016 from http://www.ft.com/cms/s/0/e347de5c-e088-11e3-9534-00144feabdc0.html#axzz42aTJgS6F

Choudhary, V. (2014). *NDA government splurges on Swachh Bharat ad campaign, Budget 2016*. Retrieved March 4, 2016 from http://www.livemint.com/Politics/pJjqckXlzJwDwvNeK81mEM/NDA-government-splurgeson-Swachh-Bharat-ad-campaign.html

Convergence India. (2016a). *24th Convergence India 2016: The ICT and Broadcast Expo, exhibitions India Group*. Retrieved March 12, 2016 from http://www.convergenceindia.org/pdf/Convergence-India-2016-Brochure.pdf

Convergence India. (2016b). *Welcome to Convergence India, Ministry of Communication and Information Technology*. Retrieved March 15, 2016 from http://www.convergenceindia.org/

Dalmia, A., Gupta, M., & Varma, V. (2015). IIIT-H at SemEval 2015: Twitter Sentiment Analysis The good, the bad and the neutral! *SemEval*, *2015*, 520.

Deloitte. (2015). *Technology, Media & Telecommunications India Predictions 2015*. Retrieved March 14, 2016 from https://www2.deloitte.com/content/dam/Deloitte/in/Documents/technology-media-telecommunications/in-tmt-india-predictions-2015-noexp.pdf

Deloitte. (2015a). *Digital India: Unleashing Prosperity, Confederation of Indian Industry*. Retrieved March 11, 2016 from https://www2.deloitte.com/content/dam/Deloitte/in/Documents/technology-media-telecommunications/in-tmt-tele-tech-2015-noexp.pdf

Deloitte. (2015b). *E-governance and Digital India Empowering Indian Citizens Through Technology, ASSOCHAM*. Retrieved March 11, 2016 from http://www2.deloitte.com/content/dam/Deloitte/in/Documents/technology-media-telecommunications/in-tmt-empowering-indian-citizens-through-technology-noexp.pdf

Department of Electronics and Information Technology. (2016). *Appstore, The National Mobile Governance Initiative, Mobile Seva, Live apps*. Retrieved March 14, 2016 from https://apps.mgov.gov.in/descp.do?appid=517&param=topapps

Dinnie, K. (2015). *Nation branding: Concepts, issues, practice*. Routledge.

Ewing, M. T., & Napoli, J. (2005). Developing and validating a multidimensional nonprofit brand orientation scale. *Journal of Business Research*, *58*(6), 841–853. doi:10.1016/j.jbusres.2003.09.012

Foreman, J., & Argenti, P. A. (2005). How corporate communication influences strategy implementation, reputation and the corporate brand: An exploratory qualitative study. *Corporate Reputation Review*, *8*(3), 245–264. doi:10.1057/palgrave.crr.1540253

Gromark, J., & Melin, F. (2013). From market orientation to brand orientation in the public sector. *Journal of Marketing Management*, *29*(9-10), 1099–1123. doi:10.1080/0267257X.2013.812134

Hankinson, P. (2001). Brand orientation in the Top 500 fundraising charities in the UK. *Journal of Product and Brand Management*, *10*(6), 346–360. doi:10.1108/10610420110406040

Haywood-Farmer, J. (1988). A conceptual model of service quality. *International Journal of Operations & Production Management*, *8*(6), 19–29. doi:10.1108/eb054839

India Today. (2016). *Zuckerberg, Modi change their Facebook profile pictures to support Digital India campaign, News, Technology*. Retrieved March 15, 2016 from http://indiatoday.intoday.in/technology/story/facebook-ceo-mark-zuckerberg-changes-his-profile-picture-to-support-digital-india-campaign/1/484366.html

Kay, M. J. (2006). Strong brands and corporate brands. *European Journal of Marketing*, *40*(7-8), 742–760. doi:10.1108/03090560610669973

Kurniawan, P., & Sidharta, I. (2016). SERVQUAL on brand image and relationship equity. *International Review of Management and Marketing*, *6*(4), 866–871.

Leijerholt, U., Chapleo, C., & O'Sullivan, H. (2018). A brand within a brand: An integrated understanding of internal brand management and brand architecture in the public sector. *Journal of Brand Management*, 1–14.

Lowndes, V., Pratchett, L., & Stoker, G. (2001). Trends in public participation: Part 1–local government perspectives. *Public Administration*, *79*(1), 205–222. doi:10.1111/1467-9299.00253

M'zungu, S., Merrilees, B., & Miller, D. (2017). Strategic hybrid orientation between market orientation and brand orientation: Guiding principles. *Journal of Strategic Marketing*, *25*(4), 275–288. doi:10.1080/0965254X.2015.1076880

Morrison, S., & Crane, F. G. (2007). Building the service brand by creating and managing an emotional brand experience. *Journal of Brand Management*, *14*(5), 410–421. doi:10.1057/palgrave.bm.2550080

Mujtaba, S. (2015). *Branding; Incredible India! Vs Make in India Ad Campaigns*. Retrieved March 7, 2016 from http://muslimmirror.com/eng/branding-incredible-india-vs-make-in-india-ad-campaigns/

MyGov. (2016). *Digital India, Government of India*. Retrieved March 4, 2016 from https://mygov.in/group/digital-india/

Napoli, J. (2006). The impact of nonprofit brand orientation on organizational performance. *Journal of Marketing Management*, *22*(7-8), 673–694. doi:10.1362/026725706778612176

Pande, S. (2014). *Just the Right Image, Case Study, Business Today*. Retrieved March 12, 2016 from http://www.businesstoday.in/magazine/case-study/case-study-strategy-tactics-behind-creation-of-brand-narendra-modi/story/206321.html

Panwar, P. (2015). *All you need to know about Digital India programme: Explained*. Retrieved March 4, 2016 from http://www.oneindia.com/feature/what-is-digital-india-programme-explained-1792279.html

Phukan, S. R. (2015). *Top Five Programmes Launched by Modi*. Retrieved March 15, 2016 from http://www.mapsofindia.com/my-india/society/top-five-programmes-launched-by-prime-minister-narendra-modi-in-2014

Pollitt, C., & Bouckaert, G. (2017). *Public management reform: a comparative analysis-into the age of austerity*. Oxford University Press.

Schmidt, H. J., Mason, R., Steenkamp, P., & Mugobo, V. (2017). Does brand orientation contribute to retailers' success? An empirical study in the South African market. *Journal of Retailing and Consumer Services*, *38*, 210–222. doi:10.1016/j.jretconser.2017.06.012

Shaikh, S. (2014). *Narendra Modi shares his vision of 'brand India' in 5 Ts, NDTV*. Retrieved March 7, 2016 from http://www.ndtv.com/cheat-sheet/narendra-modi-shares-his-vision-of-brand-india-in-5-ts-548337

Sharma, A. (2015). *Government's social media campaign claims investors spellbound, women safe & NDA better than UPA*. Retrieved March 7, 2016 from http://articles.economictimes.indiatimes.com/2015-04-01/news/60720025_1_modi-magic-modi-government-social-media-campaign

Shimp, T., & Andrews, J. C. (2013). *Advertising promotion and other aspects of integrated marketing communication*. Cengage Learning.

Siddhanta, P. (2015). *Prime Minister Narendra Modi set to launch Digital India Week today, Tech-News Technology*. Retrieved March 15, 2016 from http://indianexpress.com/article/technology/tech-news-technology/prime-minister-narendra-modi-set-to-launch-digital-india-week-today/#sthash.Bga1HObz.dpuf

Statista. (2016). *Share of mobile phone users that use a smartphone in India from 2014 to 2019, Telecommunications, Industry*. Retrieved March 14, 2016 from http://www.statista.com/statistics/257048/smartphone-user-penetration-in-india/

Tomkinson, R. (2017). *Shared services in local government: improving service delivery*. Routledge.

Urde, M. (1994). Brand orientation-a strategy for survival. *Journal of Consumer Marketing*, *11*(3), 18–32. doi:10.1108/07363769410065445

Van de Walle, S., Van Roosbroek, S., & Bouckaert, G. (2008). Trust in the public sector: Is there any evidence for a long-term decline? *International Review of Administrative Sciences*, *74*(1), 47–64. doi:10.1177/0020852307085733

Van Dooren, W., Bouckaert, G., & Halligan, J. (2015). *Performance management in the public sector*. Routledge.

Vasanti, P. N. (2012). *Awareness trap of government ads campaigns, opinion, live mint*. Retrieved March 11, 2016 from http://www.livemint.com/Opinion/zAmFNtD7QPIWN3XIHMaj3K/Awareness-trap-of-govt-ad-campaigns.html

Vedung, E. (2017). *Public policy and program evaluation*. Routledge. doi:10.4324/9781315127767

Wallin Andreassen, T. (1994). Satisfaction, loyalty and reputation as indicators of customer orientation in the public sector. *International Journal of Public Sector Management*, *7*(2), 16–34. doi:10.1108/09513559410055206

Yin Wong, H., & Merrilees, B. (2007). Multiple roles for branding in international marketing. *International Marketing Review*, *24*(4), 384–408. doi:10.1108/02651330710760982

KEY TERMS AND DEFINITIONS

Clarity: Brand recognition and differentiation start with brand clarity. Brand clarity helps the audience to identify the brand and organization and connect the customers with the brand. Clarity involves informing targeted customers about what the brand is all about, what does it talk about and what message does the brand wants to convey to the audience.

Communication: Communication is a part of marketing that helps in providing information to the consumers about the product. Communication involves crafting messages and sending them to internal and external audiences.

Competition: Competition in the global world has increased and this makes the success of the brand difficult. Competition requires the company to position the brand in the global market.

Consistency: Consistency is another important key to build a strong brand. Consistency with the message conveyed to people and goals of the organization helps in building a brand image.

Digital India Campaign: Digital India was launched by the Prime Minister of India Narendra Modi on July 1, 2015 to empower the people of the country digitally. The digital India campaign was launched with the aim of bridging India's Digital segment and to solicit investments in the technology sector.

Make in India: Make in India was launched at a global level to attract foreign investment to boost manufacturing sector of India. Global level branding, design and innovation were introduced to promote the brand in countries globally.

Swachh Bharat: Swachh Bharat campaign was launched at a national level in India with respect to cleanliness drive in the country. It was marketed through TV commercials, politicians and celebrity endorsements in the whole country.

Chapter 4
Digital Divide and Its Dimensions:
A Study in India

Vasantha Gouri Prathapagiri
National Institute of Rural Development (NIRD), Hyderabad, India

ABSTRACT

Information communication and technology (ICT) has brought about revolutionary change in the life style of common man. Usage of technology is now mandatory for every transaction made by two or more persons staying in distant places. Mobile number and e-mail ID are believed to be the genuine identities of any person or institution in the contemporary world. However, spread of ICT and its applications is uneven in developing countries with particular reference to India. While the rich and influential people make use of latest technology and its related applications, others are unable to do so. They suffer from stale and outdated technology and many more do not have access to ICT on account of their geographical position, illiteracy ignorance, and the like reasons. This gap between haves and have-nots of ICT is termed as "digital divide." While high income countries, over 90% of the population is using internet, and in lower income countries, less than 10% of the population uses it.

INTRODUCTION

Information Communication and Technology has brought about a revolutionary change in the lifestyle of a common man in this contemporary world. Every small activity or transaction today is incomplete without the aid of ICT. In fact this world

DOI: 10.4018/978-1-5225-5412-7.ch004

is reduced to a global village due to the fast developments in communication and technology. Mobile Number and Email ID have become genuine identities for people and organizations. However situation is not the same with all the countries in this world. While the rich and developed countries in the west are having access to latest ICT most of the Asian and African countries have limited or no access to ICT and its applications. India is one among those countries having limited access to ICT and many parts of India suffer from lack of ICT facilities. This gap between countries and places with high accessibility of ICT to less or no accessibility is termed as 'Digital Divide'. There is a wide gap in the pace of development between the countries having high access to ICT and the ones having low or total absence of ICT. Long time later it was identified that real issue is not so much about access to digital technology but about the usage and benefits derived from it (Arif, n.d.).

Objectives of This Chapter: Reader Should Be Able to Understand

1. The concept of digital divide
2. Digital divide and its various dimensions in India
3. Government Efforts to bridge digital divide in India
4. Barriers to bridging digital divide and thus
5. Importance of digital education

DIGITAL DIVIDE

The term 'digital divide' is said to have been coined a decade ago by a former United States Assistant Secretary for Commerce for Telecommunications, Larry Irving Jr. focus attention on "...the existing gap in access to information services between those who can afford to purchase the computer hardware and software necessary to participate in the global information network and low income families and communication that cannot……" (Dragulanescu, 2002).

DEFINITION AND MEANING OF DIGITAL DIVIDE

There are many definitions of 'Digital divide'. Some view it primarily as a technological gap in terms of access to and usage of ICT. Others however take a broader perspective, 'The Digital divide refers to social stratification due to unequal ability to access, adapt and create knowledge via usage of ICT' (Warschauer Mark, 2012).

This notion of digital divide between technological haves and have-nots has been a useful tool in efforts to bring greater, more equal access to powerful ICT like internet. In general the term "Digital-Divide" is used to describe the situations in which there is a market gap in access to use of new information and communication devices. Also there is gap between individual households, businesses and geographical areas at different socio-economic levels with regard to their opposition to access and use of new information, communication technology and internet (Kaur Kawaljeet & Jaswinder singh, 2016).

There are broadly four kinds of digital divides observed throughout the world (Keniston Kenneth & Deepak Kumar, 2004).

1. Divide that exists within every nation whether it is industrialized or developing and between those who are rich educated and powerful and those who are not. For Example, in India, despite the success of PCOs/STD/ISD booths in cities and semi urban areas and despite repeated Government promises to provide telephone connections to all the villages in India, even today many remain unconnected. As a result there are many ruralites who have never made a telephone call.
2. The second divide is less noted-linguistic and cultural divide. 60% to 80% of all websites are in English and the rest are in Japanese, German, Spanish, French, Portugal and increasingly Chinese. In India, like the rest of south Asia only 2% to 10% of population speak fluent English while the rest speak other languages. For people who do not speak English, barriers to information age are insurmountable since all widely operating systems require some knowledge of English.
3. The third divide is the growing digital gap between the rich and the poor nations. In the year 1999 UN report on human development devotes much of a chapter to the widening gap between information rich and poor nations. Information rich are countries like Sweden, Germany, Finland and Iceland where household telephone connectivity is well over 90% and computer saturation is over 50%. At the other extreme end lies most of Africa, South America, South Asia, China, Indonesia and 80% of the world where telephone connectivity is 3% less.
4. The fourth divide indicates the emergence of new elite group beneficiaries of the successful IT industry and other knowledge based sections of the economy such as biotech and pharmacy.

DIGITAL DIVIDE IN INDIA

With the advancement in New Information Communication and Technologies (**NICT**), the world today has become increasingly global village. All the developed countries are enjoying the benefits of NICT leaving behind the developing countries. In India, there is a wide gap among communities due to different languages, diverse cultures, religions and farfetched regions. Above all huge population, poverty unemployment and its related problems deny majority of rural and also urban people from benefiting from ICT and its related services. 2011 census report indicated total population growth rate to be 17.64%, Sex ratio is 940 females for 1000 males and total literacy rate is 74.04% (Male 82.14% and Female 65.46%). Rural and Urban distribution of population is 68.84% and 31.16%. Rural populace are living in more than 600,000 villages spread all over the country with poor or no minimum infrastructure like roads, water transport, clean drinking water etc. (Dr.Murthy, 2014).

According to World Bank, 'India faces shark digital divide'. India is a global IT power house but huge majority of people remain locked out of the benefits brought by digital economy. India's vibrant businesses processes outsourcing sector centred in southern hubs of Hyderabad and Bangalore has made it the leading exporter of IT services and skilled manpower in development world. However a Billion people have no internet access, biggest offline population of any country (One Library Per Village, 2017). Also, there are wide variations between people using internet in different regions. Groaning under the basic problems such as illiteracy malnutrition and sheer poverty, India's rural populace is far behind Bangalore which according to UNHDR 2001 is better off than many cities in US, Europe & Japan when it comes to technological innovations (Ranjit, 2002). 'The digital' in 2017 report compiled by Hoot suite, social media management platform demonstrates that, compared to global internet penetration rate of 50%, only 35% of Indian population uses internet ("News Headlines", 2017).Lack of sufficient infrastructure and also dearth for knowledge to use the infrastructure, both deny chances for majority of Indian crowd to avail themselves of benefits derived from access to latest ICTs. Hence, India though has been appreciated globally for providing ICT services faces a huge digital divide as it has a relatively low percentage of population with access to internet.

While one part of India is fast developing by adopting new IT in professional and informal day-to-day activities as well, we are more concerned about the other part of India where electricity is still not properly accessible and people are living in remote villages and forest terrains where network is not available. On one side of the spectrum we have the first India a nuclear and space exploration power, home to a bustling technology and start-up economic system, the world's most active user base, second largest network of Facebook users and adopters of high street western brand technology. At the same time we have second India, while still experiencing crippling poverty is now at the cusp of joining digital community, thanks to advances in mobile, Internet and increasingly affordable mobile technology (Raghav, 2016).

Apart from the digital divide, there also exists a wide gap in adoption of digital technology across different demographic groups within the country. In fact increasing penetration of digital technology by bridging the existing digital divide is associated with greater social progress of a country, it is also essential to build up the corresponding human capital necessary for making optimal use of technology (Kapoor and Mathur, 2016).

Thus the nature of Digital divide is very complex, manifested in different dimensions in India

DIMENSIONS OF DIGITAL DIVIDE

Some of the dimensions identified are as follows:

- **Ownership and Access:** Divide does exist with relation to ownership of new technologies and access to them. Those who own these technologies does not necessarily equate with using them. Those who own a personal computer at home do not necessarily have internet connection and vice versa.
- **Rural and Urban Places:** In India, there is a wide gap between people and their lifestyles in rural and urban areas. People in urban settings do have access to sophisticated modern gadgets for their daily usage and living. In contrast to it are the people in rural areas depending upon agriculture and cattle rearing. While computers and internet are widely available in urban areas it is not the same case with people in rural areas. India's moderate ICT status can partially be attributed to significant urban rural divide. Almost 3 quarters of population are living in villages where access to ICT remains very low. (Sarkar, 2015) Nature of ICT work force can be summarised as follows: Typically a software worker in India hails from an urban and semi-urban locality, follows Hinduism, belongs to upper socio-economic strata of Indian society (P.Vighneswara, 2007)
- **Literacy and Digital Literacy:** Basic literacy indicates the ability to read and write. As per UNESCO definition goes, literacy involves a continuum of learning in enabling individuals to achieve their goals, to develop their knowledge and potential and to participate fully in their community and wider society(UNESCO,2012) Digital literacy also has come a long way from what it meant - basic proficiency to use computers.. Today it is meant to comprise of a set of basic skills which include the use& production of digital media, information processing and retrieval, participation in social networks

for creation, sharing of knowledge and wide range of professional computing skills.

In India basic literacy rate is around 75% as per 2011 census. Gap between rural and urban, male (85%) and female literacy rates (65%) is still wide. In fact provision of basic literacy to its large population itself is a challenge for Indian government. Knowledge about usage of computers is therefore limited to few people living urban areas and internet penetration is still not up to the mark. Absence of basic infrastructure and knowledge to use them denies 'Digital literacy' for majority of Indian population.

- **Education Standards:** Education makes a significant impact on the ability of a person to use ICT. As the level of education rises, the gap relating to ICT

Usage between those who are highly educated and less educated widens. This is because education opens the avenues for new opportunities where the acquired knowledge can be properly utilized.

- **Gender Discrimination:** India traditionally being a patriarchal society, women were deprived of education and employment since ancient period. This is one aspect where the digital divide is predominantly expressed in Indian society. Indian women have a reduced access to ICT for a number of reasons ranging from socio-cultural attitudes. Even in IT and ITES companies, women have low representation. According to 2004 survey by India's National Association for software companies, 74% professionals are men and women constitute only 26%. In IT enabled services, women constituted 30% (2009) of the total employee base in IT-BPO industry. Thus even in IT industry, women are concentrated in those areas that require routine and discretionary skills and are less visible in back office operations. Hence fewer women are projected as managers. (Etzkowitz, Gupta, & Kemelgor, (2010))
- **Income Levels:** Increase in the income levels leads to rise in the purchase power among the people and hence access to high quality ICT becomes possible for them. At the same time low income levels leads to reduce or no access to ICT.
- **Geographical Position:** Employment and career growth of are directly related to easy access to internet technology. Country with poor internet access suffer greater economic downfall than countries with better access to internet. Within India also, there are several areas in the northeast with less or no access to internet partly due to their remote geographic position and partly due to lack of proper network for communication.

- **Age Factor:** Old age people and senior citizens do not easily adapt to changes in ICT. This is partly due to their reluctance to accept some new products in the market and also they need to learn how to use the new equipment. This hence increases the digital divide between young and old generations.
- **Language:** India is a multilingual country with 22 recognized official languages and more than 780 different languages are spoken in the country (Hindusthantimes.com). English enjoys an associate status in India. It is the most important language for national, political and commercial communication. 30% of the people speak Hindi and the rest of the languages are spoken in other regions of India are sparsely represented over the web. Therefore one of the formidable obstacle to ICT diffusion in India is language. (Dubey, (2009))
- **Race and Origin:** This kind of divide is found in USA and other western countries. Blacks and Latin Americans have less access to digital technology when compared to whites there.
- **Other Disabilities**: Both communication, use and internet access were found to be markedly low among disabled people. There is a wide range of disabling conditions that require specific approaches to information and communication. People with disabilities need to bear additional costs to obtain adaptive technology.

Despite all the above mentioned dimensions of digital divide found, India is still in the leading position when compared to other countries with regard to tech savvy man power and their interest in ICT utilization. Basic English education, availability of ICT infrastructure at urban and semi-urban setups facilitates urban and rural youth to take up careers in ICT.

BRIDGING THE DIGITAL DIVIDE IN INDIA

Although India has been one of the emerging superpowers in Information and Technology, the benefits have been remarkably slow particularly in remote and rural areas. (Singh, 2007,). Use of IT and computerization in India began in 1978 and thereby progressed slowly. In 1985 the Government of India decided to increase the pace of IT usage at district level. National Informatics Centre (NIC), a central Government organization was chosen to implement a national program called DISNIC. (Dutt, (2003)) Last but not least National e-Governance plan (NeGP) initiated in 2006 forms the base for spread of IT throughout the country.

Some Government Initiatives for bridging the digital divide in Rural India:

- **Kissan Call Centre ("A Portal of Government", 2015)**: This was initiated by Ministry of Agriculture in the year 2004, throughout the country to deliver extension services to the farming community. The purpose of these call centres is to respond to issues raised by farmers instantly in local language. Queries relating to agriculture and allied sectors are being addressed through these call centres. Just by a small call farmer comes in to contact with an agricultural graduate and allied sectors.
- **Bhoomi Project:** Karnataka government initiated this project with the aim to digitize all the farm land records in order to bring about transparency in rural India land record management. This programme implemented in 2002, was one of the pioneering e-governance programmes in the country. This programme is recognized by UN and World Bank and is lauded as landmark e-governance initiative. Absence if stake holders, management capacity building among the government servants etc. are some of the reasons behind Bhoomi s popularity (E-governance, 2010).
- **CARD:** Computer Aided Administration of Registration Department (CARD) is an e-government project launched by State Government of Andhra Pradesh. This project aimed at complete computerization of land registration process in Andhra Pradesh. (CARD - An E - Government initiative in Andhra Pradesh (India), 2003)
- **e-Seva:** Launched in the year2001, e-seva project marked yet another milestone in the march towards complete e-governance in united Andhra Pradesh. E-Seva centres opened under the project act as one-stop-shop for nearly 66 Government to Citizen Services. E-Seva services include instant money transfer, payment of mobile DTH charges, utility bill payment, electricity bill payment, bus ticket bookings and many more. Thus E-seva provides a wide spectrum of citizen friendly services ("Welcome to eSeva", 2014).
- **Gyandoot:** It is a Government to citizen Internet based service portal implemented in Dhar district of MP in Maharashtra in the year 2000. The project was designed to extend the benefits of ICT to people in rural areas by directly linking the Government and villagers through information kiosks. Gyandoot pioneered the idea of rural tele-centres in India. The project concept has been replicated by other ICT development initiatives in India. This project also received the award in 2000 for public service and democracy.
- **Friends: (Fast Reliable Instant Efficient Network)** for disbursement of services is a single window 'no queue' integrated remittance centre where the citizens have the opportunity to pay all taxes and other dues to the

government under one roof with no extra costs. Friends accept payment from Kerala University, MG University, local bodies, state electricity boards etc. Launched in the year 2000, this initiative facilitate its citizen's speedy access to government services (Kerala State IT Mission, 2017).

- **Lifeline India:** Launched in 2006, Life line India helps the rural poor to find useful information through the usage of digital technology. BT along with one world – charitable organizations are operating at village level to provide telephone based information services to the rural farmers- enabling them to record a question and soon after retrieve the recorded reply. Coverage extends up to more than 700 villages and an average of 350 calls are being received every day. What the farmers need to do is to dial the lifeline numbers from a community telephone. Life lines in India have proven the value of digital inclusion educating the rural people to use technology, find access to advice and learning to improve the future of their families and local communities. (Bansode.S.Y, 2011)
- **Voice:** Vijayawada Municipal corporation has introduced a multi-channel project VOICE (Versatile, online information for citizen empowerment) to disseminate information about government activities to citizens and to enable online service interactions. 'Voice' provides government related information like budgetary details, public notices, tourism related information etc. Voice also provides online transactions initiating services including request for water and sewage connections, birth and death certificate registration etc (eGovernment for Development, 2008).
- **VidyaVahini:** Launched in 2003, VidyaVahini programme aims to computerize all the Government schools in India. A pilot project has already undertaken in 140 schools in 7 districts across the country. Further by selecting 20 Government and aided schools in consultations with different state governments, a computer lab worth 10 lakhs is proposed to be setup. This program aims to provide a thrust to computer aided learning for rural students. (The Hindu, 2003)
- **Dristee Foundation Services** ("Wikepedia", 2018)**:** Established in the year 2000, Dristee is an Indian based organization that provides IT goods and services to rural India through village kiosks that are run and managed by local entrepreneurs and thus helping to stem the distress migration of people from rural to urban parts of the country. Partnered with ICICI, Microsoft, IFC and SBI this organization facilitates IT services to remote rural areas in the country.
- **Lokmitra Centre** (Government of Himachal Pradesh, n.d.) **:** Common service centre scheme in Himachal Pradesh is popularly known as Lokmitra Kendra project. Goal was to establish 3366 e-governance centres at Panchayat level in

the state. The centre established under Public Private Partnership (PPP) mode leverages the support of various stake holders such as state government, local bodies etc. Earlier confined to payment of bills, Lokmitra centre has become a single organ providing a large number of services through a single login id- Aadhar based services, birth death marriage registrations, BPL certificates election related services, online police complaints and so on.

- **Janmitra Common Service Centre (CSC) ("CSC.gov.in", 2017):** Initiative of Uttar Pradesh, common service centres are ICT enabled front end service delivery points at village level for delivery of government, financial, social and private sector services in agriculture, health, education, banking, insurance pension utility payments etc. This programme aims at reaching the remote villages in rural India.
- **NeGP and E-Kranti ("E-Kranti", 2006):** Launched in 2006, National e-Governance plan (NeGP) is a comprehensive programme of Government of India, designed to leverage capabilities and opportunities presented by ICT to promote good governance across the country. NeGP proposes to implement ICT projects with timeliness and responsibility allocations – in a 'mission mode.' There were 27 mission mode projects approved in this context. Vision of NeGP is to make all government services accessible to the common man, in his locality, through common service delivery outlets. The implementation strategy envisages a clear definition of service goals and metrics for each project.

Considering the shortcomings of NeGP –lack of integration among Government applications and databases, GOI approved E-Kranti with the vision to make governance more transparent. Mission mode projects also increased to 44. Many new social sector projects namely women and child development, social benefits from financial inclusion, e-Bhasha and so on are added as Mission mode projects under e-Kranti.

- **Digital India Programme (Digital India Programme", 2018):** It is a campaign launched by GOI to ensure that Government services are made available to its citizens electronically by improving online infrastructure and by increasing internet connectivity and by making the country digitally empowered in the field of technology. The journey of e governance initiatives in India took a broader dimension in mid 1990s with wider applications emphasising on citizen centric services. Despite successful implementation of many e-governance projects across the country, e-governance as a whole has not been able to make the desired impact and fulfil all its objectives.

Launched in 2015, Digital India aims to digitally connect rural areas in India with high speed internet. Its three components include:

1. Development of a stable and secured digital infrastructure.
2. Developing government services digitally.
3. Universal digital literacy

Vision of Digital India is inclusive growth in areas of electronic services products manufacturing and job opportunities. The whole programme is centred on three key areas i.e. digital infrastructure as a utility to every citizen, governance and services on demand and digital empowerment of citizens. Further Government aims to strengthen 9 pillars to Digital India and they are:

1. Broad Band highway i.e. public internet access programme
2. e-Governance: Reforming the Government through Technology
3. e-Kranti
4. IT for Jobs
5. Early Harvest programmes
6. Electronics manufacturing
7. Information for all

Digital India provides various services to citizens like

1. **Digital Locker:** In order to implement the idea of paperless governance, digital locker is a platform for issuance and verification of documents in a digital way thus preventing the use of any physical documents. However Indian students who sign up for digital locker and get a dedicated cloud storage space. They can get access to their documents wherever possible.
2. **E-Education:** All schools in India are to be connected with broadband and free Wi-Fi is to be setup in all the schools. Further it aims as developing a massive online courses in pilot basis.
3. **e-Health:** It covers online medical consultation, medical records, online medical supply and pan-India exchange of patient information. Further it aims at providing full medical coverage to the citizens within three years since 2015.
4. **National Scholarship Portal:** It is a one stop solution through which various services starting from student application receipt, processing and sanction of scholarships to students are enabled. It works under Mission Mode project and aims to provide a common portal for various scholarship schemes of Central Government and state Government.

5. **E-Chaupal:** Despite massive industrialization since the past decade, India is still dependent on agriculture. The farmers are often exploited by unreasonable intermediaries at every stage involved

Some More Initiatives:

1. **UTS Mobile Ticketing:** Government of India in its effort to moving towards cashless economy initiated e-ticketing on IRCTC for booking reserved tickets. More than 58% of train accommodation is reserved through
2. **E-Ticketing:** Facility of for purchasing unreserved ticket through mobile phone is also available in some metro cities like – Delhi, Mumbai, Kolkata and Hyderabad. Further automatic vending machines dispensing unreserved tickets using smart cards are provided in over thousand locations
3. **Sugamya Pusthakalaya:** This is a one shop stop for disabled people like blind & print disability. Books of diverse languages from various libraries across India can be assessed. Users access a collection of over 3.28.900books with their individual reading shelves online and download facilities.
4. **Start-up India Portal and Mobile App:** Start-up India portal is a flagship initiative of Government of India (GOI) intended to build a strong eco-system for nurturing innovations and start-ups in the country that will drive sustainable economic growth and generate large scale employment opportunities. Government through this initiative aims to empower start-ups to grow through innovation and design.
5. **Soil Health Card:** It aims at promoting Integrated Nutrient Management through judicious use chemical fertilizers including secondary and micro nutrients in conjunction with organic manures & bio-fertilizers for improving soil health, its productivity and ensuring quality control requirements of fertilizers and promoting organic farming practices.
6. **SMS Based Mid-Day Meal Monitoring Scheme:** Mid-day meal mobile application is meant for effective monitoring of daily and monthly mechanism for MDM in charge teacher who has to send the daily /monthly data using SMS. The authorities can send SMS alerts to all the defaulters using single button available on the app.
7. **UMANG (Unified Mobile App for New Age Governance):** This application facilitates a single point of access to all government services. 1200 services of various government departments, centre state and local bodies- which aim to abridge inconvenience faced by users in managing multiple mobile applications and avail one stop solution to varied government services.

8. **SWAYAM (Study Webs of Active–Learning for Young Aspiring Minds):** This app seeks to introduce digital technology among the students who remained untouched with it earlier and hence were not able to join the mainstream knowledge economy. This is done through an indigenously developed IT platform that accommodates all courses right from 9th Standard to PG to be assessed by everyone.
9. **PMVY (Pradhan Mantri Kushal Vikas Yojana):** It is a flagship scheme of Ministry of Skill development and Entrepreneurship (MSDE). Objective of this scheme is to enable a large number of Indian youth to take up industry relevant skill training that will help them to secure a better livelihood.
10. **PMJDY (Pradhan Mantri Jan-Dhan Yojana):** It is a national mission on financial inclusion that aims at an integrated approach towards inclusion of all households within the country within the preview of mainstream financial services. - Access to financial literacy, credit, insurance and pension facility. This initiative facilitates channelling of Government benefits to the beneficiaries accounts and pushes ahead the direct benefit transfer scheme of the union government.
11. **PMGDSA (Pradhan Mantri Gramin digital Saksharata Abhiyaan):** Main objective of this scheme is making all the people in the rural areas across the states and union territories as digitally literate by March 31st 2019. The scheme aims to bridge the digital divide specifically training the rural youth including the marginal sections of the society.
12. **E-Pathshala:** This is developed by NCERT and hence is showcasing and disseminating all educational e-resources including text books audio, video and a variety of other print and non-print material through website and mobile application. This application serves the dual purpose of reaching the remote areas of the country and also contributing towards bridging digital divide and offering comparable quality of e contents. All stake holders- students, parents and teachers can access to these e-books through the net.
13. **E-Marketplace:** Government e-Market place (GeM) is single window solution for online procurement of common use goods and services required by various government departments, organizations and public sector undertakings. GeM aims to enhance transparency, efficiency and speed in public procurement. The portal offers online registration facilities for all stake holders- Government users, Product sellers and service providers.
14. **E-Basta:** This project has created a framework to make school books accessible in digital form and e-books to be read and used on tablets and laptops. Main idea is to bring various publishers and schools together on one platform.

15. **E-District:** This is a mission mode program envisaged to strengthen the district administration of the state by providing ICT support to the participatory departments and district administration through centralized software applications for selected category of citizen services. Community Service centres (CSC) were proposed to be established at Gram Panchayat level under this programme.
16. **DISHA:** (Digital Saksharata Abhiyaan) National digital literacy mission has been formulated to impart IT training to 52.5 lakh persons including Asha Workers, Anganwadi teachers and authorised ration dealers in all states /Union Territories across the country. The initiative aims at training non- IT literate citizens to become IT literate to enable their active and effective participation in democratic and developmental processes and enhance their livelihoods also ("Government of India", 2016).
17. **(PMKVY (Pradhan Mantri Krishi Vikas Yojana):** It is a flagship programme of ministry of skill development and entrepreneurship. Objective of this scheme is to ensure large number of Indian youth to take up industry relevant skill training that will help them in securing better livelihood.
18. **MyGov:** This is a unique initiative undertaken to encourage participative governance involving the common citizen at large. The idea of MyGov brings Government closer to common man by using online platform for exchange of ideas and views with experts contributing for socio economic transformation of India.
19. **RAS (Rapid Assessment System):** Initiated by Digital India for continuous feedback on e-services delivered by State Governments and Government of India. This system has multiple channels for receiving feedback and is backed by analytics. These analytics will help in integrating departments for continuous system improvement.

Innovative ICT applications By Media Lab Asia for Rural Development

(Media Lab Asia, (n.d.):

- **Interactive Information Dissemination System (IIDS):** It has been designed to facilitate the farmers with information regarding latest scientific farming methods whenever they require. It is a pull and push based system, there is mobile interface at the front end and web interface at the back end. Data can be transmitted through voice, text, images and videos from both ends. This is an integrated model, largely integration of toll free IVRS, Smart phone application and interactive portal. Current implementation of IIDS is spread across 3 states- Andhra Pradesh& Telangana as 'Annapurna Krishi Prasar Seva (AKPS) and Meghalaya as m4agriNEI.

- **Digi-Bunai:** (Open source Cad tool for Weaving) Aim of this initiative is to reduce 'Effort and Time' of manual processes design making, creating graph and punching the jacquard cards. The user can see the complete cloth digitally to experiment with different parameters of design. The software will aid the weavers to create the artwork and translate the sari design to be loaded on the looms. Features of this application include-create and edit the designs based on handloom parameters, convert artwork into graph based on the weavers assigned, fabric quality and loom parameters, 2 D simulation of the fabric to get a feel of the real fabric also calculate the bill material with existing yarn database.

With the support of DC-Handloom (Ministry of Textiles, GOI) the application and services are pilot tested at National Centre for Textile design (NCTD) and at Weavers service centres and four common service centres at Varanasi under active engagement of weaving community over there.

- **Punarjjani:** It is a web based tool to assist special teachers in assessment of children (6-18 years) with mental retardation (MR). It enables the teacher for easy, efficient, quick and regular assessment of MR children. 21 traininig workshops were conducted at Delhi, Ahmedabad etc. on using this tool for MR children assessment and monitoring their progress. 820 special teachers representing 485 special schools and 122 Sarva Siksha Abhiyaan blocks in Tamilnadu were trained under this initiative
- **Punarbhava:** This is a web portal to provide information regarding disability field. Wide range of segregated information about persons with disabilities and other stake holders in this field is made available here.
- **Bharat Net Project to Gram Panchayats ("Press Trust of India", 2017):** 'Bharat Net Project' is the new name given to 'National Optical Fibre Net' (NOFN) which was launched in 2011 to provide broad band connectivity to all 2.5 lakh Gram Panchayats in the country. It is an ambitious project of national importance aimed to establish by 2017 a highly scalable network infrastructure accessible on a non-discriminatory basis that can provide on demand affordable broad band connectivity for all households in rural India. The entire project is being funded by Universal service obligation fund (USOF) setup to improve telecom services in rural and remote areas of the country. Its objective is to facilitate – e- governance, e-health, e-education, e-banking, internet and other services to rural India. By Nov 2016 Bharat Net

reached 80,000 Gram Panchayats across rural areas. Government also set up Wi-Fi hotspots across all connected villages.

- **Vishveswariah PhD Scheme for Electronics and IT:** This was initiated by Ministry of Electronics & IT scheme in June 2014 to enhance the number of PhDs in Electronic system Design and Manufacturing (ESDM) and IT/ITES sectors in the country.

This scheme is providing fellowship support to 1500 PhD scholars. Also identify and support 200 bright young faculty members involved in research and technology development in ESDM and IT ("To Give Real Service", 2012)

- **ITRA (Information Technology Research Academy):** It is an enabling programme launched by Ministry of Electronics, to help build a national resource for advancing the quality and quantity of Research and Development (R&D) in ICT and IT related institutions across India. So far ITRA conducted R&D in three focus areas- Mobile computing, networking and applications (ITRA-Mobile), IT based innovations in water resources sustainability (ITRA-Water) and IT based transformations in Indian agriculture and food (ITRA-AG and Food). Further, 17 technologies with potential start up possibilities are being pursued. These technologies include solutions to society important problems in the areas of disaster management, urban floods, remote health care transport and drought management (ITRA, 2011)
- **BHIM (Bharat Interface for Money and Aadhar based Mobile payment Application):** Government with the ambition to encourage cashless economy introduced BHIM for retail merchants. This new service allows the customers to make purchases using their Aadhaar numbers linked with their bank accounts. The transaction will require customer's fingerprint for authentication. Thus BHIM is a smart mobile phone application based on unified payments interface that allows simple easy and quick payment transactions ("Digital India", n.d.).
- **Rural Connect:** This is another unique ICT initiative to capture all best and innovative practises by sharing the experiences of policy and project directors as well as rural development and Panchayati raj field functionaries. This web based rural connect application is aimed to capture all grass root realities, best practices and initiatives which are not popularly available across the country due to lack of proper documentation, sharing, replicability and lessons learnt from them.

National Institute of Rural Development and Panchayati Raj (NIRDPR) hosting the rural connect platform urges all the development functionaries' policy and program directors researchers and PRI functionaries to take a few minutes and share your experience, knowledge expertise, ideas and new ways of doing things for rural development. Through documentation of best practises and case studies from different regions would help the stakeholders to plan effectively and implement the need based local region specific programmes. Also this documentation would take up research and action research based on field inputs to bring in faster development and to address the emerging needs of rural people and thereby bridging the digital divide. Any department or an agency or individuals can access to Rural Connect with the link available on NIRD website ("Share your Story", n.d.)

- **SMS (Centralized Smart Meeting System for Effective Governance):** Smart Meeting System is a web based online application that empowers the administrative system for effective functioning and improving governance. In order to create an easy ICT system for organizing, conducting and capturing minutes and monitor the decisions taken, smart meeting system is developed by NIRDPR as a part of their mandate to improve the governance for Nation's prosperity. SMS aims at bringing more accountability and provide improved governance to the citizens ("Smart Meeting System: NIRDPR", n.d.).

There are several other mobile applications introduced as a part of Digital India programme facilitating the citizens to make use of online Government services.

Despite all the above efforts made by GOI there are certain barriers in the way of effective implementation of these programmes. Some of them as listed below:

BARRIERS TO BRIDGING DIGITAL-DIVIDE

- **Illiteracy and Digital Illiteracy:** Education and information literacy play an important role in keeping society from fragmenting into information haves and have not's. From the perspective of digital divide, IT literacy is very important to allow access to digital information. In India where approximately $1/4^{th}$ of its population is illiterate digital literacy cannot be expected out of them. Government schools in the villages lack in basic infrastructure like benches and chairs and washrooms for their students. Access to and usage of computers is therefore something out of question for them. Hence there are people in India who are literate but not digitally literate and hence are denied access to digital information.

- **Indian Education System**: Traditional class room teaching methods in vernacular languages, emphasising more on theoretical aspects of all the subjects prevents them from getting practical exposure to concepts which IT education can contribute.
- **Poverty:** There is a strong correlation between digital divide and poverty. Almost 40% of world's population lives in low income countries. About 1 billion have no access to ICT. (Stoiciu, 2011) Similarly in India also the rural poor have very little or no access to ICT. Nevertheless, given that, digital services are the vehicle for production and participation, the need to be connected is real and significant. Being disconnected from the digital services pushes people into exclusion and poverty (W.Muschart, (2013)
- **Language**: India being a land of cultural and ethnic diversity there exist multiple languages since ancient times. But access to ICT requires some knowledge of English as majority of ICT packages are in English. Access to IT through unrecognized local languages is not possible. But in India, these kind of languages are more in number.
- **Gender Discrimination:** India being a traditionally patriarchal society women have less access to education when compared to men. Even so in the case of digital education. Most of the Indian women particularly from rural areas remain digitally illiterate. Lack of IT knowledge hampers their education and employment opportunities.
- **Other Economic and Geographic Barriers:** Lack of money to invest on digital literacy is one reason why digital divide deepens among the middle class and poor community in India. Staying in remote villages where net connection is unavailable and cannot afford to go to another place for digital education is another reason contributing for deep digital divide.

CONCLUSION AND SUGGESTIONS

India is the world's largest sourcing destination for the information technology (IT) industry, accounting for approximately 67 per cent of the US$ 124-130 billion market. The industry employs about 10 million workforces. More importantly, the industry has led the economic transformation of the country and altered the perception of India in the global economy (IBEF, 2017). India is fast developing in ICT sector as is evident that largest number of IT professionals today are from India but there are many areas in the country not accessible to ICT. Lack of quality net services and gender based digital divide are some of the issues which require serious concern. The following are some workable solutions to reduce digital divide and contribute to build strong digital India

THE WAY FORWARD

Government must take all measures to increase Internet access and usage in rural areas.

- Design and offer appropriate software and short courses for those who have no digital literacy
- Involve NGOs and private corporate sectors in provision of infrastructure and teaching the digital illiterates.
- Establish free kisoks for public usage in semi-rural and rural areas.
- Schools, Libraries and community halls can be utilized to impart digital literacy among the rural areas.
- Formulate new software that can connect with rural people in their local languages.
- Encourage competition among the telecom providers to facilitate digital technology at cheaper rates to the community.
- Encourage local farmers and self-help groups to use digital technology to market their produce online.
- Panchayats must use digital technology to provide services to the public like collection of revenue, birth and death registration etc. This is already under implementation.
- Women must be particularly taught to use digital technology for making household remittances and other economic transactions.
- Children from primary school level onwards must be inculcated with digital education in every village.

REFERENCES

A Portal of Government of India for Farmer Centric Mobile Based Services. (2015). Retrieved from http://mkisan.gov.in/

ArifD. T. (n.d.). Retrieved from www.Iasj.net

Bansode, S. Y. D. (2011). Bridging the Digital Divide in India: Some Initiatives. *Asia Pacific Journal of Library and Information Science, 1*(1), 108-121.

CARD - An E-Government initiative in Andhra Pradesh (India). (2003). Retrieved from www.icmrindia.org/casestudies/catalogue/IT%20and%20Systems/

CSC.gov.in. (2017). Retrieved from https://www.csc.gov.in/

Digital India Power to Empower. (n.d.). *BHIM (Bharat Interface for Money): Digital India Programme*. Retrieved from https://digitalindia.gov.in/content/bhim-bharat-interface-money

Digital India Programme, Department of Electronics & Information Technology, Government of India. (2018, May 19). Retrieved from http://digitalindia.gov.in/

Dragulanescu, N. (2002). Social Impact of the "Digital Divide" in a Central–Eastern European Country. *The International Information & Library Review*, *34*(2), 139–151. doi:10.1006/iilr.2002.0190

Dr.Murthy, N. N. (2014). Digital Divide, Access and use of New Information Communication Technologies among Indian Rural Females. *ISOR Journal of Humanities and Social Sciences, 19*(8), 35–43.

Dubey, P. (2009). *Study of Development of Machine Translation System from Hindi to Dongri language: An important tool to bridge digital divide*[REMOVED HYPERLINK FIELD]. Retrieved from www.shodhganga.inflibnet.ac.in

Dutt, S. (2003). Impact of Information Communication Technology on Society. *Yojana*.

E-Governance. (2010, March). *Learnings from Bhoomi*. Retrieved from http://egovkarnataka.blogspot.com/2010/03/learnings-from-bhoomi-march5th2010.html

E-Kranti. Welcome to NeGD: National eGovernance Division (NeGD). (2006). Retrieved from https://negd.gov.in/e-kranti

eGovernment for Development. (2008). *ETransparency Case Study No.16*. Retrieved from http://www.egov4dev.org/transparency/case/voice.shtml

Etzkowitz, H., Gupta, N., & Kemelgor, C. (2010). The Gender Revolution in Science and Technology. *Journal of International Affairs*.

Government of Himachal Pradesh, Department of IT State Information Portal. (n.d.). *Lokmitra Kendra - CSC Scheme*. Retrieved from http://hp.gov.in/hp/

Government of India: National Institute of Electronics & Information Technology. (2016, May 20). *National Digital Literacy Mission - NDLM*. Retrieved from http://beta.nielit.gov.in/calicut/content/national-digital-literacy-mission-ndlm

IBEF. (2017). *IT & ITeS Industry in India*. Retrieved from https://www.ibef.org/industry/information-technology-india.aspx

India, G. O. (2012). *Kisan Credit Cards*. Retrieved from http://mkisan.gov.in

ITRA. (2011). Retrieved from https://itra.medialabasia.in/

Kapoor, A., & Mathur, D. (2016, July 28). Bridging the digital divide. *The Hindu*. Retrieved from https://www.thehindu.com/opinion/op-ed/Bridging-the-digital-divide/article14511451.ece

Kawaljeet & Singh. (2016). ICT Diffusion &Digital Divide in India: Implications for economic policies. *Pacific Business Review International, 1*(2).

Kenneth & Kumar. (2004). IT Experience. In *India: Bridging the Digital Divide*. Sage Publications.

Kerala State IT Mission. (2017). *Friends*. Retrieved from http://www.itmission.kerala.gov.in/friends.php

Mark, W. (2012). Smart Policies to close the Digital Divide: Best Practises from around the world. In W. Mark (Ed.), *Report of Economic Intelligence Unit Limited*. The Economist.

Media Lab Asia. (n.d.). *Digital India Corporation*. Retrieved from https://medialabasia.in/

Muschart, W. R. M. (2013). The internet and social in equality in international perspective. New York: Routledge, Taylor & Francis Group.

News Headlines, English News, Today Headlines, Top Stories. (2017). Retrieved from https://www.hindustantimes.com/

One Library Per Village. (2017). *Bridging Digital Divide*. Retrieved from https://www.mygov.in/sites/default/files/mygov_144229659619673.pdf

Press Trust of India. (2017, February 8). *Internet to be available in 2.5 lakh gram panchayats by 2018-end: Govt*. Retrieved from https://www.business-standard.com/article/pti-stories/net-to-be-available-in-all-gram-panchayats-by-next-year-govt-117020800525_1.html

Raghav, B. (2016, November 3). *A tale of two Indians: An emerging technological superpower or future digital colony*. Retrieved from http://mashable.com/: http://mashable.com/2016/11/03/a-tale-of-two-indias/#HIDxJ1WNqsqA

Ranjit, D. (2002, October 5). *Mr. India's Digital Divide: An ever widening chasm*. Academic Press.

Sarkar, P. (2015). *The Global Digital Divides: Explaining change*. Springer.

Share Your Story. (n.d.). *Rural Connect*. Retrieved from http://nird.gov.in/RC/

Singh, D. N. (2007). *Bridging the Digital Divide in India: Some Challenges and Opportunities*. Retrieved from http://unpan1.un.org/intradoc/groups/public/documents/un-dpadm/unpan042671.pdf

Smart Meeting System, NIRDPR. (n.d.). Retrieved from http://nird.gov.in/sms/

Stoiciu, A. (2011, October). The Role of e-Governance in Bridging the Digital Divide. *UN Chronicle*. Retrieved from https://unchronicle.un.org/article/role-e-governance-bridging-digital-divide

The Hindu. (2003, June 12). *The Prime Minister launches Vidyavahini*. Retrieved from https://www.thehindu.com/thehindu/2003/06/12/stories/2003061203581100.htm

To give real service, you must add something which cannot be bought or measured with money. (2012). *Visvesvaraya PHD Scheme for Electronics & IT*. Retrieved from https://phd.medialabasia.in/

Vighneswara, P. I. (2007). Digital Divide in India: Inferences from the Information and Communication Technology workforce. In M. A. Ragnedda (Ed.), Digital Divide: Internet and Social Inequality in International Perspective. London: Routledge.

Welcome to eSeva: Government of Telangana. (2014). Retrieved from https://www.esevaonline.telangana.gov.in/

Wikepedia: The Free Encyclopedia. (2018). *Drishtee*. Retrieved from https://en.wikipedia.org/wiki/Drishtee

Chapter 5
Digital-Locker Services in India:
An Assessment of User Adoption and Challenges

Sumangla Rathore
https://orcid.org/0000-0001-9626-1544
Suyash College, Udaipur, India

Avinash Panwar
Mohanlal Sukhadia University, Udaipur, India

ABSTRACT

On 1st July 2015, Government of India launched a Digital India campaign which is a flagship program of the government with an objective to transform India into a digitally empowered society. One key initiative of the program is digital locker service which aims at sharing and storing of electronic documents at one place in a digital locker. A study was undertaken to assess the awareness level of citizens regarding this service, to identify the problems and challenges associated with its implementation, to identify factors that affect adoption of such initiatives, and to make recommendations to various stake holders. The data analysis revealed that main concerns associated with the service include security, confidentiality, and ease of use. The survey data also revealed that the behavioral intention regarding adoption of this service is mainly determined by the user innovativeness and ease of use, usefulness, and compatibility do not seem to have an impact on the behavioral intention to adopt the service.

DOI: 10.4018/978-1-5225-5412-7.ch005

INTRODUCTION

What Is Digital India Programme?

On 1st July 2015, Government of India launched a Digital India campaign which is a flagship programme of the government with an objective to transform India into a digitally empowered society. Digital India programme covers multiple digitization ideas and projects under a common umbrella. The program has been conceptualised by the Department of Electronics and Information Technology, Government of India. The Digital India program was expected to be implemented in phases until 2018 and shall be a transformational journey towards making sure that government services are available to all citizens electronically.

Vision of Digital India Programme (as per the Press Information Bureau, Government of India)

The Digital India programme aims to achieve following objectives as per its vision statement:

1. Infrastructure as Utility to Every Citizen:
   a. Making available high speed internet as a core utility in all Gram Panchayats.
   b. Digital identity throughout the lifecycle of an individual – unique, lifelong, online and authenticable.
   c. Enable participation for digital and financial services through Mobile phones and Bank accounts.
   d. A Common Service Centre within the locality for easy access.
   e. Private space on a public Cloud which is shareable.
   f. Ensuring safety and security in Cyber-space of the country.
2. Governance and Services on Demand:
   a. Easy and single window access to all persons through seamlessly unified departments or jurisdictions.
   b. Real time availability of Government services through online and mobile platforms.
   c. Easy access to all citizen privileges by making them available on the Cloud.
   d. Digitally enabling government services with an objective of improving ease of doing Business.
   e. Cashless financial transactions by making them electronic, above a threshold.
   f. Decision support systems and development through GIS.

Table 1. Products and services unveiled during Digital India Week

Products • Digital Locker • National Scholarship Portal • e-Hospital • e-Sign • Digitize India	**Portal/Apps** • Digital India Portal and Mobile Apps • MyGov mobile app • Swachh Bharat Mission app	**DoT** • Bharatnet in 11 states • Wi-fi hot spots • NGN
Institutions • Centre for flexible electronics • Centre of excellence IoT	**Policies** • Policy document on EDF • Policy document on e-governance policy initiatives under Digital India	

Source: https://trak.in/tags/business/2015/07/02/digital-locker-bharatnet-e-sign-10-initiatives-digitalindiaweek/

3. Digital Empowerment of Citizens:
    a. Providing universal digital literacy.
    b. Making all digital resources universally accessible.
    c. Availability of all Government documents/ certificates on the Cloud.
    d. Availability of digital resources / services in Indian languages.
    e. Participative governance through digital platforms that encourage collaboration.
    f. Portability of all entitlements for individuals through the Cloud.

The Digital India programme was promoted through a Digital India Week event which was inaugurated by the Prime Minister of India, Mr Narendra Modi, in capital city of Delhi. During this programme various products and services were unveiled by the Government to address the issues of digital divide, to bring transparency in government operations and to leverage the power of technology for overall upliftment of lives of Indian citizens.

The main projects launched during the event are as given in Table 1.

A brief summary of the main projects proposed by the government is given below:

1. **Digital Locker:** Government of India launched a beta version of the Aadhaar linked Digital Locker in February of 2015. The digital locker scheme has been envisaged to allow the Indian citizens to place all educational, medical, passport and PAN card details in a digital form over a cloud storage system so that it can be accessed from anywhere in the world without having to carry all the documents physically. The Digital Locker also has functionality where users can directly submit their documents to Government departments while submitting their applications online.

2. **e-Sign:** E-Sign is a component of Digital Locker which enables the users to electronically Sign and attest Digital documents using their Aadhaar card number and PAN card. The application can contribute towards making the process of submitting any government application completely paperless.
3. **National Scholarship Portal:** A one stop solution in the form of National Scholarships Portal is envisaged which shall offer end to end scholarship process right from submission of student application, verification, sanction and disbursal to end beneficiary for all the scholarships provided by the Government of India.
4. **e-Hospital:** e-Hospital shall connect all hospitals across India to provide services such as appointment booking with hospital through Online Registration System (ORS), lab reports and blood availability in any government hospital. All these services can be availed online and will be Aadhaar based.
5. **Digitise India:** The main objective of Digitise India is to convert all the important documents and services in Government offices and record rooms in digital format so that these documents can be made available online in the form of a library and can be searched online. The Government proposes to carry out the digitization process through Crowd sourcing wherein citizens can earn money by participating in this activity.
6. **MyGov Mobile App:** MyGov mobile app shall be a mobile app version of the MyGov portal. Through this app, citizens can offer ideas and suggestions and thus contribute towards Government Policy making. The app shall also be used to disseminate information regarding various initiatives and services launched by the Government.
7. **Swachh Bharat Mission App:** Swachh Bharat Mission app aims to increase citizen awareness and participation in Clean India mission. The app users can share public toilet photographs across India along with their locations so that this information when once collated in centralized place can be used by ordinary citizens.
8. **BharatNet:** BharatNet is related to providing broadband networking in the country which shall be the world's largest rural broadband connectivity project using optical fibre to connect each of 2.5 lakh gram panchayats with a minimum of 100 Mbps bandwidth. Eventually, this project will serve as an infrastructure backbone of Digital India, to facilitate delivery of various e-Governance initiatives along with e-Health, e-Education, e-Banking, internet and various other services.

9. **WiFi Hotspots:** Wifi hotspots shall be launched across 2500 towns and cities in India by Government of India in partnership with Bharat Sanchar Nigam Limited (BSNL), the public sector Indian telecom company.
10. **Next Generation Network (NGN):** NGN is another project that aims to bring high-speed broadband connectivity in India. It will congregate public switched telephone network, data network and wireless mobile network to offer high-speed broadband network access. Value Added Services such as video chats, video conferencing and other services will be made available on mobile phone or fixed line telephone at affordable prices.

Programmes Covered Under Digital Initiative

The proposed digital initiatives under the Digital India programme will be implemented and monitored through a programme management structure. The management structure comprises of the Cabinet Committee on Economic Affairs (CCEA) for according approval to projects, a Monitoring Committee headed by the Prime Minister, a Digital India Advisory Group chaired by the Minister of Communications and IT, an Apex Committee chaired by the Cabinet Secretary and the Expenditure Finance Committee (EFC) / Committee on Non Plan Expenditure (CNE).

Experts believe that the digital technologies can bring about social and economic transformation which is comparable with the industrial revolution. Terms such as 'The Internet Economy' or "Internet of Everything (IoE)" have been coined to represent the new age Internet technologies which have the potential to generate immense business opportunities, employment and development of society. Similar transformation is expected from the 'Digital India' programme which can act as a driving force of progress of new India.

The following pillars of opportunities shall be implemented to further enhance public behavior and expectations in digital way (Digital India: Unleashing Prosperity, 2015):

1. Broadband Highways
2. Digital Locker
3. Mobile connectivity
4. e-Kranti
5. Jobs
6. Manufacturing
7. MyGov
8. Information for all

9. Scope with Foreign Universities

Benefits

Digital India is a programme to transform India into a digitally empowered society and knowledge economy. It is expected to bring following benefits with its implementation:

- **Easy Access to Citizen Services:** Digital technologies will help in offering services like banking at the doorstep of citizens with the help of high speed broadband connectivity.
- **E-Governance:** The citizens shall be able to access government services in real time with increased transparency and efficiency. It will also promote easy availability of cloud based services through cloud infrastructure.
- **Centralized Document Management:** The digital revolution will benefit the citizens by providing easy mechanism to access digital resources such as documents.

CONCEPTUAL FRAMEWORK OF DIGI-LOCKER SERVICES

A digital locker is an online space on servers for storing data files that can be accessed across the Internet. These servers are generally privately owned and offer their storage space to users for storing data for a fee. Since these files are centrally stored over a remote server, it helps the users to access these files from anywhere over the Internet, through any device. This ensures anytime, anywhere access to data and resolves the issues of data localization, wherein data is stored locally on a single physical hard disk drive that can only be reached by accessing the computer directly.

The term "digital locker" was first used by Microsoft for part of its proprietary Windows Marketplace service (Masters, T., 2019). The Microsoft's service was meant to enable customers to download proprietary software from servers of the company. A Digital Locker was provided to the customer for retaining a copy of the software for downloading in case of future need, for example in case of restoring Microsoft applications when migrating to a new computer. It was envisaged as a replacement of the software delivery in physical form of CDs and DVDs. This service also helped in providing a better customer service by hosting programs on a company-controlled server which enabled direct access to application purchases, protection against accidental loss of a physical disc, and easy upgradation to new systems.

Digi locker service in India, introduced by the Prime Minister of India in July 2015 is similar to the Digital Locker concept introduced by Microsoft. It is a dedicated personal storage space, linked to each resident's Aadhaar number.

Most of the government documents are issued in physical paper based form by the various agencies across the country. As a result, whenever a citizen has to submit any of these documents alongwith any application to a government department or agency, h/she has to use a photocopy or a scanned copy of the document. This leads to lot of manual paper work, file storage, document checking, verification, etc. resulting in high cost, inefficiencies and inconvenience in the system. Since the entire system is not fool-proof, it also leads to various incidents involving forged documents and certificates. Hence, there was a need to develop a system that can help in not only storing and issuing these documents electronically, but also attaching a strong identity to them, so that they cannot be misused or forged.

Digi Locker Service is an online cloud based data repository, offered as a service from Department of Electronics & Information Technology, Ministry of Communications & IT, Government of India. It allows citizens of India to store their government issued documents such as PAN (Permanent Account Number), Voter Identity, Degree Certificates in an online repository. To avail this service, the user must have a valid Aadhaar card, or unique identification (UID) number. The service will consolidate data from different government agencies centrally, linked by the Aadhaar number, thereby enhancing the ease of access and usage of the document for the people. In order to ensure the authenticity of these e-documents, the task of document sharing will be done through registered repositories only. It will also eliminate the problems such as the loss and damage of important documents like birth certificate etc. The Digital Locker shall also be linked with a facility for e-signing the documents.

The main purpose of this service is to reduce the use of physical paper based documents and to enable sharing of verified electronic documents across various government departments. The document/certificate issuing organizations are required to register on Digital Locker so that they can directly upload electronic versions of certificates of citizens in their Digital Locker. This enables the citizens to access and share these electronic certificates online with various departments and agencies registered on Digital Locker while applying for the services provided by them, thereby eliminating the need of forwarding photocopies of the documents. Thus, Digital Locker integrates the citizens, issuing organisations and requesting organisations on one platform so as to reduce administrative overhead of agencies by eliminating paperwork. It will also reduce the effort and time taken by the residents in receiving the services from various government agencies.

In order to receive public feedback on the concept before its implementation, a beta version of the service was launched on 10th February 2015. The department of electronics and information technology invited comments from users on the government's idea crowd sourcing platform myGov.in. Doubts had been raised about the security of the documents thus stored but according to Mr R.S. Sharma,

Secretary, Department of Electronics and IT, the system has been designed to be totally safe and secure.

Objectives of Digi-Locker Service

There are three key objectives of the Digital India programme, i) to establish the requisite digital infrastructure for digital identification, mobile phone connectivity and banking, (b) to provide and maintain a real-time online financial transaction platform, and (c) to enable residents to access all their documents and records digitally on a real-time basis. Digi-Locker service is an attempt to achieve the third objective and is aimed at minimizing the use of physical documents and to provide authenticity of the e-documents. Following are the objectives of the digi-locker service, as announced by the government:

1. To ensure digital empowerment to citizens of India by providing them with Digital Locker on the cloud.
2. To reduce the use of paper documents.
3. To develop a system that can ensure validity of the e-documents and thereby eliminating usage of counterfeit documents.
4. To make available a web portal and mobile application for secure access to Govt. issued documents.
5. To reduce cost and other administrative overheads for providing citizen services and to ensure ease of access for the residents to receive these services.
6. Anytime, anywhere access to the documents.
7. Enable e-Signing of documents.

Benefits of Digi Locker Service

The government has envisaged the following key benefits of the service:

1. It will enable digital empowerment of residents.
2. It will minimize the use of physical documents. For example, when a candidate is applying for job or education, the certificates like those related to birth, marriage, income, etc. will not be required to be carried and can be downloaded from the digital locker. The documents can be easily verified on the basis of his/her Aadhaar number.
3. The electronic version of the documents can be shared easily, online with any registered agency or department which requires them.

4. The authentication of the electronic documents can be carried out easily through the registered Aadhaar Number and digital signature of the user. This shall reduce the risk of forged documents.
5. The Govt. departments can issue electronic documents directly to the Digital Lockers of the citizens through a web based or mobile application. To understand this, let us consider a scenario. The driving licence of the citizens can be issued directly by the RTO (Regional Transport Office) in the designated repository. The certificate from here will be sent to the concerned resident's Digital Locker based on his/her Aadhaar number. In this case RTO can be called as an 'Issuer.' Similarly, other government agencies or educational institutions can issue certificates and upload them to digital locker system.
6. The service shall be available 24x7 and can be reached from anywhere.
7. The Digital Locker will also come with e-Signing facility. This shall ensure the authentication of documents.
8. A dedicated personal storage space of 10MB shall be offered which may be increased to 1 GB in future.
9. In order to ensure consistency, a uniform architecture shall be developed to support a well-structured standard document format. This will support easy sharing of documents across departments and agencies, while ensuring privacy and authorized access to residents' data.
10. A user shall be notified of the names of issuers which have issued e-documents to him and those of requesters which have accessed his documents.

BACKGROUND

Adoption of technology has always been an area of interest for researchers. There have been several studies that have attempted to apply, extend and integrate models of technology adoption and diffusion so as to provide better explanation of user and community behavior with respect to specific application areas of technology.

Fichman (1999) has given two categories of the innovation studies: Adopter studies and Diffusion Modeling studies. Adopter studies are aimed at understanding differences in the adopter innovativeness whereas the diffusion modeling studies are related to the rate, pattern and extent of technology diffusion. Downs and Mohr (1976) opine that early adoption of an innovation does not necessarily ensure a systematic pattern of early adoption (as cited in Fichman, 1999).

E-governance initiatives are generally targeted at the entire population and are expected to be a continual phenomenon. Hence, the nature and characteristics of adopters play a crucial role in adoption of these initiatives and also to make predictions about the future course of a particular digital initiative by the government so that necessary remedial plans can be undertaken. The second category of studies given by Fichman(1999) i.e. diffusion modeling studies represent a very small fraction of IT innovation research particularly in the area of e-governance.

However, there is no dearth of literature on the studies related to user adoption of Internet, e-commerce and Information Systems. In fact there are some well-established theories and models that explain user adoption of aforementioned technologies; such as Theory of Reasoned Action(TRA), Technology Acceptance Model (TAM), Diffusion of Innovation(DOI), and Web Trust Models(Davis, 1989; Rogers, 1962; Moon & Kim, 2001; Cheung, Zhu, Kwong, Gloria, & Limayem, 2003; Gefen, Elena & Straub, 2003; Gefen & Straub, 2000; Pavlou, 2001). However there are very few researches in the area of e-governance adoption as this is a relatively young area of research.

Since, e-governance is implemented through the use of Information and Communications Technology, it is important to understand the adoption of technology first and this understanding can be then further extended to form a basis for explaining e-governance adoption. Although, research on e-governance adoption, in particular, is very limited; the literature that is available has been discussed with special reference to use of theories and models in explaining the e-governance adoption with Technology Acceptance Model (TAM) by Davis (1989) and Diffusion of Innovation (DOI) Theory by Rogers (1995), being the popular ones.

Carter and Belanger (2004) conceptualized a theoretical model of factors that influence citizen adoption of e-government initiatives by integrating constructs from TAM, DOI and Web Trust Model. While proposing this model, they have discussed how similar and different e-commerce and e-governance domains are and have given sufficient clarifications for the theories chosen for the model that are more commonly followed in the field of e-commerce research. The findings indicate that perceived usefulness, relative advantage and compatibility are significant indicators of citizens' intentions to use e-government initiatives. However, trustworthiness was not found to have a direct impact on intention to use e-government services.

Al-adawi, Yousafzai and Pallister (2005) have opined that although a lot has been discussed about the benefits of e-governments to offer better citizen services, very little has been researched on whether citizens are likely to use e-government. Their paper presents the citizens perspective of e-government. The research done by the authors is aimed at understanding the citizens' perception of e-government as a primary government interaction channel and the factors that affect their level of usage. A conceptual model of citizen adoption of e-government is proposed in the study that includes constructs from the Technology Acceptance Model (TAM), trust and risk literature. The paper also throws light on the differences between citizen's intention to get government information and citizen's intention to conduct government transactions on e-government website. As per the authors, the model shall help the governments in assessing the citizens' adoption of their online services and take remedial actions. In addition, it also contributes to the existing literature by proposing a unique model of citizens' e-government adoption that also considers trust and risk issues.

Tan, Pan and Lim (2005) examined the impact of e-government from stakeholders' perspective. To assess the significance of e-governance for organisations and individuals this study pursued its influence from the three critical aspects of stakeholder management: "(1) identifications of stakeholders:(2) recognition of differing interests among stakeholders:and (3) how an organisation caters to and furthers these interests." The study has three major findings: (1) It is important to discard the traditional preference for controls to develop instead a proactive attitude towards the identification of all relevant collaborators for successful implementation of e-governance (2) By carrying out careful assessments of the technological feasibility, stakeholders should strive towards transforming public services to define the scope for as well as put a control and collaboration mechanism in place and (3) The ultimate objective of government should be to develop strategies for proper alignment of stakeholder interests with e-governance implementation so that a self-governing and self-sustaining system can be evolved.

Al-adawi, Yousafzai and Pallister (2005) have also presented a model that proposes four direct determinants of e-governance adoption viz. perceived usefulness, perceived ease of use, trust and perceived risk by taking constructs from TAM, trust and risk literature. However, these determinants were hypothesized to influence the user intentions towards two focal behaviors –getting information and conducting transactions.

A study by Kumar, Mukerji, Butt and Persaud (2007) provides a conceptual framework for e-government adoption in Canada. The study emphasizes on the fact that users are to be considered the pivotal point for e-government adoption strategy. The model is based on the theories borrowed from the vast marketing and information systems literature and proposes that user characteristics and website design have a direct influence on egovernment adoption. In addition to these factors, they have also included service quality in their model which has a direct influence on user satisfaction which in turn affects the adoption of e-governance. The main theories and literature that are referred to in their model include TAM and literature related to perceived risk, trust and service quality.

The Kumar et al.'s (2007) conceptual model was further extended by Bwalya (2009) by adding culture awareness and need of adequate and inexpensive IT infrastructure to the e-governance adoption model.

According to Bwalya (2009) Zambia started implementing e-government model of government since 2006. The Government of Zambia realised the potential of digital technologies in offering transparent, efficient and participatory governance. The e-governance model there is expected to control red tapism and corruption in public service delivery by curbing inefficient practices. According to the researcher, the adoption of e-Governance will introduce a paradigm shift wherein public institutions will be more responsive and transparent and will promote efficient Public Private Partnerships (PPP) for citizen empowerment.

According to Chuns. Shulman, Sandoval, Hovy, (2010), the reach of Information and Communication Technologies (ICT) has moved beyond the daily lives of people and has started influencing the interactions between governments and citizens. The digital governance or e-governance has resulted in creating a new form of ecosystem that has transformed the existing technology based communication with various stakeholders such as citizens and businesses dealing with the Government, particularly with the help of the Internet and Web technologies. A lot of improvement has been observed with respect to performance of government bodies and various processes.

The authors describe the e-government implementation as a process of modernization of the public sector from paper based manual tasks to digitally empowered ones in the first three stages of the entire process. These stages as discussed in the research paper are based on the "information delivery model" and the "public administrative process automation model". As a result of this implementation of e-government model, the citizens have anytime and anywhere access to government information and services. This also helps to achieve more efficiency in government processes through computerised services which result in automation of tasks.

Barua, Thapar(2012), have claimed that India has been very quick in adopting and implementing e-governance. For example, the Government of West Bengal (federal unit of India) implemented a Pension Management System (PMS) as a part of e-governance initiatives in its pension office for faster and efficient delivery of citizen services. The empirical analysis of the adoption of PMS revealed that one of the factors responsible for successful implementation of PMS is the adoption of application by the employee. This study also used the Technology Acceptance Model (TAM) and Trust to build a conceptual framework. Regression analyses were carried out on the data gathered from 60 employees working on the system to assess the proposed model. The findings of the study prove that the determinants of the research model are significant. The study also elucidate that there are errors in the tasks performed by the system which the Government of West Bengal should address. This is claimed to be the first study of employee adoption of e-governance in pension office of India.

Digital locker being a new concept, very few studies have been done on its implementation and related aspects. One of such studies is in the form of a research article published by Pfister and Schwabe(2013) that describes the concept of digital data safes for managing personal data and the landscape of existing services. The authors have followed an exploratory research approach to propose a model of hierarchical service layers. In addition to this, Pfister and Schwabe(2013) also identify factors and areas of interest that are relevant for the adoption of electronic data safes in e-government and e-business using the Unified Theory of Acceptance and Use of Technology as a theoretical base. The authors conclude that key enablers for the adoption of electronic data safes by end-users include clearly perceivable benefits for them.

The literature review indicates that although there is some good amount of work done in adopting theoretical models from Information Systems research and developing frameworks that describe e-governance adoption(adopter studies), but the task of empirical confirmation has not been widely done. Hence, there exists a gap in terms of conducting vigorous empirical research to validate the applicability of these well-established models of Information Systems and e-commerce research to e-governance adoption.

RESEARCH METHODOLOGY

Objectives of the Study

1. To assess the awareness level of citizens regarding this programme.
2. To identify the problems and challenges associated with the implementation of the scheme.
3. To identify factors that affect adoption of such initiatives.
4. To make recommendations to various stake holders regarding implementation of the service.

Methodology

The study was mainly carried out in three stages:

1. To begin with, extensive review of literature was carried out to understand the adoption of such e-governance initiatives in various countries and the main issues related to such initiatives.
2. In the second phase, data from the government crowdsourcing platform, mygov.in was collected. This data comprised of the comments that were made by people regarding Digilocker service. A total of 105 comments were collected that were organised into three categories namely: Benefits perceived, Problems faced and Suggestions.
3. In the third stage, a research model was developed that comprised of constructs from TAM (Technology Acceptance Model) and DOI (Diffusion of Innovation)

Figure 1. Research model

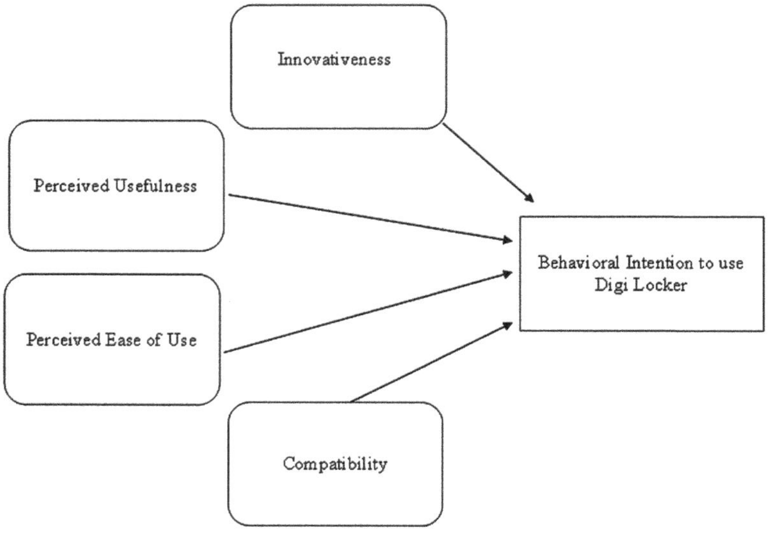

theory. The model was aimed at analysing the relationship between perceived ease of use, perceived usefulness, compatibility, innovativeness (independent variables) and Behavioural Intention to use Digilocker service(dependent variable). In order to validate this model, a survey was then carried out on 100 respondents.

Research Model

On the basis of the review of literature, following research model (Figure 1) was proposed for the study. The model comprises of constructs from IS theories such as Technology Acceptance Model and Diffusion of Innovation theory. It also includes Innovativeness as one of the constructs that can act as precursor to behavioural intention to use Digi-locker service.

Research Design

Data Sources

- Secondary Data: Newspapers, journal articles, magazines and online sources.
- Primary Data: Primary data was mainly collected from two sources viz.:
    - The government crowd-sourcing platform, www.Mygov.in

- Survey of Indian residents. A well-structured questionnaire was used as the Survey Instrument.

Sampling Plan for Survey

- Sample Size – 100
- Sample Unit – Residents of Udaipur, Jaipur, Agar, Ajmer and Neemuch.
- Sampling Method – Convenience sampling.

Development of Questionnaire

The Questionnaire was divided into 3 sections i.e. (Part A, Part B, and Part C)

Part A i.e. 1st Section of the questionnaire comprised of questions pertaining to Personal Information of the respondents.
Part B i.e. 2nd Section of the questionnaire comprised of questions pertaining to computer skills and Internet skills.
Part C i.e. 3rd Section of the questionnaire comprised of questions pertaining to awareness of digilocker service, its usage, problems, suggestions and behavioural intention, innovativeness, compatibility, perceived ease of use and perceived usefulness.

The constructs related to behavioural intention, innovativeness, compatibility, perceived ease of use and perceived usefulness were measured using a Likert scale and were adopted from following researchers as given in Table 2.

DATA ANALYSIS AND FINDINGS

Sample Profile

The sample comprised of 66 male and 34 female respondents. 43% of the respondents belonged to the age group of 15-24 years, 15% were from the age group of 25-34 years, 24% from 35-45, 14% from the age group of 44-55 and only 4% of the respondents were above 55 years of age.

More than 60% of the respondents were graduates, 19% were post graduate and 20% of the respondents had academic qualification up to school level. Out of 100 respondents, 40 were service class people, 20 had their own business, 29 women were housewives and 11 were students; 45% were single and 55% were married.

Table 2. Development of constructs

Construct	Source
Behavioural Intention Given a chance, I intend to use the Digilocker service It is likely that I will use the Digilocker service in future I intend to increase my use of Digilocker service in the future.	**Pavlou(2003)**
Perceived Usefulness Using the Digilocker service will help me to accomplish my related tasks more quickly. Using Digilocker would improve my performance. Using Digilocker would increase my productivity Using Digilocker would make it easier to do my daily activities. I would find Digilocker useful in my life .	**Davis(1989)**
Perceived Ease of Use Learning to operate Digilocker would be easy for me . I would find it easy to do what I want to do with the Digilocker. My interaction with Digilocker service would be clear and understandable I would find Digilocker to be flexible to interact with. It would be easy for me to become skillful at using Digilocker service. I would find Digilocker service easy to use.	**Davis(1989)**
Compatbility Using a Digilocker fits well with my lifestyle. I think that using Digilocker fits well with the way I live my life. Using Digilocker is completely compatible with my current situation. Using the Digilocker for my routine activities is compatible with how I like to do things.	**Slyke, Belanger and Comunale (2004)**
Innovativeness I am among the first in my circle of friends to try some new technology when it appears. If I heard that some new service were available online, I would be interested enough to obtain it. Compared to my friends, I use the latest of technologies and online services. I like to obtain a new service online before other people do.	**Goldsmith and Hofacker (1991)**

Assessment of Computer and Internet Skills

It was found that out of 100 respondents, only 16 had never used a computer, 38 rated themselves as beginners and 45 considered themselves to be competent. Of those who have used a computer, 52% people use it every day, 18% monthly and 14% use it every week. It was also observed that majority of people(more than 75%) use Internet everyday, and only 2% use it less than once a month. Most of the time people use internet for more than 3 hours a day. As per the survey majority of people use Internet on their mobile phones and at their school, college or office.

Awareness About Safety Measures on Internet

Out of 100 respondents it was found that 75% of people said yes they know about staying safe on internet and 25% said that they don't know about it.

Awareness and Intention to use the Digital-Locker service.

57% of people were aware about the service and 43% were not aware about the service.

The remaining questions were answered by only those respondents who knew about the service.

Source of Awareness

Out of 57 respondents who were aware about the service most of the people came to know about this service by friends & family, newspaper and internet, and others by TV channels and other sources.

Usage of Service

Out of 57 respondents who were aware about the service, we found that 71% of people had used this service and 28% had never used this service

User Experience with the Service

When asked about the experience while using the service it was found that out of those who had used Digi-locker service (41 people), 25 were extremely satisfied and satisfied and very less no. of people were dis- satisfied. The satisfied users amount to almost 60% of people who actually used the service.

Reasons for not Using the Service

An open-ended question was included in the questionnaire to know about the reasons for not using the service. Most of the respondents said that they did not use the service due to lack of knowledge and interest. Others said that they do not find it much useful for them as they have alternative methods for uploading their documents online.

Suggestions

Several suggestions were received for this service in which out of 57 respondents 20 people agreed that there should be a mobile application for the digital locker service and 10 said it should be more secure and the process of attachment of digital signature should be made more easy.

Data Analysis Regarding Behavioural Intention to Adopt the Service and Factors Affecting the Adoption

Multiple regression analysis was used for testing the dependence of Intention to use Digilocker on four variables as proposed in the research model. The purpose of a regression analysis is to relate a dependent variable to a set of independent variables. Regression analysis was seen as the most appropriate analytical technique since the goal of this study was to determine the relationship between use intention (dependent variable) and users' characteristics as well as perceptions of Digital locker (Independent variables).

The test revealed that the overall model was found to be significant ($p<.05$). Out of four independent variables i.e. perceived ease of use, perceived usefulness, compatability and innovativeness, only innovativeness was found to be significant($p<.05$). Hence other variables were excluded from the analysis.

The detailed results of the test are discussed in Table 3.

Analysis of Data Collected From www.mygov.in

In order to understand the opinion of the masses regarding the digital locker service, comments which were posted on the government crowdsourcing platform, www.mygov.in were collected over a period of 3 months (August to October, 2015). A total of 105 comments were collected that were organised into three categories namely: Benefits perceived, Problems faced and Suggestions. Further, the comments were also analysed to identify major issues related to the service. A compilation of these comments, segregated as per the issues is presented below:

Benefits Perceived

1. Ensuring transparency and fairness in government dealings

This step will lead to consumption of time and money and the corruption will definitely be controlled.

Table 3. Regression Analysis

ANOVA[b]						
Model		Sum of Squares	df	Mean Square	F	Sig.
1	Regression	3.185	1	3.185	6.674	.013[a]
	Residual	24.815	52	.477		
	Total	28.000	53			

a. Predictors: (Constant), INOV
b. Dependent Variable: BI

Coefficients[a]						
Model		Unstandardized Coefficients		Standardized Coefficients	t	Sig.
		B	Std. Error	Beta		
1	(Constant)	2.586	.598		4.326	.000
	INOV	.383	.148	.337	2.583	.013

a. Dependent Variable: BI

Excluded Variables[b]						
Model		Beta In	T	Sig.	Partial Correlation	Collinearity Statistics
						Tolerance
1	PU	.206[a]	1.601	.116	.219	.997
	PEOU	.054[a]	.400	.691	.056	.937
	Com	-.005[a]	-.039	.969	-.006	.976

a. Predictors in the Model: (Constant), INOV
b. Dependent Variable: BI

There is a racket of fake certificates To curb this, digital locker can be of great help.

Digital locker makes it easier to validate the authenticity of documents as they are issued directly by the registered issuers.

2. Reducing paper work

Digital locker is a very great step towards India. It's a good thought to reduce the paperwork.

It reduces the administrative overhead of Government departments by minimizing the use of paper.

Digital Locker is aimed at eliminating the use of physical documents and enables sharing of verified electronic documents across government agencies.

Digi Lock will reduce the administrative overheads of government departments and agencies created due to paper work.

3. Preservation of records

Digital library is good concepts for preserving precious data in digital format, also it help in maintaining governmental licencing mapping if digitization possible.

The concept of digital lock is very good. It can preserve the important documents digitally and it can used from anywhere by using the password at any time.

Digital library is good concepts for preserving precious data in digital format, also it help in maintaining governmental licencing mapping if digitization possible.

4. Convenient and Time saving

Citizens can now access their digital documents anytime, anywhere and share it online. This is convenient and time saving.

It will also make it easy for Indian citizens to receive services by saving time and effort as their documents will now be available anytime, anywhere and can be shared electronically

Anyone wants documents at any place anytime with the help of digi locker he/she can get it

Easy to use by just username and password and all the documents are with you anytime you don't have to take bunches of paper everywhere.

Its good movement toward digitalization. Digital locker concept is good concept of making your personal/Govt. docs all under one roof. It will help all of us to be paper free. It will save Environment too.

Digital locker is a time saving concept you don't have to take bunch of papers everywhere you go just with one concept digital locker you can do your work.

Problems Faced

1. Website and Interface Related

I tried to login to the Digital locker. It does not open up. Very sad that we are not able to design a robust website in spite of great publicity.

Citizens may make several errors while uploading the documents in the Ditigal locker which would lead to the documents getting rejected later.

There should be clear instructions on the sign up page about the acceptable format of passwords, i.e. at least one upper case letter, lower case letter symbol and number should be used in password. Without instructions it becomes irritating to modify and retype two-passwords every time after hitting the "submit" button.

Test of availability of a username should be done right after an username is entered.

Process of Signing Up is complex many peoples can't sign up so it should be made easy to sign up for peoples.

2. Document Sharing

If we share a document link with other we have no option to track that user using my shared document link or share it with another users.

The ownership of the scanned documents, lies with the individual who has uploaded it. In that case, how can the Government agencies can access an individual's document, once they are removed from his / her account.

3. Lack of Awareness

Digital locker was poorly marketed and people still dont know what to do with it, A clear idea for the same needs to be made available to general public

i can understand this great effort... but i dont feel it will reach everyone.. Basic education about cloud computing lacks in the rural areas. Try to eradicte this first.

Digital Locker is not so popular among peoples like many people are still not aware about the digital locker because of lack of promotion so govt. should pay attention to this issue.

4. Security

Information can be hacked very easily so, important document should not be digitized. Documents related to defense matter should not be digitized and even it is digitized then it should be within the computer of defense. These information should not be put on website as there is great chances of hacking this information. Public administration matter, hospital matter, educational matter etc can be digitized.

The only worry that people have is what if the service gets hacked? All the personal information of people would get leaked and it could cause serious problems for people.

If a person lost his mobile and other one take it and misused then he/she get a chance to access his/her digital locker with the use of mobile. That I mean using OTP there is no security. Almost user use windows as a platform they can also may take our secret keys entering with our system.

People privacy must be ensured. Because illiterate villagers may be cheated. All post offices must be re-designate as Govt-People channel & ensure more safety & responsibility. Pvt. parties may misuse -like PAN CARD & voters card for selfish use & anti national activities with poor illiterate villagers documents.

5. Linking with Aadhaar Card

Digital Locker is a good one. But linking with Aadhar / Mobile is some what problem. Though I linked my mobile number with my Aadhar card, Digital locker website says that my mobile is not linked and I am not able to go through it.

Please don't make aadhar card based mandatory login system. Open it for non-aadhar users.

Aadhar card is the only document is needed to generate digi locker rather than govt. should accept other documents also so it may help people more

For registering other than Aadhaar number other choice should also be given like PAN card number or Passport number or Voter ID card number.

Digital Locker" a good idea to store all important documents of a individual. But this good idea will go to scrap if the login method not changed. Please note that most of the citizens changed their mobile numbers after Aadhar enrollment. So a person will not get to login until he has the enrolled mobile number. Please give some alternative options to login.

It is not possible for anyone to register without having phone number registered with aadhar number. Neither it is easy to update the phone number in UIDAI website.

6. Network Related

Before thinking of Digital locker, we should have to think about network services provided by service provider i.e. it's too slow & expensive for lower middle class.

How useful it is will depend on infra at Government offices, Edu.Institutes,finance companies, banks etc. How are they going to access the documents stored in Digilocker? Till today many banks do not accept Aadhar Card as proof of residence.

7. Training

For those who're uneducated they feel difficult to use so it may be drawback of digi locker

Suggestions

1. Enhancing Security

It can be best if you add more security like 128bit SSL encryption.

A more advanced security system & cloud system should be developed to prevent it from hacking.

Digital Locker must be more secure. It can be done as follows:

a. *Adding Two Step verification during signing in sessions.*

   b. *Linking account to valid ID like Aadhar card no. Passport etc.*
   c. *Use of 256 bit encryption*
2. Alternative to Aadhaar Card

Open it for non-aadhar users because there are many people in the country who doesn't have the aadhar card.

Aadhar card should not be the the only base of registration. It cannot be made compulsory and the honorable supreme court of India has also clarified this. No citizen can be deprived from any government scheme/benefit just because he/she does not have an aadhar card. An alternative should be available. Eg - Passport, election card, driving licence, ration card, etc. Aadhar cards have not yet reached many talukas of India. e.g. Jafarabad taluka of Amreli district of Gujarat.

3. e-Sign Availability

Digital Signature should be linked to Aadhar Number and should be given to every citizen of India free of cost. This will mitigate the problem of fake signatures and fraudulently signed documents ultimately leading to a reduction in filing of court cases.

I have uploaded e aadhar, but its not doing esign for the same. So, Eaadhar must be downloaded here directly with esign.

4. Document Uploading and Verification

Documents Uploaded on Digital locker must be verified and they can be accepted by all govt agencies without further verification.

Currently, documents are verified through AADHAR. There is a need to create a centralised repository of Universities, HR departments of all major companies/ Govt. department and Financial institutions, through which the authenticity of a document be verified in a little frame of time.

In some cases students yet have not obtained their graduation or PG degree, for them there should be option to upload year/semester wise mark sheets under one category

Loaded document must be verified by government for 100% authenticity.

5. Proper Promotion of the Service

There need to be more FAQs about tech errors.

Make Digital Locker Center Help desk in every city so that people will get to know about the benefits of digital locker and they can upload there documents on digital locker.

I have one more to add- Once the technical work is complete and project is ready to be launched - Promote it well.

Make people realize its importance and if possible make it compulsory for several issuing authorities to issue an electronic copy of the document into digital lockers of people, whose Aadhaar number is available to them.

6. Making it Mandatory for Government Organisations

For any document generated by government in any person's name then that document copy should be directly loaded to that person digital locker with govt. label. So no duplicate, its real, original and can be blindly accepted for any other reference.

We need to make all departments digital to accept the softcopy documents. One of the biggest concerns of a common man is piles of paper that he needs to submit at all the govt. offices.

7. Technical Suggestions

Define Fixed document types

Define Fixed Metadata/Taxonomy of the documents,

Multiple distributed repositories, Archival of metadata information in database and document in Image Server to ensure the scalability.

There should be proper Document Management System in the back end for proper archival of citizen documents. Compliance with Open industry standards such as PDF/A for long term archival

Here could be a compression software integrated which will automatically compress the uploaded documents in case they are over 1MB.

There should be provision for account holder to include mail id.

8. Mobile App

You must also make a digital locker app so that people can access it from their mobile phones and tabs those who do not know how to link with their identities.

CONCLUSION AND RECOMMENDATIONS

Digital Locker is a useful online initiative. Citizens can now access their digital documents anytime, anywhere and share it online. The present study aimed at understanding the awareness level of citizens as regards this service. The main conclusions of the study are as presented below:

Major Findings

1. As per the survey, computer literacy and usage is on a rise. Majority of the respondents know how to use a computer and are working on it regularly.
2. Majority of the people who were surveyed said that they use Internet everyday and are spending more than three hours a day on Internet.
3. Most of the people access Internet on their mobile phones. This can be considered as an important finding in order to target a large number of mobile Internet users.
4. People are becoming aware about the safety issues related to Internet usage.
5. There is a lack of awareness regarding the Digi-locker service. Out of the total people surveyed, nearly about 50% are aware about this initiative.
6. Friends and family, newspapers and Internet were the main sources of information regarding the service.
7. The people were mostly satisfied with the experience regarding Digi-locker service.
8. Most of the respondents said that they did not use the service due to lack of knowledge and interest. Others said that they do not find it much useful for them as they have alternative methods for uploading their documents online.
9. The survey data also helped in analysing the proposed research model and it was found that the behavioural intention regarding adoption of this service in

mainly determined by the user innovativeness, implying that mainly people who are inclined towards trying new technological initiatives are the ones who are the early adopters of the service. Ease of use, usefulness and compatibility do not seem to have an impact on the behavioural intention to adopt the service.

10. Most of the people remarked that the government needs to promote this service in a more effective manner so that people can understand and benefit from the service. A summary of the most significant suggestions is presented below:
    a. Proper and more effective promotion of the service.
    b. Ensure better security measures for the online platform.
    c. Having an alternate option other than the Aadhaar number
    d. Verification and validation of documents by government agencies.
    e. Making it mandatory for government agencies to upload documents into the digital locker of the citizens
    f. Developing a mobile app.
11. The problems that were highlighted by the users can be summarised as follows:
    a. The interface and overall performance of the website needs to improve.
    b. Document tracking feature to be enabled.
    c. Proper training and guidance regarding use of the service should be provided by the government or government appointed agencies.
    d. Poor network connectivity.

RECOMMENDATIONS

1. Government should make efforts to popularise the initiative by adopting appropriate promotion strategies. As the study reveals that mostly people learnt about the service from friends, family, Internet and newspapers, these channels of communication may be emphasised more. Social media can be a very helpful tool in making this service popular through word of mouth.
2. Moreover, it was also found that people who intend to use this service are the ones who are interested in trying new technologies. Perceived ease of use, usefulness or compatibility does not seem to have an impact on the intention to use the service. This implies that the government needs to make the citizens more aware regarding the usefulness and benefits of the service so that people are attracted towards using this service because of its perceived benefits and not just because of their innovativeness.
3. Aadhaar number as the primary method of authentication does not seem to be well-accepted by the people. There were many instances where people have suggested considering other methods of identification, apart from Aadhaar card so that non-aadhaar card users can also access the service.

4. The main concerns associated with the service include security, confidentiality and ease of use of the application. There were suggestions pertaining to developing a mobile app, attaching a digital signature and making it mandatory for every government transaction in order to popularise the service. These suggestions by the users may be considered by the government to improve the adoption of the service.
5. Security remains a major concern among the users. In spite of deploying several security measures, if the government is unable to build trust regarding the service, it will severely affect its adoption. Hence, efforts must be made to make the service more secure & robust and adequate information regarding this must be shared with the public in order to develop trust and confidence in the service.

Limitations of the Study

The study was carried out in a limited geographical area and hence needs to be expanded to cover other areas in order to get a more generic view of the topic.

Due to lack of awareness about the service, almost half of the respondents did not answer the questions related to the experience, suggestions, intentions and perceptions regarding Digi-locker, making it a very small sample size for carrying out a rigorous statistical analysis. In order to enhance the overall reliability of the study, it would be advisable to replicate this study on a larger sample and particularly in those areas where digi-locker is a much accepted phenomenon.

REFERENCES

Ajzen, I., & Fishbein, M. (1972). Attitudes and Normative Beliefs as Factors Influencing Intentions. *Journal of Personality and Social Psychology*, *21*(1), 1–9. doi:10.1037/h0031930 PMID:5079550

Al-adawi, Z., Yousafzai, S., & Pallister, J. (2005). Conceptual Model Of Citizen Adoption of E-Government. *The Second International Conference on Innovations in Information Technology*. Available online at http://www.it-innovations.ae/iit005/proceedings/articles/G_6_IIT05-Al-Adawi.pdf

Barua, M., & Thapar, L. M. (2012). E -Governance Adoption In Government Organization Of India. *International Journal of Public Sector Information and Communication Technologies*, *3*(1), 20. http://airccse.org/journal/mpict/papers/3112ijmpict01.pdf

Bass, F. M. (1969). A New Product Growth Model for Consumer Durables. *Management Science*, *15*(5), 215–227. doi:10.1287/mnsc.15.5.215

Bwalya, K. J. (2009). Factors Affecting Adoption of e-government in Zambia. *The Electronic Journal on Information Systems in Developing Countries*, *38*(4), 1–13. doi:10.1002/j.1681-4835.2009.tb00267.x

Carter, L., & Belanger, F. (2004). Citizen Adoption of Electronic Government Initiatives. *Proceedings of the 37th Hawaii International Conference on System Sciences.*

Chandrashekhar, R., Dubey, S., Chawla, R., Kumar, P., Kareer, N., Verma, S., ... Bhatnagar, S. (2008). Impact Assessment of e-Governance Projects: A Benchmark for the Future. *Vikalp*, *33*(4), 69–93. doi:10.1177/0256090920080406

Cheung, C. M. K., Zhu, L., Kwong, T., Chan, G. W. W., & Limayem, M. (2003). Online Consumer Behavior: A Review and Agenda for Future Research. *Proceedings of the 16th Bled eCommerce Conference, eTransformation*, 194-218

Chun, S. A., Shulman, S., Sandoval, R., & Hovy, E. (2010). Making Connections between Citizens, Data and Government. *A Information Polity*, *15*(1-2), 1-9. http://content.iospress.com/articles/information-polity/ip000205

Davis, F. (1989). Perceived Usefulness, Perceived Ease of Use and User Acceptance of Information Technology. *Management Information Systems Quarterly*, *13*(3), 319–340. doi:10.2307/249008

Dawes, S. S. (2008). The Evolution and Continuing Challenges of E-Governance. *Public Administration Review*, *68*(Special Issue), S86–S102. doi:10.1111/j.1540-6210.2008.00981.x

Digital India. (2015). *Unleashing Prosperity*. Retrieved August 2016 from https://www2.deloitte.com/content/dam/Deloitte/in/Documents/technology-media-telecommunications/in-tmt-tele-tech-2015-noexp.pdf

Fichman, R. G. (1999). The Diffusion and Assimilation of Information Technology Innovations. In R.W. Zmud (Ed.), Framing the Domains of IT Management: Projecting the Future…Through the Past (pp. 105-128). Cincinnati, OH: Pinnaflex Educational Resources, Inc.

Gefen, D., Elena, K., & Straub, D. (2003). Trust and TAM in Online Shopping: An Integrated Model. *Management Information Systems Quarterly*, *27*(1), 51–90. doi:10.2307/30036519

Gefen, D., & Straub, D. (2000). The Relative Importance of Perceived Ease of Use in IS Adoption: A Study of Ecommerce Adoption. *Journal of the Association for Information Systems*, *1*(8), 1–28. doi:10.17705/1jais.00008

Goldsmith, R. E., & Hofacker, C. F. (1991). Measuring consumer innovativeness. *Journal of the Academy of Marketing Science*, *19*(3), 209–221. doi:10.1007/BF02726497

Kumar, V., Mukerji, B., Butt, I., & Persaud, A. (2007). Factors for Successful e-Government Adoption: A Conceptual Framework. *The Electronic Journal of E-Government*, *5*(1), 63–76. Available online at www.ejeg.com

Mahajan, V., Muller, E & Bass, F.M. (1995). Diffusion of New Products: Empirical Generalisations and Managerial Uses. *Marketing Science, 14*(3).

Masters, T. (2019). *What Is a Digital Locker?* Retrieved online from https://www.wisegeek.com/what-is-a-digital-locker.htm# on

Moon, J., & Kim, Y. (2001). Extending the TAM for a World-Wide-Web context. *Information & Management*, *38*(28), 217–230. doi:10.1016/S0378-7206(00)00061-6

Pavlou, P. (2001). Integrating Trust in Electronic Commerce with the Technology Acceptance Model: Model Development and Validation. *Seventh Americas Conference on Information Systems*.

Pavlou, P. A. (2003). Consumer Acceptance of Electronic Commerce: Integrating Trust and Risk with the Technology Acceptance Model. *International Journal of Electronic Commerce*, *7*(3), 69–103.

Pfister, J., & Schwabe, G. (2013). The Landscape of Electronic Data Safes and their Adoption in E-Government and E-Business. *System Sciences (HICSS), 2013 46th Hawaii International Conference*, 1963-1972.

Rogers, E. M. (1995). *Diffusion of Innovations*. New York: The Free Press.

Slyke, C. V., Belanger, F., & Comunale, C. L. (2004). Factors influencing the adoption of web-based shopping: The impact of trust. *ACM SIGMIS Database*, *35*(2), 32–49. doi:10.1145/1007965.1007969

Taking eGovernance to the Next Level. (2011). *Newsline*. Retrieved June 21, 2011 from http://www.nasscom.in/upload/newsline/May2011/Taking_eGovernance_Next_Level.pdf

Tan, C. W., Pan, S. L., & Lim, E. T. K. (2007). Managing Stakeholders Interests in E-Government Implementations. *Journal of Global Information Management, 13*(1), 31–53. doi:10.4018/jgim.2005010102

Teo, T. S. H., & Pok, S. H. (2003). Adoption of WAP-enabled mobile phones among Internet users. *Omega, 31*(6), 483–498. doi:10.1016/j.omega.2003.08.005

Tornatzky, L. G., & Klein, K. J. (1982). Innovation Characteristics and Innovation Adoption Implementation: A Meta-Analysis of Findings. *IEEE Transactions on Engineering Management, 29*(1), 28–45. doi:10.1109/TEM.1982.6447463

Uncles, M., Ehrenberg, A. & Hammond, K. (1995). Patterns of Buyer Behavior: Regularities, Models, and Extensions. *Marketing Science, 14*(3), G61–G70. doi:10.1287/mksc.14.3.G71

KEY TERMS AND DEFINITIONS

Diffusion of Innovation Theory: A theory proposed by Rogers that describes how, why, and at what rate new ideas and technology spread.

Digital India: A campaign launched by the Government of India, which is a flagship program of the government with an objective to transform India into a digitally empowered society.

Digital Locker: A digital locker is a file storage space on servers that are accessible across the internet.

E-Governance: The use of information and communication technologies (ICTs) to support citizen services, government administration, democratic processes, and relationships among citizens, civil society, the private sector, and the state.

Perceived Ease of Use: The degree to which a person believes that using a particular system would be free from effort.

Perceived Usefulness: The degree to which a person believes that using a particular system would enhance his or her job performance.

Technology Acceptance Model: An information systems theory given by Davis, that models how users come to accept and use a technology.

Chapter 6
Learning and Developing With Each Other:
Case of Collaborative Innovation Through ICT in India and Canada

Rajan Gupta
https://orcid.org/0000-0002-9851-4047
Department of Computer Science, University of Delhi, India

Saibal Kumar Pal
DRDO, New Delhi, India

ABSTRACT

ICT is a powerful tool which can be used by both India and Canada to harness the growth and development in the respective regions. Researchers and practitioners can come together from Indo-Canadian communities and take the association to a more meaningful level. The current research discusses the ICT tools that can be adopted from Canada by India to improve the education quality and knowledge transmission. On the other hand, Canada government can make efforts to enhance knowledge transfer and translation through ICT by adopting tools like best practices repository, communities of practice, corporate intranet/extranet, corporate yellow pages, expertise locator, online chat/instant messaging, knowledge portals, groupware-workflow and tracking system, and document/content management that are already used in India. ICT has the potential to develop the country politically, socially, and economically.

DOI: 10.4018/978-1-5225-5412-7.ch006

INTRODUCTION

India is the seventh largest country in terms of geographic area and is second largest in the world in terms of population. With population of 1,236,344,631 or 1.24 billion India is densely populated. According to its demographics, it is a young nation with 58.3% of the population under 30 years of age. The urban population, as estimated in Census 2011, accounts for 31.3% of the total population that implies majority of the population resides in rural areas. However, the urban population is increasing at the rate of 2.47%. The literacy level is 72.9% and education expenditure by the country is 3.1% of the GDP. The country ranks seventh in terms of nominal GDP (International Monetary Fund, 2016). Initially, India was an agrarian economy as agriculture and allied sector contributed almost 51.9% to the GDP but the focus changed to services. The technological boom or the push in Information & Communication Technology (ICT) in almost all the sectors after liberalization has contributed in GDP as well. ICT is being used in almost all the industries- SMEs, manufacturing, agriculture, heath, education, BFSI, infrastructure development, income tax, real estate analytics, disaster management and many more. ICT application has led to the development in many industries, thereby, contributing to the overall economic development of the nation (GOI, 2015).

Canada is the world's second largest country in terms of area with population 34,834,841 which is one-fourth of that of India. Majority of the population (54.5%) lies within the age group of 24-64 years. Approximately, 80.7% of the total population resides in urban areas which are far more as compared to that in India. The literacy level is as high as 99% and education expenditure is 5.4% of GDP which is again higher than India's (Statistics Canada, 2015). However, it ranks tenth in terms of nominal GDP behind India (International Monetary Fund, 2016). In Canada, ICT is applied in various sectors such as education, heath, agriculture, research, SMEs, disaster management, tourism etc.

The Indo-Canadian community has been making efforts to bridge the gap in the demographics of the two countries through development in ICT and its application in various industries. It recognized the potential areas where ICT can be used for the development of the overall sector.

The Indo-Canadian bilateral agreement on ICTE was signed in 2013 and was spread over five areas- B2B cooperation, R&D collaboration, E-Governance, cyber security and Investment & Innovation. An MoU on ICT and electronics has already been signed in 2012. Another meeting was held between the delegations from both the countries to discuss the India-Canada ICTE Working and majorly focused on ICT areas like- E-Governance, cloud computing, big data, 4G/LTE technologies, M2M/IoT and cyber/ mobile security. Issues like mobility, cyber security, investment, innovation and incubation in ICT were also discussed (Department of Electronics and Information Technology, 2016).

India-Canada relations are old and rooted in Westminster institutions, trade, and ties between people, common law and investments between the countries. The relations are growing but are well below the potential. These potential areas where the countries show interest are energy, infrastructure development, ICT, and biotechnology sectors. Canadian and Indian economies complement each other in many ways can very well work with each other on the development front.

Indian sectors are moving up the value-chain with the help of application of ICT. IT activity of Canada also contributes to strengthen their value added services. Since, there exist similar sensitivities in some sectors of both the countries, ICT application by the negotiators is recommended to achieve the need for balanced agreement. It is an important lever for productivity growth in both the countries (The Canadian Chamber of Commerce, 2012).

There are industries in Canada that are well flourished and their products and services can help in meeting Indian needs. These sectors include financial services, mining, energy, agri-food, healthcare, infrastructure, machinery and equipment, logistics and post-secondary education. India and other developing countries appreciate Canada's conservative way of dealing with finances. Canada has the best global mining companies. It has plentiful energy and strong expertise in hydro-power. The agri-food sector of Canada is also reliable and uses advanced technology for processing, producing and delivering food. The country has research based pharmaceuticals and advanced healthcare services that India can adopt to improve its healthcare. Canada can also lend its clean tech expertise to India for improving its infrastructure and logistics services. Engineering talent to produce machinery and equipment and technology used in developing highly competent people can also be adopted by India to improve its factor of production (The Canadian Chamber of Commerce, 2012).

Indo-Canadians possess strong Information Technology and knowledge capabilities that underpin India's economic growth. India can learn largely from ICT to improve its various sectors such as education, health, agricultural; development and food processing. A large number of Indo-Canadians are experts in areas like medicine, education and health. They can mutually benefit from the knowledge through exchange. Also, ICT based solutions in these fields can be adopted by developing countries from the developed ones. ICT tools such as nanotechnology, quantum computing, optics, solid state physics and bio-informatics can be adopted by India to improve science, engineering and technical education. Knowledge and information sharing on travel and tourism from Canada to India will also help in improvement of the Indian tourism industry (Wadhva & Woo, 2005).

There has been witnessed advanced technology usage in many industries of Canada that can be adopted in Indian industries and vice-versa. Potential areas where usage of ICT might help both the countries have been discussed in this paper. The purpose of this study is to explore the potential partnerships for both the nations with the help of ICT.

ICT APPLICATION AREAS

Small and Medium Enterprises (SMEs)

Application in Canada

Usage of Information and Communication Technology (ICT) in Canadian SMEs is quite common. 92.8% of Canadian SMEs make use of internet which is quite more than the usage of internet in India. All the companies having 100 to 499 and almost all manufacturing SMEs have internet connection (97.6%). 59.3% Canadians use smart phones, PDAs and digital tablets. Most of the Canadian SMEs make regular use of office suits. Use of Management Software Packages such as Enterprise Resource Planning, Customer Relationship Management and Supply Chain Management is also common in Canadian SMEs. E-mails, intranet and Web 2.0 are other tools used by Canadian SMEs to perform business functions (NetPME, 2011).

Cloud computing has also been introduced by The Office of the Privacy Commissioner of Canada (OPC) (2011) to SMEs to enhance transparency and accountability of the business. Canadian SMEs make use of mobile, cloud and analytics in their businesses. Canadian SMEs also make use of Virtualization, Business Intelligence and Cloud Solutions to solve their business problems. They use collaborative internet tools such as emails, videoconferencing and web meetings. Mobile websites, intranet and extranet sites and other collaborative tools are used by Canadian SMEs. Online banking, social media, online government services and project management are quite common among Canadian SMEs.

Learning for India

The SME sector of India can prove to be the primary contributor to the economy. The sector's contribution to the Indian GDP is expected to rise to 22% in 2020 from 17% in 2011. Technology has been recognized as the key business driver in this sector. However, its adoption is slow as compared to the other SME setups in different countries. Indian SME industry has adopted various ICT tools such as Enterprise Resource Planning and Business Intelligence to solve their business problems.

However, to bring in operational efficiency and transform the customer experience, the industry must make use of Social, Mobile, Analytics, and Cloud (SMAC). SMAC is the integration of Social, Mobile, Analytics and Cloud technologies that would help in optimizing cost structure and satisfying customer needs (Ernst & Young, 2014).

- **Social technologies** include powerful tools such as Facebook, twitter, YouTube and others that would allow connection, discussion and exchange of views and makes it easier for users to connect with industry participants and the diverse consumer segments. It creates positive word of mouth, generate leads and enhance sales.
- **Mobile technologies** allow people to exchange, view and act on information. Entrepreneurs are enabled to obtain a clear view of business operations and take decisions regarding, inventory, operations, financials and such. It provides remittance solutions to the owners and employees of SMEs.
- **Analytics** involve the use of tools and technologies such as data mining and others to deal with the large volume of data and to optimize business decisions. Use of analytics in business decisions increases operational efficiency and create an understanding of the customer. It helps businesses to drive innovation and respond to the fast changing customer needs in order to be competitive. The affordable BI tools encourage SMEs to focus on data-backed analytical business decision making.
- **Cloud technologies** allow technology resources to be connected through a utility model in a cost effective manner. It handles the upfront investments of businesses, in person servicing cost and issues of new charging models and technology solutions. Cloud technologies are highly useful for SMEs in the cases of disaster management, e-mail hosting and remote database management (Ernst & Young, 2014).

Disaster Management

Natural disasters can happen in any country despite it being developed, developing or under-developed. It can cause massive destruction to the lives and property of people. Disaster management includes effective response to the potential hazards through timely information and early warning systems. ICT tools and techniques like internet, remote sensing, GIS, satellite sharing data etc. help in planning for the potential disaster management. Seismic surveillance networks and sharing of data through satellites in case of disasters are used by majority of OECD countries (Australia, Canada, France, India, United States, Italy, Japan, Brazil, China, United Kingdom and others).

ICT Tools Used in India

India has been using advanced ICT tools for disaster management. The disaster management system of India has implemented improved Tsunami Early Warning System (TEWS) & monitoring and has developed Disaster Resource Network. India is currently deploying satellite system which has capabilities like weather forecasting, high resolution images, land, ocean and ice monitoring and digital terrain models. These tools are helpful in preparation, assessment and relief in disasters.

Canada can also adopt the TEWS system and develop their disaster resource network. It can develop an online inventory of emergency resources and a national emergency communication plan to prevent potential hazards (National Disaster Management Division, 2016).

- **Online Inventory of Emergency Resources** is a database of disaster management related information and resources. It is important for mobilizing equipment and skilled human resources at the time of crisis. There is a strong need to maintain a database of such resources as lack of information available about can cause delays and could be prove critical in case of sudden eventualities.
- **TEWS** is a system sending tsunami related warnings to prevent damage and save lives. It helps in detecting tsunamis in the Oceans alert the countries that are prone such accidents. The major contribution of this system is that it predicts the travel time of tsunami reaching the coast. It helps in disseminating the information about tsunami alerts to scientists, administrators and the general public helping reduction in damage to life and property. It helps in locating the tsunami, key contact persons and affected areas.

ICT Tools Used in Canada

Various ICT tools are used in disaster management programs of Canada such as satellite radio, cell broadcasting, satellite remote sensing, SMS, wireless ad-hoc mesh networks with GPS, GIS, GPS, internet (Web 2.0) and e-mail. Cell broadcasting and GPS mapping are useful ICT tools not used in Indian disaster management program. These tools can be incorporated for effective response to potential disasters.

- **Cell Broadcasting** is a text messaging service in which the user can inform the situation to many users at a time those are located in a single geographical area. It is integrated in the existing network infrastructure to avoid the cost of laying of cables, purchase of new handset or software. It is such a dedicated and geo-scalable channel that one message can reach millions in a minute. It is geo-specific in a way that the message can be broadcasted to people at risk area only and avoids widespread panic.

- **Wireless Ad-hoc Mesh Networks with Global Positioning System (GPS) Mapping** allow knowing the precise location of buildings, streets, emergency service, landmarks and disaster relief sites that can help in saving lives and saves time. This system is quite useful for disaster management teams and public safety personnel to protect life and property loss. Wireless mesh networks penetrate isolated and remote areas and help in monitoring environmental conditions such as temperature, speed etc. it is an inexpensive and reliable too which is effective in harsh environments also.

Education

ICT is being used to provide knowledge and information in a non-formal way. There is a rise in demand for enrichment learning, especially in countries where there is ageing population and people have more leisure time that they wish to spend in intellectual pursuits. The learners for pleasure usually demand a non-formal context of learning and for that use of ICT is a convenient an effective solution. The only concern is the needed skills to use the appliances, navigate through web pages and afford the digital connection. The technologies used are e-mails, presentational software, World Wide Web, multimedia, videoconferencing, and satellite broadcasting.

ICT Usage in Indian Education

Indian schools and colleges have adopted high end technology solutions (digital web based resources) to low-end technology solutions (TV/Radio). Indian schools make integrated use of new technologies with existing ones to make the learning process more effective. Older technologies such as radio, TV, books are used with new technologies such as Internet, e-mail and wireless communication. There has been increased used of mobile technology for English language learning, facilitating educational administration task and gaining other educational information. Learning technologies have been evolved from programs such as microcomputer software packages, CBT systems, bulletin boards and authoring systems to Web and internet based systems and Learning Management. Virtual learning has been introduced but lack of system of classifying such materials results in online learning materials remaining underutilized. Repositories are also equipped with ICT tools such as a Web based user interface, a search mechanism and a tool to retrieve the learning object. Several portals have also been developed for teachers to share information through networks. The 'Teachers of India' is an online portal developed to provide a forum to the teachers where they can interact freely, share thoughts and information, resources and new experiments with the teachers from all over the world (PriceWaterhouseCoopers, 2010).

ICT Usage in Canada Education

Canadian schools have been using advanced ICT techniques to support pedagogical approaches of learning. ICT tools such as models/ simulations, CSCW environments (computer-supported collaborative work), broadcasting, hypermedia resources, didactic courseware, automated testing or feedback, and Intelligent Tutoring Systems (ITSs) (adaptive courseware) are being used in Canadian schools to impart knowledge to students for better learning.

- **Hypermedia resources** are course resources that are meant for self-learning at the pace which is convenient to the user, or for private study guided by the teacher. It is the corpus of loosely structured documentation which includes multimedia such as audio, video, graphics embedded with hypertext links.
- **Didactic courseware** involves Computer Based Training (CBT) and Computer-Assisted Learning (CAL) resources used in didactic format with sequential lessons for self-paced learning that may replace or supplement convenient learning.
- **Automatic testing or feedback** is the way of assessing the knowledge of learners. It is a tool to test systematic objective testing. It is useful for large class groups and the subject matter is favorable to testing. It includes test questions, automated marketing, feedback generation and summary information on performance of students.
- **Intelligent Tutoring Systems (ITSs) (adaptive courseware)** is also a self -paced learning course which is adaptive and extends to CBT/CAL approach. It seeks to customize lessons on the basis of dynamically modeling individual student performance.
- **Satellite Broadcasting** is another way to carry lessons which involve two-way learning environment. It allows educational providers to reach remote and isolated parts of the world. It provides data directly to digital receivers over large geographical areas (Dhanarajan, 2002).

Knowledge Translation and Transfer

Knowledge translation and transfer (KTT) is the process of transformation of knowledge into use for research purposes through synthesis, dissemination, dialogue, collaboration and exchange. Knowledge translation and transfer involves spreading and use of knowledge through various processes to speed up the research process

(Ontario, 2016). KTT is used in improving health, agriculture, education, social sciences and other sectors. Modern information and communication technology is quite useful for knowledge transfer and translation. The concept of transforming research knowledge into action has recently been adopted in many countries. Technology Enabled Knowledge Translation (TEKT) is a growing field which uses varied capacity of ICT to support the stages of Knowledge transfer- knowledge generation, knowledge storage and knowledge application (Ho et al, 2012). India can adopt such technological advances and apply in education field to get better results and provide quality knowledge to future human resources.

ICT in Canada

There has been a rapid growth in the KTT industry of Canada and other associated processes (McKibbon, Lokker, Mathew, 2014). ICT plays a major role in knowledge translation and transfer. The ideas and information are transferred in graphic or visual mode through web, radio, TV, print or in person. The strategic communication tools used are mass media campaign, direct mail, publications, newsletters, press releases, speeches, social media and opinion leaders. ICT gives access to latest information and knowledge and helps in transmission of such knowledge to people using the most efficient tools.

In Canada knowledge dissemination relies on various mediums to communicate research findings such as print (brochures, newspapers, press releases etc.), video (television public service announcements, self-help video tapes), audio (radio public service announcements, self- help audio tapes) and electronic (newsletters, websites and softwares). Researchers use seminars, emails, articles and web to communicate information to the people. Providers/ administrators use conferences, popular media, electronic users and groups. Consumers and families transfer information through community lectures, web sites and other popular media (Morris, 2003).

Knowledge transfer in Canada involves building of a network having like-minded individuals that belong to different constituencies such as policy makers, ICT technology experts, and industrial professionals in order to enable mutual exchange of ideas and future collaboration using technology enabled knowledge transfer (KT). Other communication methods used to transfer research results are pamphlets, social marketing, focus groups, partnerships and outreach programs (Pecku, 2012).

ICT in India

Information technology is a means to extend the knowledge resources beyond the limitations existing in the system. The ICT techniques and tools used in transfer of information include following (Krishnaveni & Raja, 2012):

- **Best Practices Repository**: It is a collection of best practices and lessons learnt from different kind of projects. It may be stored in the form of documents, graphs, pictures, models, presentations and diagrams etc.
- **Communities of practice/ purpose**: A formal team representation is there in every organization. Apart from this, informal communities of practices exist in the organization based on interests, technology etc. These communities enable knowledge sharing and enrichment of organization's capability of using the technology.
- **Corporate Intranet/ Extranet/ Internet**: Internet is the major source of knowledge sharing. It is difficult to perform activities efficiently without internet in today's world. It allows identifying knowledge across the world, assimilating it and using it according to the need of the project. Also, organizations have intranet facilities that they use according to their individual needs. Extranet is the web application that is used within the organization for knowledge and information transfer.
- **Corporate Yellow Pages**: Corporate yellow pages are intranet applications that allow identification of various people within the organization. It is also used to locate the resource availability from the resource pool.
- **Expertise Locator**: It allows identification of various expertise with various skill set and helps in fetching new projects while preparing some proofs of concepts.
- **Online Chat/ Instant Messaging**: It is the most convenient tool for sharing the information within the teams of the organization and among organizations located at different places.
- **Knowledge Portals**: Knowledge portals are repositories for organization wide information and act as a process enabler for the team members.
- **Groupware-Workflow and Tracking System**: These are workflow systems that include leave management applications, time sheet maintenance application and project milestone applications etc.
- **Document/ Content Management**: It is the repository for the contents of the projects and related documents. Every organization has their own set of processed documents that needs to be maintained in servers in order to transfer information between onsite and offshore teams. Such applications can also track various versions of documents like the archival of it (Krishnaveni, & Raja, 2012). Canadian Knowledge Transfer and Translation (KTT) industry should adopt the ICT tools used in KTT industry of India to facilitate transfer of knowledge.

Summary of ICT learning for India and Canada is shown in Figure 1.

Figure 1. Summary of ICT Learning for India and Canada
Source: Self-Authored

Learning for India	Learning for India & Canada	Learning for Canada
Small & Medium Enterprises Social technologies Mobile technologies Analytic technologies Cloud technologies	**Disaster Management (CAN)** Online Inventory of Emergency Resources TEWS	**Knowledge Translation & Transfer** Best Practices Repository Communities of practice Corporate Intranet/ Extranet Corporate Yellow Pages Expertise Locator Online chat/ instant messaging Knowledge Portals Groupware-workflow and tracking system Document/ Content Management
Education Hypermedia resources Didactic courseware Automatic testing or feedback Intelligent Tutoring Systems (ITSs) (adaptive courseware)	**Disaster Management (IND)** Cell Broadcasting Wireless Ad-hoc Mesh Networks with Global Positioning System (GPS) Mapping	

LEARNINGS

India and Canada differ in terms of geographic and demographic features. They differ in terms of area, population, GDP, urban-rural ratio and technological advancement. The ICT application in industries also varies due to infrastructure facilities, computer literacy, governance policies, maturity of industries and financial constraints.

Since there exist differences in the application of Information and Communication Technology (ICT) in industries within both countries, the successful use of ICT tools in a country can be replicated in another. The paper discussed the potential areas in India where successful ICT techniques of Canada can be replicated for advancement in that sector and vice-versa. It was discussed that SME and education sector is more advanced in Canada due to application of advanced Information and Communication Technology (ICT) such as social and mobile technology, analytics, cloud computing, hypermedia resources, automatic testing or feedback etc. on the other hand, advanced ICT tools used in KTT industry of India can be adopted by Canada for improvements in the knowledge transfer sector.

Collaboration among Indian & Canadian government and a concentrated effort is required to align the E-Governance policies of both the nations keeping in mind the difference between the country-specific factors. The advancement in technology applied to industries in a particular country can be adopted by another country to improve its economic growth. Governments of both the countries must develop a strategic partnership to facilitate advancement in areas like agriculture, science & technology, health, education and tourism. The paper suggests the potential areas where ICT needs to be developed- SMEs (Canada), education (Canada), disaster management (Canada & India) and knowledge translation and transfer (KTT) (India).

CONCLUSION AND WAY AHEAD

ICT has the potential to develop the country politically, socially and economically. Developmental decisions, these days, depends on the ability to gather, analyze and utilize information and knowledge. ICT transmits information to individuals for their economic and social empowerment. Government of both the countries has the objective to allow citizen-government interaction at all levels through electronic interaction mode (E-Governance). The paper described the current scenario of ICT application in various areas of India and Canada. It also assessed the success of information technology in specific areas in a country and that the other country can also benefit from such application.

Much of the population of India resides in rural areas and majority of the people in the country are young. So, there is a high potential of social and mobile technologies, analytics to exploit the markets since it is not so popular in such areas and the young population can adopt it easily. Therefore, SMEs in India have been suggested to adopt social and mobile technologies, analytics and cloud computing as ICT tools to capture the market and facilitate economic growth.

The paper also discussed the ICT tools that can be adopted from Canada by India to improve the education quality and knowledge transmission. On the other hand, Canada government must make efforts to enhance Knowledge Transfer & Translation through ICT by adopting tools like best practices repository, communities of practice, corporate intranet/ extranet, corporate yellow pages, expertise locator, online chat/ instant messaging, knowledge portals, groupware-workflow and tracking system and document/ content management which are already used in India. India possesses a wide skill gap and large illiterate population, therefore, transfer of knowledge is deemed important and practiced widely using advanced technology. Canada, where population is on the rise and the number of expatriates is increasing, also demands advancement in knowledge transfer and translation which can be achieved through the use of ICT.

Disaster Management has different ICT applications, so both the countries need to learn from each other in this respect. Online Inventory of Emergency Resources and Tsunami Early Warning Systems (TEWS) must be adopted by Canadian government and Cell broadcasting must be used to broadcast disaster occurrence to prevent loss of life and property.

ICT is a powerful tool which can be used by both the countries to harness the growth and development in the respective regions. Researchers and Practitioners can come together from Indo-Canadian Communities and take the association to a more meaningful level.

REFERENCES

CIHR. (2014). *More about knowledge translation.* Retrieved June 12, 2016 from http://www.cihr-irsc.gc.ca/e/39033.html

Department of Electronics and Information Technology. (2016). *Country wise Status*. Bilateral Cooperation, Ministry of Communication and IT, Government of India. Retrieved June 13, 2016 from http://deity.gov.in/content/country-wise-status

Dhanarajan, G. (2002). Objectives and strategies For effective use of ICTs. In Technologies for Education (pp. 58-74). Academic Press.

Ernst & Young. (2014). *SMAC — the next growth driver for SMEs in India, ASSOCHAM*. Retrieved June 8, 2016 from http://www.ey.com/Publication/vwLUAssets/EY-SMAC-the-next-growth-driver-for-SMEs-in-India/$FILE/EY-SMAC-the-next-growth-driver-for-SMEs-in-India.pdf

GOI. (2015). *India in Figures 2015, Ministry of Statistics and Programme Implementation, Central statistics Office*. Retrieved June 13, 2016 from http://mospi.nic.in/Mospi_New/upload/India_in_figures-2015.pdf

Ho, K., Jarvis-Selinger, S., Lauscher, H. N., Cordeiro, J., & Scott, R. (Eds.). (2012). *Technology Enabled Knowledge Translation for EHealth: Principles and Practice*. Springer Science & Business Media. doi:10.1007/978-1-4614-3495-5

International Monetary Fund. (2016). *World Economic Outlook Database*. Retrieved June 13, 2016 from http://goo.gl/Q3me27

Krishnaveni, R., & Raja, C. S. (2012). Factors that enable Knowledge Management in Information Technology Organizations–a Statistical Study. *Journal of Contemporary Research in Management, 3*(4), 1–6.

McKibbon, K. A., Lokker, C., & Mathew, D. (2014). *List of KT terms evaluated. What is KT?* Retrieved June 9, 2016 from http://whatiskt.wikispaces.com/List+of+KT+terms+evaluated

Ministry of Agriculture, Food and Rural Affairs. (2016). *Understanding Knowledge Translation and Transfer (KTT).* Author.

Ministry of Home Affairs. (2016). *ICT for Disaster Risk Reduction the Indian Experience, National Disaster Management Division, Government of India.* Retrieved June 11, 2016 from http://www.undp.org/content/dam/india/docs/ict_for_disaster_risk_reduction_indian_experience.pdf

Morris, J. (2003). *Technology Enabled Knowledge Translation (TEKT): Current Best Practices in Innovation, Evaluation, and Future Directions*. The Division of Continuing Medical Education. Retrieved June 11, 2016 from http://catalogue.iugm.qc.ca/GEIDEFile/15939.PDF?Archive=193678091185&File=15939_PDF

NetPME. (2011). *Use of ICT by Canadian SMEs, Cefrio*. Retrieved June 8, 2016 from http://www.cefrio.qc.ca/media/uploader/NetPME2011_UseofICT-anglHW.pdf

Pecku, G. M. (2012). *Knowledge Transfer Project* (Master of Health Informatics Program). Dalhousie University. Retrieved June 11, 2016 from http://www.omafra.gov.on.ca/english/research/ktt/indexktt.html

PriceWaterhouseCoopers. (2010). *Information and Communication Technology in for education in India and South Asia*. Retrieved June 9, 2016 from http://www.infodev.org/infodev-files/resource/InfodevDocuments_1016.pdf

Statistics Canada. (2015). Canada Population Estimates: Age and sex. *The Daily*. Retrieved June 13, 2016 from http://www.statcan.gc.ca/daily-quotidien/150929/dq150929b-eng.htm

The Canadian Chamber of Commerce. (2012). *Canada-India: The way forward.* Author.

The Office of the Privacy Commissioner of Canada. (2011). *Introduction to Cloud Computing, Fact Sheets*. Retrieved June 8, 2016 from https://www.priv.gc.ca/resource/fs-fi/02_05_d_51_cc_e.asp

Wadhva, C. D., & Woo, Y. P. (2005). *Asian Regionalism, Canadian and Indian Perspectives*. APH Publishing.

West, P. (2004). *Applied Health Research: A briefing paper on knowledge transfer, Disseminaation and Utilization.* Retrieved June 11, 2016 from http://www.continuousinnovation.ca/AppliedHealth-KTDU.html

KEY TERMS AND DEFINITIONS

Automatic Testing or Feedback: It is a way of assessing the knowledge of learners in Canada. It is a tool to test systematic objective testing. It is useful for large class groups and the subject matter is favorable to testing. It includes test questions, automated marketing, feedback generation and summary information on performance of students.

Best Practices Repository: It is a collection of best practices and lessons learnt from different kind of projects in India. It may be stored in the form of documents, graphs, pictures, models, presentations, and diagrams, etc.

Didactic Courseware: It involves computer-based training (CBT) and computer-assisted learning (CAL) resources used in didactic format with sequential lessons for self-paced learning that may replace or supplement convenient learning in Canada.

Hypermedia Resources: They are course resources in Canada that are meant for self-learning at the pace which is convenient to the user, or for private study guided by the teacher. It is the corpus of loosely structured documentation which includes multimedia such as audio, video, graphics embedded with hypertext links.

Intelligent Tutoring Systems (ITSs) (Adaptive Courseware): It is a self -paced learning course which is adaptive and extends to CBT/CAL approach in Canada. It seeks to customize lessons on the basis of dynamically modeling individual student performance.

Online Inventory of Emergency Resources: A database of disaster management related information and resources in India. It is important for mobilizing equipment and skilled human resources at the time of crisis.

TEWS: A system sending tsunami related warnings to prevent damage and save lives in India. It helps in detecting tsunamis in the Oceans alert the countries that are prone such accidents.

Wireless Ad-hoc Mesh Networks With Global Positioning System (GPS) Mapping: A system in Canada which allows knowing the precise location of buildings, streets, emergency service, landmarks and disaster relief sites that can help in saving lives within time. This system is quite useful for disaster management teams and public safety personnel to protect life and property loss.

Chapter 7
Participatory Mapping, E-Participation, and E-Governance:
Applications in Environmental Policy

Pragati Rawat
https://orcid.org/0000-0002-7347-3584
Slippery Rock University, USA

Juita-Elena (Wie) Yusuf
https://orcid.org/0000-0003-3599-1417
Old Dominion University, USA

ABSTRACT

This chapter focuses on participatory mapping as an e-governance tool to facilitate public participation. Public participation is a key component of democratic governance, and there is a growing reliance on digital government tools such as the internet and social networking sites and geographic information systems (GIS). This chapter focuses on public engagement using information and communication technology, namely participatory mapping, known by a variety of terms such as participatory GIS (PGIS), public participation GIS (PPGIS), and voluntary GIS. While the analysis involves use of participatory mapping related to environmental issues, the chapter brings together seminal work from various fields of citizen engagement and participatory mapping. The idea is to create one common narrative for scholars and practitioners, bringing together various terminologies, practices, and studies in participatory mapping in the environmental arena that offers a beginner's frame of reference.

DOI: 10.4018/978-1-5225-5412-7.ch007

INTRODUCTION

Governments at all levels are increasingly adopting citizen engagement in governing decisions (UN, 2014). Environmental issues are among the issues that have been considered too technical to be understood by the average person, but there continues to be support for public participation in environmental decision making (Crow & Stevens, 2012). While different approaches have been used for citizen engagement in environmental issues, participatory mapping has gained popularity. The purpose of this chapter is to locate and organize participatory mapping in the broader field of public participation and e-government, and discuss the various participatory mapping approaches using information and communication technology (ICT), organizing them under the umbrella term e-participatory mapping.

The literature on participatory mapping and public participation is vast and spans multiple policy areas such as environmental policy, urban planning, sustainable development, e-government, and geographical information systems (GIS), in addition to encompassing multiple techniques, approaches, and technologies used. This chapter presents a structured review by synthesizing the literature, with the aim of developing an understanding of e-participatory mapping as an e-governance tool for public participation. The idea is to create one common narrative for scholars and practitioners by compiling various terminologies, practices, and studies that offers a beginner's frame of reference. The focus is on e-participatory mapping, since ICT is becoming an inevitable part of the public participation process in both developed and developing countries.

ENVIRONMENTAL ISSUES AND PARTICIPATION

Environmental issues are concerned with human actions that affect the biosphere, including species, habitats, or landscapes. Environmental policy is aimed at governing the relationship between humans and their natural environment. Decisions regarding technical issues such as the environment are generally thought to be best left in the hands of experts and scientists (Rowe & Frewer, 2000). Environmental policy is the definitive example of technocratic policymaking (Fischer, 2000), as the technical nature of environmental policy makes it difficult for the average citizen to comprehend (Crow & Stevens, 2012). Yet, growth in citizen science suggests that citizens are interested in science and complex topics (Crow & Stevens, 2012; Dickinson et al. 2012; Brown & Donovan, 2014).

Environmental problems are complex and dynamic, leading the policy field to embrace diverse sources of knowledge and values, and embed participation in environmental decision making (Reed, 2008). For example, the United Nations

Framework Convention on Climate Change (UNFCCC) calls on member countries to implement educational and public awareness programs, provide public access to information, and seek public participation in addressing climate change and its effects (1992). ICTs, including GIS technologies, are widely used to support public participation in environmental issues (Al-Kodmany, 2002; Bojórquez -Tapia, Diaz-Mondragón, & Ezcurra, 2001; Gonzalez et al., 2008; Jordan & Shreshtha, 2000; Kingston, Carver, Evans, & Turton, 2000).

Public Participation

Public participation refers to the involvement of the public in policy making activities on a regular and ongoing basis (Lukensmeyer & Torres, 2006). It involves a range of activities such as public sharing of government information and activities, consulting with the public on policy issues, and involving them in decision making (UN, 2008; UN, 2014; Smith, 1983). Smith (1983) defines public participation as procedures for consulting, involving, and informing those affected by a decision in the decision-making process. "Authentic participation," defined as "deep and continuous involvement" that potentially allow participants to affect the situation (King, Feltey, & Susel, 1998, p. 320), can be achieved with targeted public information, active solicitation of public opinion, delegation of decision-making authority to the public, and opportunities for citizens to exercise their knowledge in policy and program development (Rowe & Frewer, 2000; Lukensmeyer & Torres, 2006).

Public participation is a democratic ideal (Rowe & Frewer, 2000) that gained importance when trust in government decreased and the demand for public accountability increased (Parr & Gates, 1989; King et al., 1998). It is considered especially useful in areas that lack official, continuous, and local data, and for effective collaboration between scientists, the community, and policy decision makers (Andrade & Szlafsztein, 2015). Public administrators have come to realize the importance of public participation for effective decision making and increased citizen buy-in (Burby, 2003; King et al., 1998; Webler, 1999). Yet, the same administrators may block participation efforts that challenge the status quo (King et al., 1998). Clear identification of relevant interest groups and stakeholders is critical for enabling participation (Brown, Adger, & Tompkins, 2002). However, some scholars are skeptical that more participation means more democracy (Parry & Moyser, 1994). Concerns have been raised about who decides the agenda for participation, whether participants are representative of the larger population, if participation impacts decision making, and the legitimacy of such decision-making activities (McLaverty, 2011; Parry & Moyser, 1994; Verba, Schlozman, Brady, and Nie, 1993).

Individuals who receive information and are encouraged to engage are more likely to increase their engagement (Lewandowski & Oberhauser, 2015). In hazard mitigation planning, having targeted plans, coordinating these plans with broader community concerns, connecting them to more immediate quality of life concerns, and preparing small area plans so that residents can relate to these as issues impacting their own neighborhood, will help planners obtain citizen input and support (Godschalk, Brody, & Burby, 2003).

Public participation in environmental issues generally involves two types of discourse between the government and the public. One type involves problem solving that seeks agreement among diverse interests to decide a course of action, and the other type involves sensemaking to overcome technical dominance, build understanding and overcome dissent (Hamilton & Wills-Toker, 2006). Various approaches have been used to enable public participation in environmental issues (e.g. Davies, Selin, Gano, & Pereira, 2012; Gray et al., 2015). Examples include focus groups, open meetings, informal questionnaires, facilitated discussions, ranking exercises, and policy mapping tools (Brown et al., 2002; Brown, Few, Tompkins, Tsimplis, & Sortti, 2005; Few, Brown, & Tompkins, 2007). While multiple approaches and tools are used for public participation in environmental studies, the current review is focused on participatory mapping, which has gained popularity in the field.

Participatory mapping is any participation-based method for generating and recording spatial data (Vajjhala, 2005). Participatory mapping emerged around the 1990s (Chambers, 1994), concurrently with the advent of the Internet and World Wide Web. ICT and Web-based applications have since gained momentum as a platform for public participation. The next section discusses the use of ICT in public participation and connects it to participatory mapping.

Role of ICT: E- Government, E-Participation, and GIS

E-government, defined as the "public sector use of the Internet and other digital devices to deliver services, information, and democracy itself" (West, 2005, p. 1), includes ICT use "for the provision of information and public services to the people" (UN, 2014, p.61) and "that improves citizen access to government information, services and expertise to ensure citizen participation in, and satisfaction with the government process" (United Nations and the American Society for Public Administration, as cited in Moon, 2002, p. 425). E-participation is defined as "the process of engaging citizens through ICTs in policy and decision-making in order to make public administration participatory, inclusive, collaborative and deliberative for intrinsic and instrumental ends" (UN, 2014, p.61). E-participation is integral to e-government's purpose and utilizes e-government infrastructure for public participation activities. Some models of e-government incorporate e-participation as an advanced stage of e-government

(Hiller & Belanger, 2001; West, 2005; Marchionini, Samet, & Brandt, 2003), one that is in need of greater effort from the government and is the least developed in practice (Hiller & Belanger, 2001; Moon, 2002).

E-participation can be conducted over a variety of platforms such as via phone, email, and Web 2.0 tools like social networking sites (e.g., Facebook, Twitter, and YouTube) and other internet-based tools (Delli Carpini, Cook, & Jacobs, 2004; Fredericks & Marcus, 2013; Tolbert & Mossberger, 2006; Mossberger, Tolbert, & McNeal, 2008). One online participatory tool claimed to have far-reaching consequences is the mapping application (Tulloch, 2007). Online mapping interfaces have become sufficiently user-friendly to allow amateurs to participate in decision making and present their ideas in meaningful ways (Tulloch, 2007; Ganapati, 2011). The Internet has encouraged citizen science by enabling personal e-devices such as computers, mobile phones, and global positioning system (GPS) receivers to work as scientific instruments that citizen scientists can use to make observations (McCall, Martinez, & Verplanke, 2015). GIS has evolved in three phases from desktop GIS to Web GIS to geo-spatial Web 2.0 platforms (Ganapati, 2010). Web GIS is developed specifically for the Web to communicate real-time data (McCall et al., 2015). Google Earth, an example of a Web 2.0 geospatial application, allows user uploading of captions, photo images, videos, audio, links, and metadata that can be geo-tagged (McCall et al., 2015).

PARTICIPATORY MAPPING

Participatory mapping is any process where individuals share in the creation of a map (Goodchild, 2007). It emerged as one of the techniques of participatory rural appraisal (PRA) and includes activities such as sketch mapping, scale mapping, and transect walking (Chambers, 1994). The working hypothesis behind participatory mapping is that local people have mental maps that can be drawn as a way to convey information through spatial representation (Chambers, 1994). In recent years, participatory mapping has been used in a variety of fields such as health (Lowe, Gaudion, McGinley, & Kew, 2014; Skinner, Hanning, & Tsuji, 2006), urban planning (Kim, 2015; Smith & Jenkins, 2015) and migration (Lingel, 2011).

Participatory mapping methods vary from using sticks, dirt, and paper to highly technical Internet crowdsourcing, GIS, and 3-D modeling (Corbett, 2009). Ground maps, sketch maps (or paper maps) are simple, inexpensive and not technology dependent, but are static and not geo-referenced (IFAD, 2009; IPAD, 2009). Mapping using GPS and multimedia maps linking digital video, photos and text with maps have the advantage of storing data in digital format but can be expensive and require user training (IFAD, 2009). Aerial and remote sensing is effective for mapping large, difficult to reach areas but is very expensive and may not be easily accessible (IFAD, 2009). Online maps have the advantage of being inexpensive and compatible with GIS, but have limited functionality and require computer access and software (IPAD, 2009). Geospatial software such as ArcGIS are interactive, flexible, and thorough, but require expert intervention and can be costly (IPAD, 2009).

Participatory mapping is an unconventional alternative for collecting spatial data for large landscape areas (Beverly, Uto, Wilkes, & Bothwell, 2008). It helps situate local observations in the wider geographic context, and has potential for exploring human dimensions of environmental issues and examining local perspectives and priorities (Joyce & Canessa, 2009). Local knowledge is considered unique, reflective of local identity and encompasses the manifestation of cultural values placed on land and place in imprecise, emotional, and holistic terms (Hoole & Berkes, 2010; Levine & Feinholz, 2015), but that may not fit neatly into a spatial format. Furthermore, exact spatial boundaries using participatory mapping are generally difficult and public administrations may question the validity of anecdotal information obtained from local community members (Levine & Feinholz, 2015).

Participatory mapping puts human experiences into a spatial context, and is a process-driven, vibrant and vital way of knowing that fosters deliberation in complex science system (Tschakert et al., 2016). The mapping process is considered more important than the resulting map because it provides an opportunity for participants to engage in new ways, learn from each other, and share concerns held by different stakeholder groups (Levine & Feinholz, 2015). At the same time, participatory mapping is criticized for its dualistic approach to power and culture, and for reifying material and discursive forms of domination pervasive in the Western culture (Sletto, 2009).

In the area of environmental issues, participatory mapping has been used in monitoring, reporting, and verifying environmental policies and problems. Examples include applications that focus on natural resource management (Hoole & Berkes, 2010; Lubis & Langston, 2015), environmental degradation (Chagumaira, Rurinda, Nezomba, Mtambanengwe, & Mapfumo, 2016), and human-nature interactions (Cocks, Dold, & Vetter, 2012; Woodhouse, Mills, McGowan, & Milner-Gulland, 2015). Other applications have addressed issues of ecosystem management (Andrade & Szlafsztein, 2015), disasters and adaptation (Kaul & Thornton, 2014; Levine & Feinholz, 2015), ecotourism (Chakrabarty, 2011), and marine spatial planning (Stelzenmüller, Lee, South, Foden, & Rogers, 2013).

ICT supports every phase of participatory mapping, such as in data collection and processing, data search and presentation, data validation, and community building that consists of advocacy activities and sharing of views and information (Gouveia & Fonseca, 2008). This chapter combines all ICT-based participatory mapping techniques and organizes them under the umbrella term of e-participatory mapping.

Participatory Mapping, GIS and E-Participatory Mapping

GIS is a core ICT tool that can facilitate e-government processes and public participation (Ganapati, 2010; Kingston et al., 2000; Tulloch, 2007). GIS has the ability to visually represent numerous aspects of a location collectively and precisely, but this ability is not sufficient for public participation (Vajjhala, 2005). Technological advancements in GIS have progressively improved GIS accessibility for ordinary citizens (Ganapati, 2011). GIS, coupled with 3D visualization, allows governments to manage assets and perform day-to-day operations, collaborate, and develop and implement sustainable solutions (Bergeron, Barbara, & Stiller, 2010). These developments, combined with decreasing computer costs, low-cost GPS, and open data access over the Internet, have led to community-based organizations and individuals utilizing GIS in community initiatives (Corbett et al., 2006). The ability of GIS to synthesize a wide variety of data including spatial representations has made it an essential planning tool (Vajjhala, 2005). Simultaneously, participatory mapping has emerged as a participatory method for collecting spatial data, but one that is time-consuming and generates unwieldy information (Vajjhala, 2005). Due to the complementary nature of GIS and participatory mapping, scholars have integrated the two approaches (e.g. Craig, Harris, & Weiner, 2002; Mapedza, Wright, & Fawcett, 2003; Mbile, DeGrande, & Okon, 2003; Robiglio, Mala, & Diaw, 2003; Vajjhala, 2005; Weiner & Harris, 2003) into what can be called e-participatory mapping.

E-participatory mapping has been used to promote inclusive decision making in environmental issues (Vajjhala, 2005). Examples include mapping environmental changes (Aswani, Vaccaro, Abernethy, Albert, & Pablo, 2015), documenting landscape-related knowledge (Barlindhaug & Corbett, 2014), planning sustainable infrastructure development (Forrester & Snell, 2007), and mapping land use and land cover change (Bauer, 2009; Garrard et al., 2016; Malek & Boerboom, 2015). Across these studies, multiple terms are used in the literature to refer to e-participatory mapping approaches, including participatory GIS, public participation GIS, voluntary GIS, community GIS, bottom-up GIS, qualitative GIS, and grassroots mapping.

FOUR APPROACHES TO E-PARTICIPATORY MAPPING

Four approaches to e-participatory mapping feature prominently in the environmental literature: participatory GIS, public participation GIS, voluntary GIS, and human sensors. This section introduces and discusses these approaches.

Participatory GIS (PGIS)

The integration of GIS technology and community initiatives has led to participatory GIS (PGIS) that uses geo-spatial information as a vehicle for interaction, discussion, and analysis in support of advocacy and decision making (Corbett et al., 2006). The practice of PGIS developed out of participatory approaches that combine a range of geo-spatial tools and methods such as aerial photographs, sketch maps, satellite imagery, participatory 3D models, and GPS "to represent peoples' spatial knowledge in the forms of virtual or physical, 2 or 3 dimensional maps used as interactive vehicles for spatial learning, discussion, information exchange, analysis, decision making and advocacy" (Rambaldi, Kwaku Kyem, Mbile, McCall, & Weiner, 2006, p.2).

PGIS begins with the preliminary appraisal stage that includes gathering information (such as existing policies, GIS datasets, imagery and maps), identifying and understanding stakeholders, and building relationships necessary for collaborative partnerships (Baldwin, Mahon, & McConney, 2013; Pozzebon, Tello Rozas, & Aguilar Delgado, 2015). Stakeholders are identified and selected based on interest in or knowledge of the issue, or based on results of stakeholder assessment exercises that obtain information on demographics, livelihood, use of resources, and environmental practices.

Mapping exercises are carried out with stakeholders to document local spatial knowledge (Baldwin et al., 2013). The mapping exercise can be carried out with individuals or small groups using interviews or focus groups (Baldwin et al., 2013; Asare-Kyei, Forkuor, & Venus, 2015; Pozzebon et al., 2015; Bracken et al., 2016; Cinderby, Snell, & Forrester, 2008; Pozzebon et al., 2015), during formal or informal meetings, using brainstorming sessions (McBride et al., 2017), by recording oral history (Cullen, 2015) or by taking a walk in the area (Pozzebon et al., 2015; Sletto, Muñoz, Strange, Donoso, & Thomen, 2010). Often the first round of mapping exercise is used to create a base-map and subsequent exercises used to add details such as identifying distribution of resources and areas of threat (Baldwin et al., 2013; Cullen, 2015). In other applications, the first mapping cycle can be aimed at identifying the pre-existing issue or historical occurrence of events such as floods, and the second iteration to identify where solutions must be implemented (Bracken et al., 2016). Sometimes initial base maps are created by the researchers themselves and are then further refined using community input (Sletto et. al., 2010).

Mapping and stakeholder assessment data are translated into GIS by scanning, geo-referencing, and digitizing the resulting maps (Baldwin et al., 2013; Cullen, 2015). Some studies use validation exercises with a wider community (Bracken et al., 2016; Cinderby et al., 2008; Sletto et. al., 2010) to refine and finalize the map. This stage of PGIS may include discussion on issues such as relevant geospatial data types or visualization techniques, supplementary end products, and means of accessing data (Baldwin et al., 2013; Cinderby et al., 2008). The final stage involves use of the PGIS products such as for assessing coastal vulnerability, identifying areas of concern for planning or environmental protection, and obtaining stakeholders' evaluation of the PGIS process and products (Baldwin et al., 2013; Cinderby et al., 2008; Cullen, 2015; Jordan & Shrestha, 1998).

PGIS has been found to be effective at co-producing knowledge by eliciting high quality local experiential knowledge compatible with experts' knowledge and generating products that are understood by locals. Simultaneously, PGIS promotes spatial learning and builds capacity to access and use information produced by a variety of stakeholders through processes that generate positive emotions and bonding among participants, ultimately empowering disadvantaged groups (Balderas Torres, Santos Acuña, & Canto Vergara, 2014; Baldwin & Oxenford, 2014; Bracken et al., 2016; Cinderby et al., 2008; Cullen, 2015; McBride et al., 2017; Rambaldi et al., 2006; Young & Gilmore, 2013).

Public Participatory GIS (PPGIS)

Public participatory GIS (PPGIS) is an innovative GIS-based decision-making system that integrates GIS with the Internet, encourages public participation, and seeks to empower communities and individuals by integrating local knowledge into decision making (Weiner & Harris, 2003). Although there is ambiguity in the terms PGIS and PPGIS, scholars have attempted to clarify the distinction between the two. First, PGIS has its roots in participatory approaches used in rural areas of developing countries while PPGIS is generally applied in developed countries (Brown, 2012; Brown & Kyttä, 2014; Dunn, 2007; Tulloch, 2008; Rambaldi et al. 2006). PGIS applications generally use purposive sampling and do not require digital mapping technology (Brown, 2012; Brown & Kyttä, 2014), while PPGIS uses random sampling techniques and digital mapping with high quality spatial data as a major objective (Schlossberg & Shuford, 2005; Brown & Kyttä, 2014; Brown & Fagerholm, 2015).

Brown (2012) analyzed 17 PPGIS studies in the areas of environmental and regional planning, and found that all used random sampling of the general public. The representativeness of the sample impacts the attributes and preferences identified in PPGIS (Brown, 2012; Brown, Kelly, & Whitall, 2014). It is argued that without the component of random sampling, PPGIS will not improve the quality of public participation (Brown et al., 2014), as there can be variations in spatial results by community.

Data collection can take multiple forms, such as using online surveys (Brown & Donovan, 2013; Pocewicz, Nielsen-Pincus, Brown, & Schnitzer, 2012; Beverly et al., 2008). Multiple mapping methods have been used in PPGIS, ranging from paper maps with markers, pen, or sticker dots; participatory 3-dimensional modeling where participants create 3D models; to digital and Internet-based applications such as Google Maps (Brown, 2012; Leon et al., 2015; Gaillard, Hore, & Cadag; 2015; Cadag & Gaillard, 2012). In Internet PPGIS, a website is created that allows participants to enter textual and spatial information such as by using an online map interface (Brown & Weber, 2013; Brown & Donovan, 2013; Brown et.al., 2014; Fonji, Larivee, & Taff, 2014).

As a decision-making tool PPGIS is considered a transparent alternative especially for complex issues such as those related to the environment (Drew, 2003). PPGIS helps decision-making agencies to spatially identify community values (Brown, 2012), integrate complex spatial information and local knowledge into solutions and decisions, and empower local stakeholders in decision making (Sieber, 2006). PPGIS has been used in the field of environmental and regional planning in countries such as the U.S., Canada, New Zealand, and Australia. These include forest and landscape planning (Brown & Donovan, 2013; Thompson, Prokopy, Floress, & Weinkauf, 2011); conservation (Brown & Weber, 2013); and forest and land management (Brown et al., 2014; Beverly et al., 2008).

Public agencies have only minimally adopted PPGIS beyond initial trials (Brown, 2012). Furthermore, despite the emphasis on random sampling, many studies have been found to use systematic, convenience or voluntary samples (Brown, 2012; Fonji et al., 2014; Thompson et al., 2011). Even PPGIS projects using random sampling have been critiqued for having a biased sample with older, educated, and higher-income male participants (Brown et al., 2014), but Brown (2012) argues that it can still produce results that differ from those obtained by governmental organizations or interest groups. While PPGIS generally requires high quality spatial information and digital data, Pocewicz et al. (2012) found that traditional paper-based PPGIS surveys resulted in a higher response rate and greater participation compared to an Internet survey. Furthermore, web-based GIS is criticized for lacking the important face-to-face PPGIS intermediaries and exacerbates skill gaps of different participant groups (Wong & Chua, 2000).

PPGIS has been promoted more by academicians than by the government and it is difficult to find a bureaucratic champion for a PPGIS project (Brown, 2012). There are several reasons for this. First, PPGIS is resource intensive and implementing it in resource-poor communities, especially those with limited access to computers and the Internet, is not very feasible (Weiner & Harris, 2003). Second, use of PPGIS is largely hampered by institutional reasons and not technical reasons (Ganapati, 2011). Agency capacity (financial, technical, and personnel), lack of agency experience in engaging the public, unsupportive organizational culture, and regulatory review requirements are barriers to participatory methods such as PPGIS (Barndt, 1998; Brown, 2012; Ganapati, 2011). Asymmetrical power and political relationships may further result in unequal participation in and support for PPGIS efforts (Laituri 2003; Sieber, 2006). For example, public agencies may withdraw support for PPGIS if the results appear to legitimize public opposition (Brown, 2012). Environmental and industry stakeholders may also be reluctant as they do not always have a control over the outcomes of the PPGIS (Brown, 2012).

Voluntary GIS (VGIS)

Voluntary GIS (VGIS) is a term introduced by Goodchild (2007) to refer to approaches where individuals, untrained in geography or cartography, voluntarily provide geographic data by harnessing new Internet technologies such as bi-directional collaborative Web 2.0 tools. Although there are similarities between PPGIS and VGIS, in PPGIS an individual may be accessing a dataset about a location as a participant in public policy decision making, while in VGIS the individual may be creating a spatial dataset about a location regardless of the policy or decision (Tulloch, 2008). On the other hand, Brown et al. (2014) argue that in the Web 2.0 environment the differences may be more semantic than real.

VGIS, rather than being based on scientific knowledge, is driven by user-generated content, information volunteered by citizens, and citizen journalism that generates the popular knowledge that can be in conflict with authoritative knowledge (McCall et al., 2015, p. 793). VGIS platforms consist of internet- and GIS-enabled devices, and is driven by technological advancements such as mashups, dynamic GIS, cybercartography and geotagging (McCall et al., 2015). An example is OpenStreetMap that started with the goal of creating a free digital map of the world using volunteer participants to collect information that is then stored in a central database and distributed in multiple digital formats using the Web (Haklay, 2010). Volunteered information can be disseminated over the Internet using applications such as My Maps and Wikimapia (Goodchild & Glennon, 2010; McCall et al., 2015).

Although VGIS is based on the same premise as PGIS or PPGIS – that local people have knowledge of their environment and socio-economic conditions – scholars claim that VGIS is generating so much information far more rapidly and at lower cost through crowdsourcing (Goodchild & Glennon, 2010; Tulloch, 2008) that it undermines the practices of participatory GIS that are limited, slower, and on a smaller scale (McCall et al., 2015). During times of emergency, government agencies are particularly stretched with limited staff and resources, and citizens' eyes and ears can be utilized to assist emergency managers and other residents (Goodchild & Glennon, 2010). VGIS augments existing data and can generate early warning signs, in addition to creating a more informed and educated public and promoting cooperation between agencies and citizens (Gouveia & Fonseca, 2008).

The challenges of VGIS are that its actors are unknown, operating under no institutional or legal framework, and following non-transparent processes that can negatively affect information credibility (Goodchild & Glennon, 2010; Gouveia & Fonseca, 2008; McCall et al., 2015). VGIS efforts are often isolated, ad-hoc initiatives and the level of commitment of the volunteers is unknown (Gouveia & Fonseca, 2008). The degree of participation is low compared to PGIS and the flow of information is usually one-way, restricting any interaction (McCall et al., 2015). In addition, the data produced using VGIS is unlikely to be rich in information (McCall et al., 2015), and there is an ongoing debate on whether crowdsourced data results in crowd wisdom (McCall et al., 2015; Haklay, 2010). Nevertheless, some scholars believe in the quality of VGIS data as it is more current and complete compared to authoritatively-produced data (Goodchild & Glennon, 2010; Haklay, 2010). In fact, Jokar Arsanjani, Helbich, Bakillah, Hagenauer, and Zipf (2013) compare collaboratively-collected free VGIS data of land use patterns with European Environmental Agency data and find above 76 percent agreement between the two.

Human Sensors

The term *human sensors* overlaps with PGIS, PPGIS, and VGIS. The human sensor web is defined as a publicly-available web that people (humans) with mobile phones or tablets (the human sensors) use to share information and report issues by enabling their mobile devices to record quantitative and qualitative parameters (Georgiadou, Budhathoki, & Nedovic-Budic, 2011; Meo, Roglia, & Bottino, 2012). Human sensors are the individuals, particularly mobile phone and social media users, who act as a distributed data collection network. ICT developments in terms of increased computational power, storage, miniaturization, multiplicity of communication channels, and remote sensing have promoted new approaches to environmental monitoring via human sensors (Gouveia & Fonseca, 2008).

Society today faces new kinds of threats such as from various manmade and natural disasters. These require effective communication, such as those provided using GIS and the Internet with humans as sensors, that starts before the disaster takes place and remains long after it subsides. Laituri and Kodrich (2008) argue that online communities (such as those related to disaster response) can efficiently upload and disseminate information to create an interactive information exchange. The images and text posted by these virtual communities help create a sense of urgency and foster a sense of community (Laituri & Kodrich, 2008). McCall et al. (2015) describe a research project in Zanzibar aimed at developing a human sensor web for water supply information. Citizens were asked to report water shortages through short message service (SMS) texts sent to a special reporting telephone number. A local internet provider relayed the text messages and uploaded them to an online accessible map.

There are challenges in application of human sensors. These include establishing methodologies for user registration and data collection, recognizing variations in the precision of devices used for data collection, user training requirements, recruitment of new volunteers, and maintenance of existing volunteers (Gouveia & Fonseca, 2008). The digital divide can also affect data collection that underpin the human sensors network. For example, in the Zanzibar water supply case study, the women were the ones who collected water but the men were the ones who possessed mobile phones (McCall et al., 2015). Sometimes the local culture can also create a hindrance. In the Zanzibar culture people were highly respectful of elders. This culture discouraged them from sending short text messages without context, but the human sensor web was not designed to extract information from long strings of text messages (McCall et al., 2015).

Issues, Controversies, and Problems

There are several challenges of and barriers to participatory mapping, including issues of accessibility due to the digital divide, inequity in empowerment of participants, conflicts amongst participants, lack of community support, and lack of a supporting institutional framework (Gouveia & Fonseca, 2008; Norris, 2014). Laws and policies further shape the broad conditions of who participates, how information is communicated, and who has access to data (Brown & Donovan, 2014; Ganapati, 2011). Lack of effective administrative mechanisms and structures hinder the outcomes of the initiatives from being incorporated into mainstream decision-making processes (IFAD, 2009).

There are also challenges associated with the four types of e-participatory mapping. Contextual issues such as linguistic and cultural factors, low participation rates, representativeness of the sample, citizen perceptions of and trust in government, and the digital divide are common concerns. Where public agencies are required to pursue e-participatory mapping, the major issues largely revolve around institutional reluctance to adopt the methodologies, and lack of resources such as technical and personnel capabilities. The credibility and richness of data, and the uncertainty of participation may also mar e-participatory mapping initiatives where individuals are voluntarily providing information. Furthermore, despite all efforts, the knowledge generated from such efforts cannot be expected to replace expert knowledge.

Another issue that stands out is the inconsistent use of the four categories of e-participatory mapping approaches throughout the literature. The literature review underpinning the discussion presented in this chapter found that, even though there are attempts at demarcating the various e-participatory mapping exercises (such as

PGIS, PPGIS, and VGIS), in practice, not all scholars follow the rules or attempt to categorize their research into one of the categories. Some researchers simply refer to participatory mapping and GIS, broadly, in their methodology rather than being more specific such as by calling it PGIS or PPGIS. For example, Brown et al.'s (2014) study identify the research by Beverly et al.'s (2008) as using PPGIS, but the original authors themselves use the general term of participatory mapping and not PPGIS. On the other hand, despite random sampling being a key feature of PPGIS, Fonji et al. (2014) only use voluntary participants in what they identify as an application of PPGIS.

PGIS and PPGIS are also noted by some scholars to be different according to the developed vs. developing nations dichotomy. However, this distinction is not consistently evident in actual application. For example, PPGIS studies have been conducted in developing nations such as Sri Lanka (Alagan & Aladuwaka, 2012), and PGIS studies have been conducted in developed countries such as the UK (Bracken et al., 2016; Cinderby et al., 2008). Further overlap can be seen using the example of the e-participatory mapping study by Fonji et al.'s (2014). This study shows characteristic of PGIS in that it has a strong educational component, and characteristics of PPGIS in the use of a dedicated systems architecture for data upload and collection for a specific and pre-identified purpose. At the same time, mapping participants were volunteers who monitored their environment using GPS devices, placing their study somewhere within the VGIS and human sensors categories.

SOLUTIONS AND RECOMMENDATIONS

Technology resource requirements and reluctance by public agencies to adopt e-participatory mapping methodologies pose challenges for e-participatory mapping. However, the complexity of environmental problems and the emphasis on stakeholder engagement, in parallel with increasing access to the Internet and software and hardware development, make e-participatory mapping an irresistible option in the future. Supporting institutional infrastructure, such as recommendations and guidelines to agencies for using e-participatory mapping, training and skill development initiatives for agency personnel and stakeholders, greater availability and accessibility of technology infrastructure, and transparent processes for reducing information asymmetry and building citizen trust are required for meaningful participation.

FUTURE RESEARCH

In the PGIS category, future research is called for to answer questions such as whether the mapping projects changed the way the communities represent themselves to the state and how to leverage participatory research to support marginalized stakeholders in policy decision making (Norris, 2014). The participation rates in PPGIS surveys have been low and Brown (2012) argues that PPGIS practitioners need to find ways to reverse the declining participation trends. Studies claim that paper-based map surveys result in higher response rates and greater mapping participation than Internet-based survey methods (Pocewicz et al. 2012), which is problematic for achieving PPGIS' goal of high quality digital spatial data. Thus, an effective method to increase participation using PPGIS while simultaneously maintain the quality of the spatial data needs to be identified (Brown, 2012). Future research should also examine public receptivity to alternate mapping using top-down, bottom-up or integrated approaches (Brown & Weber, 2013). Advancing knowledge in VGIS may require incorporating knowledge from the participatory, feminist and critical GIS approach, as well as drawing from multiple disciplines such as GIScience, cognition, and human-computer interaction (Elwood, 2008; Kwan, 2002; Boschmann & Cubbon, 2014; Cullen, 2015). Future research should focus on use of free and open source software for crowdsourced data and collective problem solving (Gajbe, Shankar, & Rodriguez, 2014), and take advantage of open source solutions and development in mobile GIS for establishing standards and protocols for data collection and seamless data exchange, new data exchange networks, and licensing arrangements to facilitate use of software and data (Laituri & Kodrich, 2008). Future work is also suggested on human sensors to improve the quality of metadata, to improve the quality of the tag categories, and to reduce record duplications (Meo et al., 2012).

CONCLUSION

This chapter situates e-participatory mapping as an e-governance tool to facilitate public participation. The discussion uses the umbrella term of e-participatory mapping to refer to all participatory mapping activities using ICT such as GIS, the Internet, and mobile technology. Various approaches of e-participatory mapping used in the field of environmental policy, including PGIS, PPGIS, VGIS, and human sensors, are explored. By bringing together the discussion of various terminologies, practices, and studies in participatory mapping, and approaches used in e-participatory mapping in the environmental policy domain, the chapter creates a single narrative for scholars and practitioners to serve as a beginner's frame of reference for those interested in embracing e-participatory mapping as an e-governance tool. Despite various challenges, e-participatory mapping is an important tool for public participation, policy implementation, and public management. A database with participatory geo-referenced data can facilitate decision making on policy issues. Advancements in ICT and the possibility of generating large amount of crowdsourced data such as through VGIS and human sensors makes public participation in mapping spatial data inevitable in the future.

REFERENCES

Al-Kodmany, K. (2002). GIS and the artist: Shaping the image of a neighbourhood in participatory environmental design. In D. Weiner, T. M. Harris, & W. J. Craig (Eds.), *Community participation and geographic information systems* (pp. 320–329). London: Taylor and Francis. doi:10.1201/9780203469484.ch24

Alagan, R., & Aladuwaka, S. (2012). Innovative public participatory GIS methodologies adopted to deal with the social impact assessment process challenges: A Sri Lankan experience. *URISA Journal*, *24*(2), 19–32.

Andrade, M., & Szlafsztein, C. (2015). Community participation in flood mapping in the Amazon through interdisciplinary methods. *Natural Hazards*, *78*(3), 1491–1500. doi:10.100711069-015-1782-y

Asare-Kyei, D., Forkuor, G., & Venus, V. (2015). Modeling flood hazard zones at the sub-district level with the rational model integrated with GIS and remote sensing approaches. *Water (Basel)*, *7*(7), 3531–3564. doi:10.3390/w7073531

Aswani, S., Vaccaro, I., Abernethy, K., Albert, S., & Pablo, J. (2015). Can perceptions of environmental and climate change in island communities assist in adaptation planning locally? *Environmental Management*, *56*(6), 1487–1501. doi:10.100700267-015-0572-3 PMID:26142887

Balderas Torres, A., Santos Acuña, L. A., & Canto Vergara, J. M. (2014). Integrating CBM into land-use based mitigation actions implemented by local communities. *Forests*, *5*(12), 3295–3326. doi:10.3390/f5123295

Baldwin, K., Mahon, R., & McConney, P. (2013). Participatory GIS for strengthening transboundary marine governance in SIDS. *Natural Resources Forum*, *37*(4), 257–268. doi:10.1111/1477-8947.12029

Baldwin, K., & Oxenford, H. A. (2014). A Participatory approach to marine habitat mapping in the Grenadine Islands. *Coastal Management*, *42*(1), 36–58. doi:10.1080/08920753.2013.863725

Barlindhaug, S., & Corbett, J. (2014). Living a long way from home: Communicating land-related knowledge in dispersed indigenous communities, an alternative approach. *Acta Borealia*, *31*(1), 1–24. doi:10.1080/08003831.2014.904619

Barndt, M. (1998). Public participation GIS—Barriers to implementation. *Cartography and Geographic Information Systems*, *25*(2), 105–112. doi:10.1559/152304098782594607

Bauer, K. (2009). On the politics and the possibilities of participatory mapping and GIS: Using spatial technologies to study common property and land use change among pastoralists in Central Tibet. *Cultural Geographies*, *16*(2), 229–252. doi:10.1177/1474474008101518

Bergeron, S. J., Barbara, L. M., & Stiller, A. (2010). Digital city initiatives for small municipalities and rural areas and their role in solid waste management. *Journal of Solid Waste Technology Management*, *36*(3), 918–926.

Beverly, J., Uto, K., Wilkes, J., & Bothwell, P. (2008). Assessing spatial attributes of forest landscape values: An internet-based participatory mapping approach. *Canadian Journal of Forest Research*, *38*(2), 289–303. doi:10.1139/X07-149

Bojórquez-Tapia, L. A., Diaz-Mondragón, S., & Ezcurra, E. (2001). GIS-based approach for participatory decision making and land suitability assessment. *International Journal of Geographical Information Science*, *15*(2), 129–151. doi:10.1080/13658810010005534

Boschmann, E., & Cubbon, E. (2014). Sketch maps and qualitative GIS: Using cartographies of individual spatial narratives in geographic research. *The Professional Geographer*, *66*(2), 236–248. doi:10.1080/00330124.2013.781490

Bracken, L., Oughton, J., Donaldson, E., Cook, A., Forrester, B., Spray, C., ... Bissett, N. (2016). Flood risk management, an approach to managing cross-border hazards. *Natural Hazards*, *82*(S2), 217–240. doi:10.100711069-016-2284-2

Brown, G. (2012). Public participation GIS (PPGIS) for regional and environmental planning: Reflections on a decade of empirical research. *Journal of the Urban and Regional Information Systems Association / URISA*, *24*(2), 7–18.

Brown, G., & Donovan, S. (2014). Measuring change in place values for environmental and natural resource planning using public participation GIS (PPGIS): Results and challenges for longitudinal research. *Society & Natural Resources*, *27*(1), 36–54. doi:10.1080/08941920.2013.840023

Brown, G., & Fagerholm, N. (2015). Empirical PPGIS/PGIS mapping of ecosystem services: A review and evaluation. *Ecosystem Services*, *13*, 119–133. doi:10.1016/j.ecoser.2014.10.007

Brown, G., Kelly, M., & Whitall, D. (2014). Which 'public'? Sampling effects in public participation GIS (PPGIS) and volunteered geographic information (VGI) systems for public lands management. *Journal of Environmental Planning and Management*, *57*(1-2), 190–214. doi:10.1080/09640568.2012.741045

Brown, G., & Kyttä, M. (2014). Key issues and research priorities for public participation GIS (PPGIS): A synthesis based on empirical research. *Applied Geography (Sevenoaks, England)*, *46*, 122–136. doi:10.1016/j.apgeog.2013.11.004

Brown, G., & Weber, D. (2013). A place-based approach to conservation management using public participation GIS (PPGIS). *Journal of Environmental Planning and Management*, *56*(4), 455–473. doi:10.1080/09640568.2012.685628

Brown, G. G., & Donovan, S. (2013). Escaping the national forest planning quagmire: Using public participation GIS to assess acceptable national forest use. *Journal of Forestry*, *111*(2), 115–125. doi:10.5849/jof.12-087

Brown, K., Adger, W. N., & Tompkins, E. L. (2002). *Making waves: Integrating coastal conservation and development*. London: Routledge.

Brown, K., Few, R., Tompkins, E. L., Tsimplis, M., & Sortti, M. (2005). *Responding to climate change: Inclusive and integrated coastal analysis*. Tyndall Centre Technical Report 24.

Burby, R. J. (2003). Making plans that matter: Citizen involvement and government action. *Journal of the American Planning Association*, *69*(1), 33–49. doi:10.1080/01944360308976292

Cadag, J. R. D., & Gaillard, J. C. (2012). Integrating knowledge and actions in disaster risk reduction: The contribution of participatory mapping. *Area*, *44*(1), 100–109. doi:10.1111/j.1475-4762.2011.01065.x

Chagumaira, C., Rurinda, J., Nezomba, H., Mtambanengwe, F., & Mapfumo, P. (2016). Use patterns of natural resources supporting livelihoods of smallholder communities and implications for climate change adaptation in Zimbabwe. *Environment, Development and Sustainability*, *18*(1), 237–255. doi:10.100710668-015-9637-y

Chakrabarty, A. (2011). Ecotourism development and security restructuring: A GIS based planning for peaceful dissuasion of anarchism in forest provinces of India. *Procedia: Social and Behavioral Sciences*, *21*, 108–115. doi:10.1016/j.sbspro.2011.07.006

Chambers, R. (1994). The origins and practice of participatory rural appraisal. *World Development*, *22*(7), 953–969. doi:10.1016/0305-750X(94)90141-4

Cinderby, S., Snell, C., & Forrester, J. (2008). Participatory GIS and its application in governance: The example of air quality and the implications for noise pollution. *Local Environment*, *13*(4), 309–320. doi:10.1080/13549830701803265

Cocks, M. L., Dold, T., & Vetter, S. (2012). 'God is my forest' - Xhosa cultural values provide untapped opportunities for conservation. *South African Journal of Science*, *108*(5/6), 1–8. doi:10.4102ajs.v108i5/6.880

Corbett, J. (2009). *Good practices in participatory mapping: A review prepared for the International Fund for Agricultural Development (IFAD).* Retrieved 29th July from http://agris.fao.org/agris-search/search.do?recordID=GB2013201933

Corbett, J., Rambaldi, G., Kyem, P., Weiner, D., Olson, R., Muchemi, J., ... Chambers, R. (2006). Overview: Mapping for Change – the emergence of a new practice. *Participatory Learning and Action*, *54*, 13–19.

Craig, W., Harris, T., & Weiner, D. (2002). *Community participation and geographic information systems*. London: Taylor and Francis.

Crow, D. A., & Stevens, J. R. (2012). Citizen engagement in local environmental policy: Information, mobilization, and media. In H. L. Schachter (Ed.), *State of citizen participation in America* (pp. 131–162). Charlotte, NC: Information Age Publishing.

Cullen, A. (2015). Making sense of claims across institutional divides: Critical PGIS and mapping customary land in Timor-Leste. *The Australian Geographer*, *46*(4), 473–490. doi:10.1080/00049182.2015.1080344

Davies, S. R., Selin, C., Gano, G., & Pereira, Â. G. (2012). Citizen engagement and urban change: Three case studies of material deliberation. *Cities (London, England)*, *29*(3), 51–357.

Delli Carpini, M. X., Cook, F. L., & Jacobs, L. R. (2004). Public deliberation, discursive participation, and citizen engagement: A review of the empirical literature. *Annual Review of Political Science*, *7*(1), 315–344. doi:10.1146/annurev.polisci.7.121003.091630

Dickinson, J. L., Shirk, J., Bonter, D., Bonney, R., Crain, R. L., Martin, J., ... Purcell, K. (2012). The current state of citizen science as a tool for ecological research and public engagement. *Frontiers in Ecology and the Environment, 10*(6), 291–297. doi:10.1890/110236

Drew, C.H. (2003). Transparency – Considerations for PPGIS research and development. *URISA Journal, 15*, 73-78.

Dunn, C. (2007). Participatory GIS -- A people's GIS? *Progress in Human Geography, 31*(5), 616–637. doi:10.1177/0309132507081493

Elwood, S. (2008). Volunteered geographic information: Future research directions motivated by critical, participatory, and feminist GIS. *GeoJournal, 72*(3), 173–183. doi:10.100710708-008-9186-0

Few, R., Brown, K., & Tompkins, E. L. (2007). Public participation and climate change adaptation: Avoiding the illusion of inclusion. *Climate Policy, 7*(1), 46–59. doi:10.3763/cpol.2007.0704

Fischer, F. (2000). *Citizens, experts, and the environment: The politics of local knowledge*. Durham, NC: Duke University Press. doi:10.1215/9780822380283

Fonji, S., Larrivee, M., & Taff, G. (2014). Public Participation GIS (PPGIS) for regional mapping and environmental awareness. *Journal of Geographic Information System, 6*(2), 135–149. doi:10.4236/jgis.2014.62015

Forrester, J., & Snell, C. (2007). Planning inclusive and sustainable urban regeneration: Balancing a visitor-based economy with local needs in the city of York, UK. *Journal of Urban Renewal and Regeneration, 1*(1), 69–82.

Fredericks, J. F., & Foth, M. (2013). Augmenting public participation: Enhancing planning outcomes through the use of social media and web 2.0. *Australian Plants, 50*(3), 244–256. doi:10.1080/07293682.2012.748083

Gaillard, J. C., Hore, K., & Cadag, J. R. D. (2015). Participatory mapping for disaster risk reduction: A review. *Globe, 76*, 31–38.

Gajbe, A., Shankar, A., & Rodriguez, S. (2014). Virtual coast guard: An open and crowdsourced GIS portal for stewardship of India's coast. *Transactions in GIS, 18*(4), 544–554. doi:10.1111/tgis.12066

Ganapati, S. (2010). *Using geographic information systems to increase citizen engagement*. Washington, DC: IBM Center for the Business of Government. Abstract retrieved on 12th November 2016 from http://faculty.cbpp.uaa.alaska.edu/afgjp/padm601%20fall%202010/GIS.pdf

Ganapati, S. (2011). Uses of public participation geographic information systems applications in e-government. *Public Administration Review*, *71*(3), 425–434. doi:10.1111/j.1540-6210.2011.02226.x

Garrard, R., Kohler, T., Price, M. F., Byers, A. C., Sherpa, A. R., & Maharjan, G. R. (2016). Land use and land cover change in Sagarmatha National Park, a world heritage site in the Himalayas of Eastern Nepal. *Mountain Research and Development*, *36*(3), 299–310. doi:10.1659/MRD-JOURNAL-D-15-00005.1

Georgiadou, Y., Budhathoki, N. R., & Nedovic-Budic, Z. (2011). An exploration of SDI and volunteered geographic information in Africa. In Z. Nedovic-Budic, J. Crompvoets, & Y. Georgiadou (Eds.), *Spatial data infrastructure in context: North and South* (pp. 203–218). Boca Raton, FL: CRC Press.

Godschalk, D. R., Brody, S., & Burby, R. (2003). Public participation in natural hazard mitigation policy formation: Challenges for comprehensive planning. *Journal of Environmental Planning and Management*, *46*(5), 733–754. doi:10.1080/0964056032000138463

González, A., Gilmer, A., Foley, R., Sweeney, J., & Fry, J. (2008). Technology-aided participative methods in environmental assessment: An international perspective. *Computers, Environment and Urban Systems*, *32*(4), 303–316. doi:10.1016/j.compenvurbsys.2008.02.001

Goodchild, M., & Glennon, J. (2010). Crowdsourcing geographic information for disaster response: A research frontier. *International Journal of Digital Earth*, *3*(3), 231–241. doi:10.1080/17538941003759255

Goodchild, M. F. (2007). Citizens as sensors: The world of volunteered geography. *GeoJournal*, *69*(4), 211–221. doi:10.100710708-007-9111-y

Gouveia, C., & Fonseca, A. (2008). New approaches to environmental monitoring: The use of ICT to explore volunteered geographic information. *GeoJournal*, *72*(3), 185–197. doi:10.100710708-008-9183-3

Gray, S. A., Gray, S., De Kok, J. L., Helfgott, A. E. R., O'Dwyer, B., Jordan, R., & Nyaki, A. (2015). Using fuzzy cognitive mapping as a participatory approach to analyze change, preferred states, and perceived resilience of social-ecological systems. *Ecology and Society*, *20*(2), 186–199. doi:10.5751/ES-07396-200211

Haklay, M. (2010). How good is volunteered geographical information? A comparative study of OpenStreetMap and ordnance survey datasets. *Environment and Planning. B, Planning & Design*, *37*(4), 682–703. doi:10.1068/b35097

Hamilton, J. D., & Wills-Toker, C. (2006). Reconceptualizing dialogue in environmental public participation. *Policy Studies Journal: the Journal of the Policy Studies Organization*, *34*(4), 755–775. doi:10.1111/j.1541-0072.2006.00200.x

Hiller, J. S., & Bélanger, F. (2001). Privacy strategies for electronic government. In M. A. Abramson & G. E. Means (Eds.), *E-government 2001* (pp. 162–198). Lanham, MD: Rowman & Littlefield.

Hoole, A., & Berkes, F. (2010). Breaking down fences: Recoupling social–ecological systems for biodiversity conservation in Namibia. *Geoforum*, *41*(2), 304–317. doi:10.1016/j.geoforum.2009.10.009

Integrated Approaches to Participatory Development (IPAD). (2009). *Participatory mapping*. Retrieved 21st January 2016 at https://coast.noaa.gov/digitalcoast/_/pdf/participatory-mapping.pdf?redirect=301ocm

International Fund for Agricultural Development (IFAD). (2009). *Good practices in participatory mapping*. Retrieved 6th January 2016 from http://www.ifad.org/pub/map/pm_web.pdf

Jokar Arsanjani, J., Helbich, M., Bakillah, M., Hagenauer, J., & Zipf, A. (2013). Toward mapping land-use patterns from volunteered geographic information. *International Journal of Geographical Information Science*, *27*(12), 2264–2278. doi:10.1080/13658816.2013.800871

Jordan, G., & Shrestha, B. (2000). *A participatory GIS for community forestry user groups in Nepal: Putting people before the technology. Participatory learning and action notes 39*. International Institute for Environment and Development.

Jordan, G. H., & Shrestha, B. (1998). *Integrating geomatics and participatory techniques for community forest management: Case studies from the Yarsha Khola watershed, Dolakha district*. Nepal: ICIMOD.

Joyce, A., & Canessa, R. (2009). Spatial and temporal changes in access rights to shellfish resources in British Columbia. *Coastal Management*, *37*(6), 585–616. doi:10.1080/08920750903097517

Kaul, V., & Thornton, T. (2014). Resilience and adaptation to extremes in a changing Himalayan environment. *Regional Environmental Change*, *14*(2), 683–698. doi:10.100710113-013-0526-3

Kim, A. M. (2015). Critical cartography 2.0: From "participatory mapping" to authored visualizations of power and people. *Landscape and Urban Planning*, *142*, 215–225. doi:10.1016/j.landurbplan.2015.07.012

King, C. S., Feltey, K. M., & Susel, B. (1998). The question of participation: Toward authentic public participation in public administration. *Public Administration Review*, *58*(4), 317–326. doi:10.2307/977561

Kingston, R., Carver, S., Evans, A., & Turton, I. (2000). Web-based public participation geographical information systems: An aid to local environmental decision-making. *Computers, Environment and Urban Systems*, *24*(2), 109–125. doi:10.1016/S0198-9715(99)00049-6

Kwan, M. (2002). Feminist visualization: Re-envisioning GIS as a method in feminist geographic research. *Annals of the Association of American Geographers*, *92*(4), 645–661. doi:10.1111/1467-8306.00309

Laituri, M. (2003). The issue of access: An assessment guide for evaluating public participation geographic information science case studies. *URISA Journal*, *15*, 25–32.

Laituri, M., & Kodrich, K. (2008). Online disaster response community: People as sensors of high magnitude disasters using internet GIS. *Sensors (Basel)*, *8*(5), 3037–3055. doi:10.33908053037 PMID:27879864

Leon, J. X., Hardcastle, J., James, R., Albert, S., Kereseka, J., & Woodroffe, C. D. (2015). Supporting local and traditional knowledge with science for adaptation to climate change: Lessons learned from participatory three-dimensional modeling in BoeBoe, Solomon Islands. *Coastal Management*, *43*(4), 424–438. doi:10.1080/08920753.2015.1046808

Levine, A. S., & Feinholz, C. L. (2015). Participatory GIS to inform coral reef ecosystem management: Mapping human coastal and ocean uses in Hawaii. *Applied Geography (Sevenoaks, England)*, *59*, 60–69. doi:10.1016/j.apgeog.2014.12.004

Lewandowski, E. J., & Oberhauser, K. S. (2015). Butterfly citizen scientists in the United States increase their engagement in conservation. *Biological Conservation*, *208*, 106–112. doi:10.1016/j.biocon.2015.07.029

Lingel, J. (2011). Information tactics of immigrants in urban environments. *Information Research, 16*(4). Available at http://InformationR.net/ir/16-4/paper500.html

Lowe, C., Gaudion, K., McGinley, C., & Kew, A. (2014). Designing living environments with adults with autism. *Tizard Learning Disability Review*, *19*(2), 63–72. doi:10.1108/TLDR-01-2013-0002

Lubis, M. I., & Langston, J. D. (2015). Understanding landscape change using participatory mapping and geographic information systems: Case study in North Sulawesi, Indonesia. *Procedia Environmental Sciences*, *24*, 206–214. doi:10.1016/j.proenv.2015.03.027

Lukensmeyer, C. J., & Torres, L. H. (2006). *Public deliberation: A manager's guide to citizen engagement.* Retrieved 24th January 2016 from https://www.whitehouse.gov/files/documents/ostp/opengov_inbox/ibmpubdelib.pdf

Malek, Ž., & Boerboom, L. (2015). Participatory scenario development to address potential impacts of land use change: An example from the Italian Alps. *Mountain Research and Development*, *35*(2), 126–138. doi:10.1659/MRD-JOURNAL-D-14-00082.1

Mapedza, F., Wright, J., & Fawcett, R. (2003). An investigation of land cover change in Mafungautsi forest, Zimbabwe, using GIS and participatory mapping. *Applied Geography (Sevenoaks, England)*, *23*(1), 1–21. doi:10.1016/S0143-6228(02)00070-X

Marchionini, G., Samet, H., & Brandt, L. (2003). Digital government. *Association for Computing Machinery. Communications of the ACM*, *46*(1), 24–27.

Mbile, P., DeGrande, A., & Okon, D. (2003). Integrating participatory resource mapping and geographic information systems in forest conservation and natural resources management in Cameroon: A methodological guide. *EJISDC*, *14*(2), 1–11.

McBride, B., Sanchez-Trigueros, F., Carver, S., Watson, A., Stumpff, L., Matt, R., & Borrie, W. (2017). Participatory geographic information systems as an organizational platform for the integration of traditional and scientific knowledge in contemporary fire and fuels management. *Journal of Forestry*, *115*(1), 43–50. doi:10.5849/jof.14-147

McCall, M. K., Martinez, J., & Verplanke, J. (2015). Shifting boundaries of volunteered geographic information systems and modalities: Learning from PGIS. *ACME: An International E-Journal for Critical Geographies*, *14*(3), 791–826.

McLaverty, P. (2011). Participation. In M. Bevir (Ed.), *The SAGE handbook of governance* (pp. 1–30). London: Sage. doi:10.4135/9781446200964.n26

Meo, R., Roglia, E., & Bottino, A. (2012). The exploitation of data from remote and human sensors for environment monitoring in the SMAT Project. *Sensors, 12*(12), 17504-17535.

Moon, M. J. (2002). The evolution of e-government among municipalities: Rhetoric or reality? *Public Administration Review, 62*(4), 424–433. doi:10.1111/0033-3352.00196

Mossberger, K., Tolbert, C. J., & McNeal, R. S. (2008). *Digital citizenship: The internet, society, and participation*. Cambridge, MA: MIT Press.

Norris, T. B. (2014). Bridging the great divide: State, civil society, and 'participatory' conservation mapping in a resource extraction zone. *Applied Geography (Sevenoaks, England), 54*, 262–274. doi:10.1016/j.apgeog.2014.05.016

Parr, J., & Gates, C. (1989). Assessing community interest and gathering community support. In International City Management Association (Eds.), Partnerships in local governance: Effective council-manager relations. Washington, DC: International City Management Association.

Parry, G., & Moyser, G. (1994). More participation, more democracy? In D. Beetham (Ed.), *Defining and Measuring Democracy* (pp. 44–62). London: Sage.

Pocewicz, A., Nielsen-Pincus, M., Brown, G., & Schnitzer, R. (2012). An evaluation of internet versus paper-based methods for public participation geographic information systems (PPGIS). *Transactions in GIS, 16*(1), 39–53. doi:10.1111/j.1467-9671.2011.01287.x

Pozzebon, M., Tello Rozas, S., & Aguilar Delgado, N. (2015). Use and consequences of participatory GIS in a Mexican municipality: Applying a multilevel framework. *Uso y consecuencias de un SIG participativo en un município mexicano: aplicando un modelo multinivel, 55*(3), 290-303.

Rambaldi, G., Kwaku Kyem, A. P., Mbile, P., McCall, M., & Weiner, D. (2006). Participatory Spatial Information Management and Communication in Developing Countries. *EJISDC, 25*(1), 1-9. Retrieved from http://www.ejisdc.org/ojs/include/getdoc.php?id=246&article=263&mode=pdf

Reed, M. (2008). Stakeholder participation for environmental management: A literature review. *Biological Conservation, 141*(10), 2417–2431. doi:10.1016/j.biocon.2008.07.014

Robiglio, V., Mala, W. A., & Diaw, C. M. (2003). Mapping landscapes: Integrating GIS and social science methods to model human-nature relationships in Southern Cameroon. *Small-scale Forest Economics. Management and Policy, 2*(2), 171–184.

Rowe, G., & Frewer, L. J. (2000). Public participation methods: A framework for evaluation. *Science, Technology & Human Values*, *25*(1), 3–29. doi:10.1177/016224390002500101

Schlossberg, M., & Shuford, E. (2005). Delineating 'public' and 'participation' in PPGIS. *URISA*, *16*, 15–26.

Sieber, R. (2006). Public participation geographic information systems: A literature review and framework. *Annals of the Association of American Geographers*, *96*(3), 491–507. doi:10.1111/j.1467-8306.2006.00702.x

Skinner, K., Hanning, R. M., & Tsuji, L. J. S. (2006). Barriers and supports for healthy eating and physical activity for First Nation youths in northern Canada. *International Journal of Circumpolar Health*, *65*(2), 148–161. doi:10.3402/ijch.v65i2.18095 PMID:16711466

Sletto, B. (2009). 'Indigenous people don't have boundaries': Reborderings, fire management, and productions of authenticities in indigenous landscapes. *Cultural Geographies*, *16*(2), 253–277. doi:10.1177/1474474008101519

Sletto, B., Muñoz, S., Strange, S. M., Donoso, R. E., & Thomen, M. (2010). El Rincón de los Olvidados: Participatory GIS, experiential learning and critical pedagogy in Santo Domingo, Dominican Republic. *Journal of Latin American Geography*, *9*(3), 111–135. doi:10.1353/lag.2010.0022

Smith, H., & Jenkins, P. (2015). Trans-disciplinary research and strategic urban expansion planning in a context of weak institutional capacity: Case study of Huambo, Angola. *Habitat International*, *46*, 244–251. doi:10.1016/j.habitatint.2014.10.006

Smith, L. G. (1983). *Impact assessment and sustainable resource management*. Harlow, UK: Longman.

Stelzenmüller, V., Lee, J., South, A., Foden, J., & Rogers, S. I. (2013). Practical tools to support marine spatial planning: A review and some prototype tools. *Marine Policy*, *38*, 214–227. doi:10.1016/j.marpol.2012.05.038

Thompson, A., Prokopy, L., Floress, K., & Weinkauf, D. (2011). A method for incorporating community priorities into GIS: Challenges, choices, and directions for landscape planners. *Landscape Journal: Design, Planning, and Management of the Land*, *30*(2), 299–312. doi:10.3368/lj.30.2.299

Tolbert, C. J., & Mossberger, K. (2006). The Effects of e-government on trust and confidence in government. *Public Administration Review*, *66*(3), 354–369. doi:10.1111/j.1540-6210.2006.00594.x

Tschakert, P., Ricciardi, V., Smithwick, E., Machado, M., Ferring, D., Hausermann, H., & Bug, L. (2016). Situated knowledge of pathogenic landscapes in Ghana: Understanding the emergence of Buruli ulcer through qualitative analysis. *Social Science & Medicine*, *150*, 160–171. doi:10.1016/j.socscimed.2015.12.005 PMID:26761375

Tulloch, D. L. (2007). Many, many maps: Empowerment and online participatory mapping. *First Monday*, *12*(2). doi:10.5210/fm.v12i2.1620

Tulloch, D. L. (2008). Is VGI participation? From vernal pools to video games. *GeoJournal*, *72*(3/4), 161–171. doi:10.100710708-008-9185-1

UN. (2008). *World public sector report*. Retrieved 21st January 2016 from http://www.unpan.org/Directories/UNPublicAdministrationGlossary/tabid/928/language/en-US/Default.aspx#

UNFCCC. (1992). *UN convention on climate change*. Available at https://unfccc.int/resource/docs/convkp/conveng.pdf

United Nations (UN). (2014). *E-Government survey 2014*. Retrieved 11th October 2015 from, http://unpan3.un.org/egovkb/Portals/egovkb/Documents/un/2014-Survey/E-Gov_Complete_Survey-2014.pdf

Vajjhala, S. P. (2005). *Integrating GIS and participatory mapping in community development planning*. Paper for the ESRI International User Conference, Sustainable Development and Humanitarian Affairs Track, San Diego, CA.

Verba, S., Schlozman, K., Brady, H., & Nie, N. H. (1993). Citizen activity: Who participates? What do they say? *The American Political Science Review*, *87*(2), 303–318. doi:10.2307/2939042

Webler, T. (1999). The craft and theory of public participation: A dialectical process. *Journal of Risk Research*, *2*(1), 55–71. doi:10.1080/136698799376989

Weiner, D., & Harris, T. M. (2003). Community-integrated GIS for land reform in South Africa. *Journal of the Urban and Regional Information Systems Association / URISA*, *15*(2), 61–73.

West, D. (2005). *Digital government: Technology and public sector performance (Safari tech books online)*. Princeton, NJ: Princeton University Press.

Wong, S., & Chua, Y. (2000). Data intermediation and beyond: Issues for web-based PPGIS. *Cartographica*, *38*(3/4), 63–80.

Woodhouse, E., Mills, M., McGowan, P., & Milner-Gulland, E. (2015). Religious relationships with the environment in a Tibetan rural community: Interactions and contrasts with popular notions of indigenous environmentalism. *Human Ecology: an Interdisciplinary Journal*, *43*(2), 295–307. doi:10.100710745-015-9742-4 PMID:25983377

Young, J. C., & Gilmore, M. P. (2013). The spatial politics of affect and emotion in participatory GIS. *Annals of the Association of American Geographers*, *103*(4), 808–823. doi:10.1080/00045608.2012.707596

ADDITIONAL READING

Chambers, R. (1997). *Whose reality counts? Putting the first last*. London: Intermediate Technology. doi:10.3362/9781780440453

Flanagin, A., & Metzger, J. (2008). The credibility of volunteered geographic information. *GeoJournal*, *72*(3), 137–148. doi:10.100710708-008-9188-y

Gould, W., & White, R. R. (1986). *Mental maps* (2nd ed.). Boston: Allen & Unwin.

Haklay, M., & Tobón, C. (2003). Usability evaluation and PPGIS: Towards a user-centred design approach. *International Journal of Geographical Information Science*, *17*(6), 577–592. doi:10.1080/1365881031000114107

Pickles, J. (1995). *Ground truth: The social implications of geographic information systems (mappings)*. New York: Guilford Press.

Renn, O., Webler, T., & Wiedemenn, P. (1995). *Fairness and competence in citizen participation: Evaluating methods of environmental discourse*. Dordrecht, The Netherlands: Kluwer Academic Publishers. doi:10.1007/978-94-011-0131-8

Sui, D., Elwood, S., & Goodchild, Ml. (2012). *Crowdsourcing geographic knowledge*. Dordrecht: Springer.

Surowiecki, J. (2004). *The wisdom of crowds: Why the many are smarter than the few and how collective. wisdom shapes business, economies, societies, and nations* (1st ed.). New York: Doubleday.

KEY TERMS AND DEFINITIONS

E-Government: Use of information and communication technology for delivery of government services.

E-Participation: Use of ITCT for engaging the public in policy making activities.

E-Participatory Mapping: E-governance tool for public participation that utilizes ICT to engage the public in participatory mapping activities.

Geographic Information Systems (GIS): A set of information technology tools to collect, store, analyze, and display spatial information.

Human Sensors: General publics' use of ICT tools for sensing and sharing data relevant for policy making.

Information and Communication Technology (ICT): Range of hardware and software associated with communication of information using digital data.

Participatory GIS (PGIS): Participatory mapping activities involving the use of GIS technology. It is associated with use of purposive samples and focus on empowerment of indigenous people.

Participatory Mapping: Activities that involve the general public in map-making activities.

Public Participation: Engagement of the general public in policy-making activities. It includes activities such as sharing of government information, seeking comments on issues and policies, and using public inputs in decision making.

Public Participation GIS (PPGIS): Participatory mapping activities using GIS and the Internet. It relies on random sampling and focuses on high data quality.

Voluntary GIS (VGIS): Participatory mapping where the public voluntarily provides spatial data using ICT tools.

Related Readings

To continue IGI Global's long-standing tradition of advancing innovation through emerging research, please find below a compiled list of recommended IGI Global book chapters and journal articles in the areas of public administration, e-government, and citizen engagement. These related readings will provide additional information and guidance to further enrich your knowledge and assist you with your own research.

Agostino, D., Arnaboldi, M., & Azzone, G. (2018). Social Media Data Into Performance Measurement Systems: Methodologies, Opportunities, and Risks. In G. Azevedo, J. da Silva Oliveira, R. Marques, & A. Ferreira (Eds.), *Handbook of Research on Modernization and Accountability in Public Sector Management* (pp. 254–275). Hershey, PA: IGI Global. doi:10.4018/978-1-5225-3731-1.ch012

Aladalah, M., Cheung, Y., & Lee, V. C. (2018). Towards a Model for Engaging Citizens via Gov2.0 to Meet Evolving Public Value. *International Journal of Public Administration in the Digital Age*, *5*(1), 1–17. doi:10.4018/IJPADA.2018010101

Anand, D., & Khemchandani, V. (2017). An Analytical Method to Audit Indian e-Governance System. *International Journal of Electronic Government Research*, *13*(3), 18–37. doi:10.4018/IJEGR.2017070102

Anthony, S. M., & Zhang, W. (2017). Alternative Tweeting: A Comparison of Frames in Twitter's Political Discourse and Mainstream Newspaper Coverage of the Singapore General Election of 2011. In M. Adria & Y. Mao (Eds.), *Handbook of Research on Citizen Engagement and Public Participation in the Era of New Media* (pp. 324–343). Hershey, PA: IGI Global. doi:10.4018/978-1-5225-1081-9.ch018

Bandeira, A. M., Meira, D., & Tomé, B. (2018). Reflections on the Accounting Framework of Public Interest Cooperatives in Portugal. In G. Azevedo, J. da Silva Oliveira, R. Marques, & A. Ferreira (Eds.), *Handbook of Research on Modernization and Accountability in Public Sector Management* (pp. 433–445). Hershey, PA: IGI Global. doi:10.4018/978-1-5225-3731-1.ch020

Boachie, C. (2017). Public Financial Management and Systems of Accountability in Sub-National Governance in Developing Economies. In E. Schoburgh & R. Ryan (Eds.), *Handbook of Research on Sub-National Governance and Development* (pp. 193–217). Hershey, PA: IGI Global. doi:10.4018/978-1-5225-1645-3.ch009

Bolívar, M. P. (2018). Governance in Smart Cities: A Comparison of Practitioners' Perceptions and Prior Research. *International Journal of E-Planning Research*, *7*(2), 1–19. doi:10.4018/IJEPR.2018040101

Borrego, A. C., Lopes, C. M., & Ferreira, C. M. (2018). The Perception of Tax Complexity Within Local Authorities' VAT Framework: Evidence From Portugal. In G. Azevedo, J. da Silva Oliveira, R. Marques, & A. Ferreira (Eds.), *Handbook of Research on Modernization and Accountability in Public Sector Management* (pp. 384–405). Hershey, PA: IGI Global. doi:10.4018/978-1-5225-3731-1.ch018

Buyana, K., & Lwasa, S. (2017). Infrastructure Governance at Sub-National Level: The Case of Kampala City in Uganda. In E. Schoburgh & R. Ryan (Eds.), *Handbook of Research on Sub-National Governance and Development* (pp. 324–342). Hershey, PA: IGI Global. doi:10.4018/978-1-5225-1645-3.ch015

Carini, C., Teodori, C., & Giacomini, D. (2018). A New Useful Tool or a Further Misunderstood Obligation?: Perceptions on the LG Consolidated Report. In G. Azevedo, J. da Silva Oliveira, R. Marques, & A. Ferreira (Eds.), *Handbook of Research on Modernization and Accountability in Public Sector Management* (pp. 55–76). Hershey, PA: IGI Global. doi:10.4018/978-1-5225-3731-1.ch004

Chigwata, T. C. (2017). Fiscal Decentralization: Constraints to Revenue-Raising by Local Government in Zimbabwe. In E. Schoburgh & R. Ryan (Eds.), *Handbook of Research on Sub-National Governance and Development* (pp. 218–240). Hershey, PA: IGI Global. doi:10.4018/978-1-5225-1645-3.ch010

Costanza, F. (2018). Governing Patients' Mobility to Pursue Public Value: A System Dynamic Approach to Improve Healthcare Performance Management. In G. Azevedo, J. da Silva Oliveira, R. Marques, & A. Ferreira (Eds.), *Handbook of Research on Modernization and Accountability in Public Sector Management* (pp. 276–299). Hershey, PA: IGI Global. doi:10.4018/978-1-5225-3731-1.ch013

Cruz, A. C. (2018). Portal for Employees in the Public Sector: A Tool for Knowledge Management in Human Resources. In G. Azevedo, J. da Silva Oliveira, R. Marques, & A. Ferreira (Eds.), *Handbook of Research on Modernization and Accountability in Public Sector Management* (pp. 342–362). Hershey, PA: IGI Global. doi:10.4018/978-1-5225-3731-1.ch016

Cunha, A. M., Ferreira, A. D., & Fernandes, M. J. (2018). The Impact of Accounting Information and Socioeconomic Factors in the Re-Election of Portuguese Mayors. In G. Azevedo, J. da Silva Oliveira, R. Marques, & A. Ferreira (Eds.), *Handbook of Research on Modernization and Accountability in Public Sector Management* (pp. 406–432). Hershey, PA: IGI Global. doi:10.4018/978-1-5225-3731-1.ch019

del Mar Gálvez-Rodríhuez, M., Haro-de-Rosario, A., & Caba-Pérez, M. D. (2017). A Comparative View of Citizen Engagement in Social Media of Local Governments from North American Countries. In M. Adria & Y. Mao (Eds.), *Handbook of Research on Citizen Engagement and Public Participation in the Era of New Media* (pp. 139–156). Hershey, PA: IGI Global. doi:10.4018/978-1-5225-1081-9.ch009

Demirbas, T. (2018). The Role of Annual Reports in Ensuring Accountability: The Case of Development Agencies in Turkey. In G. Azevedo, J. da Silva Oliveira, R. Marques, & A. Ferreira (Eds.), *Handbook of Research on Modernization and Accountability in Public Sector Management* (pp. 446–469). Hershey, PA: IGI Global. doi:10.4018/978-1-5225-3731-1.ch021

Dhamija, A., & Dhamija, D. (2018). Motivational Factors and Barriers for Technology-Driven Governance: An Indian Perspective. In A. Manoharan & J. McQuiston (Eds.), *Innovative Perspectives on Public Administration in the Digital Age* (pp. 194–211). Hershey, PA: IGI Global. doi:10.4018/978-1-5225-5966-5.ch010

Drulă, G. (2017). Citizen Engagement and News Selection for Facebook Pages. In M. Adria & Y. Mao (Eds.), *Handbook of Research on Citizen Engagement and Public Participation in the Era of New Media* (pp. 122–138). Hershey, PA: IGI Global. doi:10.4018/978-1-5225-1081-9.ch008

During, R., Pleijte, M., van Dam, R. I., & Salverda, I. E. (2017). The Dutch Participation Society Needs Open Data, but What is Meant by Open? In M. Adria & Y. Mao (Eds.), *Handbook of Research on Citizen Engagement and Public Participation in the Era of New Media* (pp. 304–322). Hershey, PA: IGI Global. doi:10.4018/978-1-5225-1081-9.ch017

Fernandes, T. M., Gomes, J., & Romão, M. (2017). Investments in E-Government: A Benefit Management Case Study. *International Journal of Electronic Government Research, 13*(3), 1–17. doi:10.4018/IJEGR.2017070101

Ferreira, A. D., Santos, C., Azevedo, G. M., Gonçalves, J., & da Silva Oliveira, J. (2018). Performance Indicators and Accountability in Portuguese Public Universities: Socio-Economic Perspective. In G. Azevedo, J. da Silva Oliveira, R. Marques, & A. Ferreira (Eds.), *Handbook of Research on Modernization and Accountability in Public Sector Management* (pp. 210–233). Hershey, PA: IGI Global. doi:10.4018/978-1-5225-3731-1.ch010

Gatchair, S. D. (2017). Collaborative Governance and the Implementation of Fiscal Responsibility Frameworks. In E. Schoburgh & R. Ryan (Eds.), *Handbook of Research on Sub-National Governance and Development* (pp. 463–482). Hershey, PA: IGI Global. doi:10.4018/978-1-5225-1645-3.ch021

Gomes, J. P., & Laureano, R. M. (2018). Impacts of Electronic Public Procurement in the Portuguese Construction Sector: Several Years After Implementation. In G. Azevedo, J. da Silva Oliveira, R. Marques, & A. Ferreira (Eds.), *Handbook of Research on Modernization and Accountability in Public Sector Management* (pp. 363–383). Hershey, PA: IGI Global. doi:10.4018/978-1-5225-3731-1.ch017

Grant, B., Woods, R., & Tan, S. F. (2017). Subnational Finance in Australia and China: The Case for Municipal Bond Banks. In E. Schoburgh & R. Ryan (Eds.), *Handbook of Research on Sub-National Governance and Development* (pp. 150–166). Hershey, PA: IGI Global. doi:10.4018/978-1-5225-1645-3.ch007

Gray, N., & Pugalis, L. (2017). Place-Based Subnational Development: Unpacking Some of the Key Conceptual Strands and Normative Dispositions. In E. Schoburgh & R. Ryan (Eds.), *Handbook of Research on Sub-National Governance and Development* (pp. 34–53). Hershey, PA: IGI Global. doi:10.4018/978-1-5225-1645-3.ch002

Groshek, J. (2017). Organically Modified News Networks: Gatekeeping in Social Media Coverage of GMOs. In M. Adria & Y. Mao (Eds.), *Handbook of Research on Citizen Engagement and Public Participation in the Era of New Media* (pp. 107–121). Hershey, PA: IGI Global. doi:10.4018/978-1-5225-1081-9.ch007

Guarini, E., & Pattaro, A. F. (2017). Fiscal Responsibility and Multi-Level Governance: Bridging the Gap between Policy and Management. In E. Schoburgh & R. Ryan (Eds.), *Handbook of Research on Sub-National Governance and Development* (pp. 167–192). Hershey, PA: IGI Global. doi:10.4018/978-1-5225-1645-3.ch008

Hansson, K., & Ekenberg, L. (2018). Embodiment and Gameplay: Situating the User in Crowdsourced Information Production. In A. Manoharan & J. McQuiston (Eds.), *Innovative Perspectives on Public Administration in the Digital Age* (pp. 239–255). Hershey, PA: IGI Global. doi:10.4018/978-1-5225-5966-5.ch013

Heaton, L., & Días da Silva, P. (2017). Citizen Engagement in Local Environmental Issues: Intersecting Modes of Communication. In M. Adria & Y. Mao (Eds.), *Handbook of Research on Citizen Engagement and Public Participation in the Era of New Media* (pp. 1–19). Hershey, PA: IGI Global. doi:10.4018/978-1-5225-1081-9.ch001

Heisler, E. (2017). Measuring Enclosures and Efficacy in Online Feminism: The Case of Rewire. In M. Adria & Y. Mao (Eds.), *Handbook of Research on Citizen Engagement and Public Participation in the Era of New Media* (pp. 389–409). Hershey, PA: IGI Global. doi:10.4018/978-1-5225-1081-9.ch021

Hodgson, J., McKinlay, P., & Knight, B. (2017). Subnational Governance and Development: A New Perspective. In E. Schoburgh & R. Ryan (Eds.), *Handbook of Research on Sub-National Governance and Development* (pp. 407–431). Hershey, PA: IGI Global. doi:10.4018/978-1-5225-1645-3.ch019

Ismailova, R., Muhametjanova, G., & Kurambayev, B. (2018). A Central Asian View of E-Government Services Adoption: Citizens' Trust and Intention to Use E-Services. In A. Manoharan & J. McQuiston (Eds.), *Innovative Perspectives on Public Administration in the Digital Age* (pp. 212–226). Hershey, PA: IGI Global. doi:10.4018/978-1-5225-5966-5.ch011

Iwasaki, Y. (2017). Youth Engagement in the Era of New Media. In M. Adria & Y. Mao (Eds.), *Handbook of Research on Citizen Engagement and Public Participation in the Era of New Media* (pp. 90–105). Hershey, PA: IGI Global. doi:10.4018/978-1-5225-1081-9.ch006

Jackson, T., Nel, E., & Connelly, S. (2017). A Comparison of Resource Equalization Processes for Subnational Rural Governance and Development: Case Studies of England, Scotland, Canada, Australia, and New Zealand. In E. Schoburgh & R. Ryan (Eds.), *Handbook of Research on Sub-National Governance and Development* (pp. 117–149). Hershey, PA: IGI Global. doi:10.4018/978-1-5225-1645-3.ch006

Ji, Q. (2017). A Comparative View of Censored and Uncensored Political Discussion: The Case of Chinese Social Media Users. In M. Adria & Y. Mao (Eds.), *Handbook of Research on Citizen Engagement and Public Participation in the Era of New Media* (pp. 269–282). Hershey, PA: IGI Global. doi:10.4018/978-1-5225-1081-9.ch015

Jovita, H., Mutiarin, D., & Nurmandi, A. (2018). Covering the Cost of the Past: Disaster Management in the Most Typhoon-Affected Region in the Philippines. *International Journal of Disaster Response and Emergency Management, 1*(2), 49–63. doi:10.4018/IJDREM.2018040104

Kang, W., & Wang, Y. (2018). China Digital Governance Development Review Over the Past Two Decades. *International Journal of Public Administration in the Digital Age, 5*(3), 92–106. doi:10.4018/IJPADA.2018070107

Kassen, M. (2017). E-Government Politics as a Networking Phenomenon: Applying a Multidimensional Approach. *International Journal of Electronic Government Research, 13*(2), 18–46. doi:10.4018/IJEGR.2017040102

Lawrie, A. (2017). The Subnational Region: A Utopia? The Challenge of Governing Through Soft Power. In E. Schoburgh & R. Ryan (Eds.), *Handbook of Research on Sub-National Governance and Development* (pp. 96–115). Hershey, PA: IGI Global. doi:10.4018/978-1-5225-1645-3.ch005

Luk, C. Y. (2018). The Impact of Digital Health on Traditional Healthcare Systems and Doctor-Patient Relationships: The Case Study of Singapore. In A. Manoharan & J. McQuiston (Eds.), *Innovative Perspectives on Public Administration in the Digital Age* (pp. 143–167). Hershey, PA: IGI Global. doi:10.4018/978-1-5225-5966-5.ch008

Ma, L. (2018). Digital Divide and Citizen Use of E-Government in China's Municipalities. *International Journal of Public Administration in the Digital Age, 5*(3), 16–31. doi:10.4018/IJPADA.2018070102

Madsen, C. Ø., & Kræmmergaard, P. (2018). How to Migrate Citizens Online and Reduce Traffic on Traditional Channels Through Multichannel Management: A Case Study of Cross-Organizational Collaboration Surrounding a Mandatory Self-Service Application. In A. Manoharan & J. McQuiston (Eds.), *Innovative Perspectives on Public Administration in the Digital Age* (pp. 121–142). Hershey, PA: IGI Global. doi:10.4018/978-1-5225-5966-5.ch007

Maulana, I. (2017). Social Media as Public Political Instrument. In M. Adria & Y. Mao (Eds.), *Handbook of Research on Citizen Engagement and Public Participation in the Era of New Media* (pp. 231–247). Hershey, PA: IGI Global. doi:10.4018/978-1-5225-1081-9.ch013

Maxwell, S., & Carboni, J. (2018). Foundations' Civic Engagement With Stakeholders: Leveraging Social Media Strategies. In A. Manoharan & J. McQuiston (Eds.), *Innovative Perspectives on Public Administration in the Digital Age* (pp. 25–41). Hershey, PA: IGI Global. doi:10.4018/978-1-5225-5966-5.ch002

McNeal, R. S., Schmeida, M., & Bryan, L. D. (2017). Smartphones and their Increased Importance in U.S. Presidential Elections. In M. Adria & Y. Mao (Eds.), *Handbook of Research on Citizen Engagement and Public Participation in the Era of New Media* (pp. 283–303). Hershey, PA: IGI Global. doi:10.4018/978-1-5225-1081-9.ch016

Melo, A. I., Santinha, G., & Lima, R. (2018). Measuring the Quality of Health Services Using SERVQUAL: Evidence From Portugal. In G. Azevedo, J. da Silva Oliveira, R. Marques, & A. Ferreira (Eds.), *Handbook of Research on Modernization and Accountability in Public Sector Management* (pp. 300–318). Hershey, PA: IGI Global. doi:10.4018/978-1-5225-3731-1.ch014

Mensah, I. K. (2017). Tackling the ICT Infrastructure Gap for the Successful Implementation of E-Government Projects. *International Journal of Strategic Information Technology and Applications*, *8*(2), 40–56. doi:10.4018/IJSITA.2017040104

Mensah, I. K. (2018). E-Government Services Adoption: The Important Elements of Trust and Transparency. *International Journal of Electronic Government Research*, *14*(3), 12–31. doi:10.4018/IJEGR.2018070102

Miller, K. L. (2017). Local Government Reform in Jamaica: A New Paradigm for Participatory Local Governance. In E. Schoburgh & R. Ryan (Eds.), *Handbook of Research on Sub-National Governance and Development* (pp. 520–542). Hershey, PA: IGI Global. doi:10.4018/978-1-5225-1645-3.ch024

Mohammed-Spigner, D., Porter, B. E., & Warner, L. M. (2018). States' Budget Investments in Technology and Improving Criminal Justice Outcomes. In A. Manoharan & J. McQuiston (Eds.), *Innovative Perspectives on Public Administration in the Digital Age* (pp. 90–105). Hershey, PA: IGI Global. doi:10.4018/978-1-5225-5966-5.ch005

Monteiro, R. P., & Pinho, C. (2018). Cost Accounting in Brazil's Public Sector: Importance, Use, and Level of Deployment. In G. Azevedo, J. da Silva Oliveira, R. Marques, & A. Ferreira (Eds.), *Handbook of Research on Modernization and Accountability in Public Sector Management* (pp. 319–341). Hershey, PA: IGI Global. doi:10.4018/978-1-5225-3731-1.ch015

Morim, A. C., Inácio, H., & Vieira, E. (2018). Internal Control in a Public Hospital: The Case of Financial Services Expenditure Department. In G. Azevedo, J. da Silva Oliveira, R. Marques, & A. Ferreira (Eds.), *Handbook of Research on Modernization and Accountability in Public Sector Management* (pp. 77–102). Hershey, PA: IGI Global. doi:10.4018/978-1-5225-3731-1.ch005

Moura e Sá, P., Lourenço, R. P., & Veloso, S. (2018). Are Public Administration Institutions Willing to Disclose Their Performance Through Data Portals?: The Case of the Portuguese Directorates-General. In G. Azevedo, J. da Silva Oliveira, R. Marques, & A. Ferreira (Eds.), *Handbook of Research on Modernization and Accountability in Public Sector Management* (pp. 234–253). Hershey, PA: IGI Global. doi:10.4018/978-1-5225-3731-1.ch011

Mupepi, M. G. (2017). Developing Democratic Paradigms to Effectively Manage Business, Government, and Civil Society: The African Spring. In E. Schoburgh & R. Ryan (Eds.), *Handbook of Research on Sub-National Governance and Development* (pp. 432–462). Hershey, PA: IGI Global. doi:10.4018/978-1-5225-1645-3.ch020

Nam, T. (2017). Achievable or Ambitious?: A Comparative and Critical View of Government 3.0 in Korea. *International Journal of Electronic Government Research*, *13*(1), 1–13. doi:10.4018/IJEGR.2017010101

Nam, T. (2019). Does E-Government Raise Effectiveness and Efficiency?: Examining the Cross-National Effect. *Journal of Global Information Management*, *27*(3), 120–138. doi:10.4018/JGIM.2019070107

Nathai-Balkissoon, M., & Pun, K. F. (2018). E-Government of Occupational Safety and Health: Improvement Prospects for a Developing Nation. In A. Manoharan & J. McQuiston (Eds.), *Innovative Perspectives on Public Administration in the Digital Age* (pp. 65–89). Hershey, PA: IGI Global. doi:10.4018/978-1-5225-5966-5.ch004

Nemec, J., Meričková, B. M., Svidroňová, M. M., & Klimovský, D. (2017). Co-Creation as a Social Innovation in Delivery of Public Services at Local Government Level: The Slovak Experience. In E. Schoburgh & R. Ryan (Eds.), *Handbook of Research on Sub-National Governance and Development* (pp. 281–303). Hershey, PA: IGI Global. doi:10.4018/978-1-5225-1645-3.ch013

Nistor, C. S., Oprisor, T., & Crisan, A. R. (2018). Implications of Accountability Through the Prospect of Integrated Reporting Adoption in the Public Sector. In G. Azevedo, J. da Silva Oliveira, R. Marques, & A. Ferreira (Eds.), *Handbook of Research on Modernization and Accountability in Public Sector Management* (pp. 189–209). Hershey, PA: IGI Global. doi:10.4018/978-1-5225-3731-1.ch009

Noor, R. (2017). Citizen Journalism: News Gathering by Amateurs. In M. Adria & Y. Mao (Eds.), *Handbook of Research on Citizen Engagement and Public Participation in the Era of New Media* (pp. 194–229). Hershey, PA: IGI Global. doi:10.4018/978-1-5225-1081-9.ch012

Ogonek, N., & Hofmann, S. (2018). Governments' Need for Digitization Skills: Understanding and Shaping Vocational Training in the Public Sector. *International Journal of Public Administration in the Digital Age*, *5*(4), 61–75. doi:10.4018/IJPADA.2018100105

Okada, A., Ishida, Y., & Yamauchi, N. (2018). In Prosperity Prepare for Adversity: Use of Social Media for Nonprofit Fundraising in Times of Disaster. In A. Manoharan, & J. McQuiston (Eds.), Innovative Perspectives on Public Administration in the Digital Age (pp. 42-64). Hershey, PA: IGI Global. doi:10.4018/978-1-5225-5966-5.ch003

Ökten, S., Akman, E., & Akman, Ç. (2018). Modernization and Accountability in Public-Sector Administration: Turkey Example. In G. Azevedo, J. da Silva Oliveira, R. Marques, & A. Ferreira (Eds.), *Handbook of Research on Modernization and Accountability in Public Sector Management* (pp. 18–39). Hershey, PA: IGI Global. doi:10.4018/978-1-5225-3731-1.ch002

Othman, R., Nath, N., & Laswad, F. (2018). Environmental Reporting and Accounting: Sustainability Hybridisation. In G. Azevedo, J. da Silva Oliveira, R. Marques, & A. Ferreira (Eds.), *Handbook of Research on Modernization and Accountability in Public Sector Management* (pp. 130–158). Hershey, PA: IGI Global. doi:10.4018/978-1-5225-3731-1.ch007

Perelló-Sobrepere, M. (2017). Building a New State from Outrage: The Case of Catalonia. In M. Adria & Y. Mao (Eds.), *Handbook of Research on Citizen Engagement and Public Participation in the Era of New Media* (pp. 344–359). Hershey, PA: IGI Global. doi:10.4018/978-1-5225-1081-9.ch019

Pinterič, U. (2017). ICT as the Path Beyond Bureaucracy?: The Use of ICT by Ignorance of the Citizens. *International Journal of Public Administration in the Digital Age*, *4*(2), 33–42. doi:10.4018/IJPADA.2017040103

Quinn, B. C. (2017). Integration, Innovation, and Intimidation?: Linking the Third Sector and Local Government in Ireland. In E. Schoburgh & R. Ryan (Eds.), *Handbook of Research on Sub-National Governance and Development* (pp. 75–95). Hershey, PA: IGI Global. doi:10.4018/978-1-5225-1645-3.ch004

Rahman, M. S. (2017). Politics-Administration Relations and the Effect on Local Governance and Development: The Case of Bangladesh. In E. Schoburgh & R. Ryan (Eds.), *Handbook of Research on Sub-National Governance and Development* (pp. 256–279). Hershey, PA: IGI Global. doi:10.4018/978-1-5225-1645-3.ch012

Rana, T. (2018). New Public Management Reforms and Modernization Changes in Australia. In G. Azevedo, J. da Silva Oliveira, R. Marques, & A. Ferreira (Eds.), *Handbook of Research on Modernization and Accountability in Public Sector Management* (pp. 1–17). Hershey, PA: IGI Global. doi:10.4018/978-1-5225-3731-1.ch001

Reddy, P. S. (2017). Political-Administrative Interface at the Local Sphere of Government with Particular Reference to South Africa. In E. Schoburgh & R. Ryan (Eds.), *Handbook of Research on Sub-National Governance and Development* (pp. 242–255). Hershey, PA: IGI Global. doi:10.4018/978-1-5225-1645-3.ch011

Ryan, R., & Woods, R. (2017). Decentralization and Subnational Governance: Theory and Praxis. In E. Schoburgh & R. Ryan (Eds.), *Handbook of Research on Sub-National Governance and Development* (pp. 1–33). Hershey, PA: IGI Global. doi:10.4018/978-1-5225-1645-3.ch001

Ryan, R., & Woods, R. (2017). Women's Political Empowerment: Lessons for Subnational Levels of Government – Nepal, Pakistan, Rwanda, and Indonesia. In E. Schoburgh & R. Ryan (Eds.), *Handbook of Research on Sub-National Governance and Development* (pp. 385–405). Hershey, PA: IGI Global. doi:10.4018/978-1-5225-1645-3.ch018

Santos, C., Ferreira, A. D., Marques, R. P., & Azevedo, G. M. (2018). EAGLE_Index: Enhancement of an Accountability Guide for Learning E-Government. In G. Azevedo, J. da Silva Oliveira, R. Marques, & A. Ferreira (Eds.), *Handbook of Research on Modernization and Accountability in Public Sector Management* (pp. 103–129). Hershey, PA: IGI Global. doi:10.4018/978-1-5225-3731-1.ch006

Schoburgh, E. D. (2017). Challenges in Institutionalizing Democratic Governance via Popularly Elected Mayor: The Case of Jamaica. In E. Schoburgh & R. Ryan (Eds.), *Handbook of Research on Sub-National Governance and Development* (pp. 344–367). Hershey, PA: IGI Global. doi:10.4018/978-1-5225-1645-3.ch016

Schoburgh, E. D. (2017). The Institutional Imperatives of Local Economic Governance: Lessons from a Small Island Developing State. In E. Schoburgh & R. Ryan (Eds.), *Handbook of Research on Sub-National Governance and Development* (pp. 54–74). Hershey, PA: IGI Global. doi:10.4018/978-1-5225-1645-3.ch003

Serna, C. A., Pineda, A. A., & Rojas, O. A. (2017). Subnational Governance Model from the Integration of Online Media and Social Networks: The Case of Medellin City, Colombia. In E. Schoburgh & R. Ryan (Eds.), *Handbook of Research on Sub-National Governance and Development* (pp. 483–498). Hershey, PA: IGI Global. doi:10.4018/978-1-5225-1645-3.ch022

Sforza, V., Mechelli, A., & Cimini, R. (2018). Towards the Modernisation of EU Public Sector Accounting Standards: Lessons From the Reconciliation Between National and Governmental Accounting. In G. Azevedo, J. da Silva Oliveira, R. Marques, & A. Ferreira (Eds.), *Handbook of Research on Modernization and Accountability in Public Sector Management* (pp. 40–54). Hershey, PA: IGI Global. doi:10.4018/978-1-5225-3731-1.ch003

Shan, Z., & Tang, L. (2017). Social Media and the Public Sphere in China: A Case Study of Political Discussion on Weibo after the Wenzhou High-Speed Rail Derailment Accident. In M. Adria & Y. Mao (Eds.), *Handbook of Research on Citizen Engagement and Public Participation in the Era of New Media* (pp. 410–425). Hershey, PA: IGI Global. doi:10.4018/978-1-5225-1081-9.ch022

Sharma, V., & Sengar, A. (2018). Mobile Governance for Affordability and Profitability/Feasibility. In A. Manoharan & J. McQuiston (Eds.), *Innovative Perspectives on Public Administration in the Digital Age* (pp. 227–238). Hershey, PA: IGI Global. doi:10.4018/978-1-5225-5966-5.ch012

Sihi, D. (2018). Friending and Funding Through Facebook: Social Media Use of Regional Nonprofit Organizations. In A. Manoharan & J. McQuiston (Eds.), *Innovative Perspectives on Public Administration in the Digital Age* (pp. 256–283). Hershey, PA: IGI Global. doi:10.4018/978-1-5225-5966-5.ch014

Song, M. Y., & Abelson, J. (2017). Public Engagement and Policy Entrepreneurship on Social Media in the Time of Anti-Vaccination Movements. In M. Adria & Y. Mao (Eds.), *Handbook of Research on Citizen Engagement and Public Participation in the Era of New Media* (pp. 38–56). Hershey, PA: IGI Global. doi:10.4018/978-1-5225-1081-9.ch003

Soverchia, M., & Fradeani, A. (2018). The eXtensible Business Reporting Language: A Digital Tool to Enhance Public Sector Accountability. In A. Manoharan & J. McQuiston (Eds.), *Innovative Perspectives on Public Administration in the Digital Age* (pp. 106–120). Hershey, PA: IGI Global. doi:10.4018/978-1-5225-5966-5.ch006

Spada, P., & Allegretti, G. (2017). Integrating Multiple Channels of Engagement in Democratic Innovations: Opportunities and Challenges. In M. Adria & Y. Mao (Eds.), *Handbook of Research on Citizen Engagement and Public Participation in the Era of New Media* (pp. 20–37). Hershey, PA: IGI Global. doi:10.4018/978-1-5225-1081-9.ch002

Staiou, E., & Gouscos, D. (2018). The Evolution of Self-Organized Social Solidarity (SoSS) Initiatives in Greece and Their Relationship to Online Media: A Longitudinal Research. In A. Manoharan & J. McQuiston (Eds.), *Innovative Perspectives on Public Administration in the Digital Age* (pp. 168–193). Hershey, PA: IGI Global. doi:10.4018/978-1-5225-5966-5.ch009

Strekalova, Y. A., Krieger, J. L., Damiani, R. E., Kalyanaraman, S., & Wang, D. Z. (2017). Old Media, New Media, and Public Engagement with Science and Technology. In M. Adria & Y. Mao (Eds.), *Handbook of Research on Citizen Engagement and Public Participation in the Era of New Media* (pp. 57–72). Hershey, PA: IGI Global. doi:10.4018/978-1-5225-1081-9.ch004

Syväjärvi, A., Leinonen, J., Kivivirta, V., & Kesti, M. (2017). The Latitude of Information Management in Local Government: Views of Local Government Managers. *International Journal of Electronic Government Research, 13*(1), 69–85. doi:10.4018/IJEGR.2017010105

Tan, S. F. (2017). Local Representation in Australia: Preliminary Findings of a National Survey. In E. Schoburgh & R. Ryan (Eds.), *Handbook of Research on Sub-National Governance and Development* (pp. 368–384). Hershey, PA: IGI Global. doi:10.4018/978-1-5225-1645-3.ch017

Tavares, M. D., & Rodrigues, L. L. (2018). Strategic Responses of Public Sector Entities to GRI Sustainability Reports. In G. Azevedo, J. da Silva Oliveira, R. Marques, & A. Ferreira (Eds.), *Handbook of Research on Modernization and Accountability in Public Sector Management* (pp. 159–188). Hershey, PA: IGI Global. doi:10.4018/978-1-5225-3731-1.ch008

Thomas, M. A., & Elnagar, S. (2018). A Semantic Approach to Evaluate Web Content of Government Websites. In A. Manoharan & J. McQuiston (Eds.), *Innovative Perspectives on Public Administration in the Digital Age* (pp. 1–24). Hershey, PA: IGI Global. doi:10.4018/978-1-5225-5966-5.ch001

Toscano, J. P. (2017). Social Media and Public Participation: Opportunities, Barriers, and a New Framework. In M. Adria & Y. Mao (Eds.), *Handbook of Research on Citizen Engagement and Public Participation in the Era of New Media* (pp. 73–89). Hershey, PA: IGI Global. doi:10.4018/978-1-5225-1081-9.ch005

Towner, T. L. (2017). Information Hubs or Drains?: The Role of Online Sources in Campaign Learning. In M. Adria & Y. Mao (Eds.), *Handbook of Research on Citizen Engagement and Public Participation in the Era of New Media* (pp. 157–178). Hershey, PA: IGI Global. doi:10.4018/978-1-5225-1081-9.ch010

Tshishonga, N. (2017). Operation Sukuma-Sakhe: A New Social Contract for Decentralized Service Delivery and Responsive Governance in KwaZulu-Natal. In E. Schoburgh & R. Ryan (Eds.), *Handbook of Research on Sub-National Governance and Development* (pp. 304–323). Hershey, PA: IGI Global. doi:10.4018/978-1-5225-1645-3.ch014

Vie, S., Carter, D., & Meyr, J. (2017). Occupy Rhetoric: Responding to Charges of "Slacktivism" with Digital Activism Successes. In M. Adria & Y. Mao (Eds.), *Handbook of Research on Citizen Engagement and Public Participation in the Era of New Media* (pp. 179–193). Hershey, PA: IGI Global. doi:10.4018/978-1-5225-1081-9.ch011

Vrettos, K., & Gouscos, D. (2019). Evaluating the Presence of Greek Tourism-Related Public Sector Entities in Online Social Networks. *International Journal of Public Administration in the Digital Age, 6*(1), 15–40. doi:10.4018/IJPADA.2019010102

Waller, P. (2017). Co-Production and Co-Creation in Public Services: Resolving Confusion and Contradictions. *International Journal of Electronic Government Research, 13*(2), 1–17. doi:10.4018/IJEGR.2017040101

Weng, S. (2018). Internet Political Participation and Public Agenda-Setting: Social Network Analysis of PX Event in Zhangzhou. *International Journal of Public Administration in the Digital Age, 5*(3), 60–75. doi:10.4018/IJPADA.2018070105

Woods, R. (2017). Not Forgetting the Public Servants: Capacity-Building to Support Subnational Governance and Development Implementation. In E. Schoburgh & R. Ryan (Eds.), *Handbook of Research on Sub-National Governance and Development* (pp. 499–519). Hershey, PA: IGI Global. doi:10.4018/978-1-5225-1645-3.ch023

Yang, K. C., & Kang, Y. (2017). Social Media, Political Mobilization, and Citizen Engagement: A Case Study of the March 18, 2014, Sunflower Student Movement in Taiwan. In M. Adria & Y. Mao (Eds.), *Handbook of Research on Citizen Engagement and Public Participation in the Era of New Media* (pp. 360–388). Hershey, PA: IGI Global. doi:10.4018/978-1-5225-1081-9.ch020

Yavuz, N., Karkın, N., Parlak, İ., & Subay, Ö. Ö. (2018). Political Discourse Strategies Used in Twitter during Gezi Park Protests: A Comparison of Two Rival Political Parties in Turkey. *International Journal of Public Administration in the Digital Age, 5*(1), 82–96. doi:10.4018/IJPADA.2018010105

Yuan, Y. (2017). A Gradual Political Change?: The Agenda Setting Effect of Online Activism in China 1994-2011. In M. Adria & Y. Mao (Eds.), *Handbook of Research on Citizen Engagement and Public Participation in the Era of New Media* (pp. 248–268). Hershey, PA: IGI Global. doi:10.4018/978-1-5225-1081-9.ch014

About the Contributors

Fernando Luís Almeida has a PhD in Computer Science Engineering from Faculty of Engineering of University of Porto (FEUP). He holds also MSc in Innovation and Entrepreneurship and MSc in Informatics Engineering from FEUP. He has around 7 years of teaching experience at higher education levels in the field of computer science and management. He has also worked for 10 years in several positions as software engineer and project manager for large organizations and research centers like Critical Software, CICA/SEF, INESC TEC and ISR Porto. During that time he had the possibility to work in partnership with big international organizations and universities in several European projects. His current research areas include innovation policies, entrepreneurship, software development and decision support systems.

Eugénio Cunha has a BSc. in Computer Science Engineering from Polytechnic Institute of Porto. He works in the computer industry field, where he is responsible for the development of new applications for Web and mobile platforms. His current research areas include software engineering and web/mobile interfaces.

Nirmalendunath Ghosh is a graduate in electrical engineering from University of Calcutta, qualified in master of distance education, worked in power sector in monitoring and demand side management participated in international conference at IIT and IIM, other universities by presentation of research paper, published in edited books and journals.

Rajan Gupta is a Research and Analytics Professional and is the Corresponding Author of the current chapters. He has done his Ph.D. (Information Systems) in the area of E-Governance from Department of Computer Science, University of Delhi. He completed his Master in Computer Application (MCA) from University of Delhi, Post Graduate Program in Management (PGPM) from IMT Ghaziabad, and Executive Program in Business Intelligence and Analytics (EPBABI) from IIM Ranchi. He is NET-JRF qualified under University Grant Commission, India and holds a certificate in Consulting from Consultancy Development Centre (CDC),

DSIR, Ministry of Science and Technology, Government of India. He is one of the few Certified Analytics Professionals (CAP) around the world and is currently serving as CAP Ambassador in Asia Region (INFORMS, USA). He has been accredited with GStat from American Statistical Association. He has worked with firms like Samsung and Inauctus [TCF Consultancy] in their research and analytics department. He has also been associated as Assistant Professor on Ad-hoc basis with Deen Dayal Upadhyaya College, University of Delhi, Department of Computer Science (Faculty of Mathematical Science) - University of Delhi, and IMT - Ghaziabad for delivering lectures in Computer Science, Data Science, IT and Management. His area of interest includes E-Governance, Public Information Systems, Multimedia Data processing, Data Mining, and Data Analytics. He has authored 2 books on E-Governance and 1 on Data Analytics. He has over 50 publications at various national and international forums.

Saibal Kumar Pal completed his post-graduation in computer science in 1990 from University of Allahabad and PhD in Information Security from University of Delhi, INDIA. He is presently serving as the Director of Information Technology & Cyber Security at DRDO Headquarters, New Delhi. His areas of interest are Cyber Security, Cryptography, Computational Intelligence and Electronic Governance. He has published more than 200 papers in journals & international conference proceedings.

Avinash Panwar is currently working as the Head, Department of Computer Science and Director, Computer Center at Mohanlal Sukhadia University, Udaipur, Rajasthan, India. Avinash Panwar holds a PhD in e-commerce domain and a Master's degree in Computer Science and Applications. His interest areas in teaching and research include System Designing, application of IT for improvement of processes and public services, Social Network Analysis and electronic Word of Mouth. He has an experience of more than 18 years in various administrative and academic positions. Dr. Panwar has had international exposure through his visit to University of Nebraska, USA as a faculty representative for a 15 day exchange programme which included 40 students from five different countries. He is also strongly associated with academic fraternity by means of guest lectures, collaborative research, conferences, meetings and other academic initiatives. He has several national and international publications to his credit.

Vasantha Prathapagiri has attained Doctorate in Public Administration, been teaching and researching last 10 years, Developed keen interest in public policy framing and implementation in rural development and also have driven activities relating to ICT initiatives in administrative and rural developmental project initiatives.

Sumangla Rathore is currently working as Director, Suyash College, Rajasthan, India and as Adjunct Faculty Member, ICFAI Foundation of Higher Education, Hyderabad, India. She holds a PhD in e-commerce domain and a Post graduate degree in Computer Applications. Dr. Rathore has been an active participant in cross-cultural international experiences involving students and academic exchange. She has several national and international publications to her credit in the field of e-commerce and Information Technology. Her research interests are in the field of e-commerce, Social media, electronic Word of Mouth, online buying behavior, technology adoption and usability evaluation.

Pragati Rawat is an Assistant Professor at Slippery Rock University of the Pennsylvania State System of higher education in the United States. Prior to embarking on her PhD program, she worked in the Unique Identification program of the government of India that created world's largest biometric identity database. Her research interests are in the science and technology policy areas. She has published in journals such as Politics & Policy, MTS Journal, and Public Works Management & Policy.

Juita-Elena (Wie) Yusuf is Professor of Public Service in Old Dominion University's Strome College of Business. She is also Assistant Director of Education for the ODU Institute for Coastal Adaptation and Resilience. Her areas of research include sea level rise and resilience, transportation policy, public budgeting, and public finance. Her work has been published in Public Works Management and Policy, Environment and Planning Part C, Coastal Management, Journal of Environmental Studies and Sciences, and other journals.

Index

T

U

V

W

www.ingramcontent.com/pod-product-compliance
Lightning Source LLC
LaVergne TN
LVHW061533290926
849162LV00004B/783